Contemporary Social Issues

Series Editor: George Ritzer, *University of Maryland*

Sex Trafficking

The Global Market in Women and Children

Kathryn Farr
Portland State University

Worth Publishers

Acquisitions Editor: Valerie Raymond
Assistant Editor: Erik Gilg
Marketing Director: John Britch
Production Editor: Margaret Comaskey
Art Director, Cover Designer: Babs Reingold
Text Designer: Lissi Sigillo
Production Manager: Sarah Segal
Composition: Matrix Publishing Services
Printing and Binding: R. R. Donnelley and Sons Company
Cover Photo: Teun Voeten/Panos

Library of Congress Control Number: 2004110827

ISBN: 0-7167-5548-3 (EAN: 9780716755487)

Printed in the United States of America

First printing 2004

Worth Publishers
41 Madison Avenue
New York, NY 10010
www.worthpublishers.com

Sex Trafficking

The Global Market in Women and Children

Contemporary Social Issues

George Ritzer, *Series Editor*

The Wilding of America: Money, Mayhem, and the New American Dream (third edition)
Charles Derber

The Myth of Self-Esteem: Finding Happiness and Solving Problems in America
John P. Hewitt

Upcoming Volumes

Hollywood Goes to High School
Robert Bulman

Society of Risk Takers
William Cockerham

Global E-litism: Digital Technology, Social Inequality, and Transnationality
Gili Drori

Speculative Capitalism: Financial Casinos and Their Consequences
Dan Krier

Post-Industrial Peasants: The Illusion of Middle Class Prosperity
Kevin Leicht and Scott Fitzgerald

Upcoming Revisions

Urban Enclaves: Identity and Place in the World (second edition)
Mark Abrahamson

Just Revenge: Costs and Consequences of the Death Penalty (second edition)
Mark Costanzo

To my daughters—Tori, Sheila, and Erin—for always giving me their love and support and for living their lives with feminist courage and integrity.

About the Author

Kathryn Farr is professor emerita of sociology at Portland State University. Her research focuses on women, gender, and crime and has been published in a number of venues, including "Battered Women Who Were 'Being Killed and Survived': Straight Talk from Survivors" in *Violence and Victims*; "Defeminizing and Dehumanizing Female Murderers: Portrayals of Lesbians on Death Row" in *Women & Criminal Justice*; "Representations of Female Evil: Cases and Characterizations of Women on Death Row," co-authored with Sheila J. Farr in *Quarterly Journal of Ideology*; and "Classification of Female Inmates: Moving Forward" in *Crime and Delinquency*.

Farr's current research calls for a critical examination of violence against women, including its universal as well as culture-specific features. More broadly, Farr's work is rooted in a feminist sociology that features the intersections of gender, race, and class in structures of violence and oppression. Her commitment to feminist dialogue and social change is reflected in her long-term affiliation with women's studies at Portland State University.

Contents

Foreword

As we move further into the twenty-first century, we confront a seemingly endless array of pressing social issues: urban decay, inequality, ecological threats, rampant consumerism, war, AIDS, inadequate health care, national and personal debt, and many more. Although such problems are regularly dealt with in newspapers, magazines, and trade books, and on radio and television, such popular treatment has severe limitations. By examining these issues systematically through the lens of sociology, we can gain greater insight into them and be better able to deal with them. Each book in the series casts a new and distinctive light on a familiar social issue, while challenging the conventional view, which may obscure as much as it clarifies. Phenomena that seem disparate and unrelated are shown to have many commonalities and to reflect a major, but often unrecognized, trend within the larger society. Or a systematic comparative investigation demonstrates the existence of social causes or consequences that are overlooked by other types of analysis. In uncovering such realities, the books in this series are much more than intellectual exercises; they have powerful practical implications for our lives and for the structure of society.

At another level, this series fills a void in book publishing. There is certainly no shortage of academic titles, but those books tend to be introductory texts for undergraduates or advanced monographs for professional scholars. Missing are broadly accessible, issue-oriented books appropriate for all students (and for general readers). The books in this series occupy that niche somewhere between popular trade books and monographs. Like trade books, they deal with important and interesting social issues, are well written, and are as jargon free as possible. However, they are more rigorous than trade books in meeting academic standards for writing and research. Although they are not textbooks, they often explore topics covered in basic textbooks and therefore are easily integrated into the curriculum of sociology and other disciplines.

Each of the books in the "Contemporary Social Issues" series is a new and distinctive piece of work. I believe that students, serious general readers, and academicians will all find the books to be informative, interesting, thought provoking, and exciting. Among the topics to be covered in forthcoming additions to the series are the global digital divide, the problems in our high schools (and the way they are reflected in the movies), and the declining wealth and increasing indebtedness of the middle class.

—George Ritzer

Preface

Responding to queries about current projects, I have often replied in the last year or so that I was writing a book. To the "on what?" question, I tried out several descriptors—sex trafficking, trafficking women into prostitution, the global market in women and children, . . . Frequently my description led to another question—"what's that?" When I further described the sex trafficking industry and the nature of debt-bonded prostitution, I was often met with disbelief, or at the least with the belief that this must be happening to some small number of women in some far-off corner of the earth, or at the least, in some well-known "sex capital," such as Bangkok. Rarely did anyone suspect that over one million women and children are trafficked into prostitution around the world annually, or that, like many Western European countries, the United States is a huge destination site, receiving around 50,000 trafficked women each year.

In fact, there was always something about which friends and colleagues with whom I talked were aghast—from the complexity of criminal networks through which women are trafficked around the world, to the number of both criminal and legitimate profiteers and the size of their profits, to the horrific conditions under which so many women and children trafficked into enslaved prostitution are living.

Sex trafficking is one of a number of structured forms of violence against women and girls that is systematic and universal. Like some, for example, domestic battering or war rape, sex trafficking is typically against some law almost everywhere, but it operates almost everywhere with relative impunity. Moreover, unlike some forms of gender violence, sex trafficking is a huge and highly successful industry, easily rationalized by free market principles. The marketed product, of course, is human, largely female, and typically without agency in the trafficking transaction.

Through this book, I hope to spread the word about the trafficking industry—its sources, operations and structure. There is every indication that the trafficking industry grows stronger each year, and that the recruitment net is widening. Younger and younger girls are being sold, abducted, or duped into internal or international sex markets, where their chances of escape are minimal and their health is continually compromised. The devastation of victims' lives is poignantly reflected in their many stories, often communicated through human rights organizations that have come to their aid.

Because the sources of sex trafficking are economic and patriarchal, and are rooted in traditions that legitimate the exploitation and sexual use of women, the demise of the industry will require social change at many levels. Success in attacking this global problem will also require the commitment and cooperation of people and organizations around the world. Neither change nor commitment is likely to come about until the "what's that?" question becomes obsolete.

Acknowledgments

I give special thanks to my daughter Sheila Farr for her careful reading of my manuscript chapter by chapter, and for her insightful suggestions for improving the text. I used them all! My partner Ivan Clark lived with "the book" from beginning to end, and I am grateful for his willingness to listen to my research and writing frustrations and to talk with me about the pervasive problems of sex trafficking and enslaved prostitution.

I also want to acknowledge the Department of Sociology and the many colleagues at Portland State University who have encouraged and influenced me in my professional development and focus—notably, Don Gibbons, who actively supported and shaped my evolution as a criminologist-sociologist, and whose high standards of scholarship have served me well over the years; and Johanna Brenner, whose leadership of women's studies and dedication to progressive feminism are so inspiring, and whose support of my teaching and research has been steadfast.

Thanks to George Ritzer for his encouragement and direction throughout this project. Thanks also to editors and others at Worth—Valerie Raymond, Worth's sponsoring sociology editor, for seeing that the project ran smoothly; Erik Gilg, her assistant, for his supportive and useful correspondence as the production process got underway; Margaret Comaskey and Sarah Segal from the Production Department, for their attention to the details of typesetting, editing, and proofreading; and to Norma Roche, in whose superior copyediting skills I placed so much confidence. In fact, the entire Worth goup working with me on my book made the production process a pleasurable experience.

Finally, I would like to acknowledge my grandchildren—Cody Farr-Baenziger, Jesse Farr-Baenziger, and Lena Farr-Morrissey—whose joy and enthusiasm for life keeps me on track.

1

Introduction: Size and Scope

Yelena

Struggling to support herself and her daughter on meager earnings that were "not enough to live on," Yelena explained how she left her hometown in Ukraine to go to Yugoslavia, where, an acquaintance had told her, there were restaurant jobs that paid $200 a month. To Yelena, who was barely able to support herself and her young daughter on the $15 or so a month she earned selling newspapers on the street, the job in Yugoslavia seemed almost too good to be true. It was. The acquaintance, she later discovered, was a recruiter for the sex trafficking industry. Yelena left her daughter with her parents and, along with a friend and a third woman, drove with the recruiter to Yugoslavia. "We trusted her," Yelena remembered. "I was a little afraid, but the desire to have a good life was much stronger." Upon their arrival, the recruiter took them to a small, run-down restaurant and introduced them to the proprietor, who let them know that he expected them to work as prostitutes. Yelena and her companions told him that they would not work as prostitutes, and, atypically, he let them go. Fortunate to have escaped this fate, but now in a foreign country without money, the women began to look for legitimate work. Help appeared to come from a man who offered to accompany them to another town where "there were jobs." He took them to the nearby town and moved them into a small apartment where ten other women were already living. This time they were not so lucky. Their seeming benefactor was actually a Yugoslavian trafficker. The other women told Yelena and her friends that they had been imprisoned in the apartment and raped and abused there. "They were crying and afraid," Yelena said. As they talked further, the young women realized that they had all been sold into enslaved prostitution. This was just the first of a dozen or so times Yelena was sold and resold, moved by traffickers from Yugoslavia through Albania and eventually to Italy.[1]

2 Sex Trafficking

Yelena is one of the increasing number of women who are successfully lured by traffickers into the global sex trade. With few jobs available in her home country, she was open to an offer of a "better life" for herself and her daughter. Perhaps, she says in retrospect, she put too much trust in the job referral because it came from someone she knew, and who was from her hometown. Maybe she was naive, or did she, somewhere in the back of her mind, suspect the truth? Whatever her individual motives and thoughts, she found herself captured, not just by an individual recruiter, but ultimately by a multibillion-dollar trafficking industry that relies on a large supply of women for its considerable profits. Yelena's story describes an all-too-familiar scenario, whereby persons with lesser resources, usually from poor or unstable countries, are either taken by force or persuaded to migrate for jobs in a new town, country, or region. They are frequently misled—the job may not exist or, at the least, may be different from what they have been told. The job virtually always includes some kind of exploitation, usually enslaved prostitution, and almost always, deplorable work and living conditions. While many adult men are trafficked for other labor, the exploited in the sex trafficking industry are primarily women and children.

Sex trafficking is a business venture, in which traffickers trade the sexualized bodies of others for money. That is, the commodity is a person, objectified in its sale by one party to another. According to human rights researcher Donna Hughes, sex trafficking includes

> any practice that involves moving people within and across local or national boundaries for the purpose of sexual exploitation. Trafficking may be the result of force, coercion, manipulation, deception, abuse of authority, initial consent, family pressure, past and present family and community violence, economic deprivation, or other conditions of inequality for women and children.[2]

Hughes's description of sex trafficking includes a variety of recruitment situations, from those that involve force or coercion to some in which people do have a modicum of agency—that is, limited or conditional choices in making decisions about their lives, and more specifically, about their work lives.[3] However, Hughes, like most human rights researchers, chooses to focus her definition on the "practice" of sex trafficking. The degree or level of consent given by the commodified person to her trader is an issue, but not the central one; instead, consent is one of several components of recruitment into the trade.

The focus of this book is also on sex trafficking as practice. As such, it examines trafficking both as a *process* (with multiple interactions and transactions) and as an *industry* (with organizational structure and culture). Because women and girls make up the overwhelming majority of persons trafficked for prostitution, they are the commodity of emphasis in this book. Their experiences as commodities are revealed through their personal stories and testimonies. Also investigated are the activities or roles of the trafficker–entrepreneurs, most of whom are men. Finally, there is throughout an exploration of economic class, gender, and ethnicity issues central to an understanding of sex trafficking as both a process and an industry. Such issues are captured in the following research-based propositions:

- An imbalance of power and other resources shapes trafficking patterns, with more powerful and affluent countries serving largely as destination sites, and less powerful and poorer countries as the primary source sites.
- There is some underlying vulnerability in trafficked women and girls that stems from their positioning in their own culture and social structure, as well as their status in the global marketplace.
- Most of the traffickers at the top of the organizational structure are men, and most men who play the better-known trafficking roles are from source countries and/or are identified as part of criminal or underworld groups. Men from more affluent, destination countries and/or with noncriminal identities play lesser-known but important trafficking roles.
- Consumers in both destination and source countries are (mainly) men, but the greater buying power of men from affluent, destination countries makes them primary consumers. These primary consumers help shape the "commodity" in racialized ways.

The sex trafficking industry is voluminous, and it is expanding at an ever-accelerating rate. It operates in a marketplace in which supply and demand are high and risks to the traffickers are low, making it a highly profitable and enduring business.

Size and Scope of Sex Trafficking Around the World

Of the estimated 4 million people who are trafficked around the world each year, over 1 million are trafficked into the sex industry, and the volume just keeps increasing.[4] Some researchers believe that the actual numbers are much higher than these estimates, pointing out that many instances of trafficking across borders go undetected, and that official counts often do not include intracountry trafficking.[5] Also, many women and children are trafficked into indentured or enslaved work *other than* prostitution, but are often victims of sexual abuse or exploitation in the course of their jobs—for example, as domestic workers or factory workers.

Of course, whether it involves humans, drugs, weapons, or something else, estimates of the size and scope of illegal trafficking are tentative at best. But there is a growing body of research, much of it conducted by nongovernmental organizations (NGOs) such as Human Rights Watch and Global Survival Network, on the epidemiology of sex trafficking. We do have more and better data than we did just a decade ago.

Based on the findings from some of this research, Pino Arlacchi of the United Nations recently reported at an international seminar on trafficking that of the at least 1 million or so women who are sex-trafficked to other countries each year, about 225,000 come from Southeast Asia, 200,000 from the former Soviet republics, 150,000 from South Asia, 100,000 from Latin America and the Caribbean, 75,000 from Eastern Europe, and 50,000 or more from Africa.[6] While these totals are on the low end of the many estimates, the proportionate breakdowns are consistent with various regional reports.

Until recently, the most prolific sources of women for the sex trade have been poor, developing countries—especially in South Asia and Southeast Asia—struggling to meet the survival needs of their populations. Since the Soviet Union's collapse in 1991, however, its former republics, as well as other Soviet-dependent Eastern European countries undergoing economic and political transitions, have been supplying women for the sex trade at the fastest-growing rate worldwide. Like developing nations, these transitional countries are increasingly dependent on loans from global funding institutions and need additional revenues to pay back their debt.

Primary destination sites for women trafficked abroad are countries with advanced market economies and relative material affluence, such as the United States, Canada, Japan, and many countries in Western Europe. With the development of sex tourism, a number of developing countries have also become destination sites for the sex trade. In fact, virtually all countries and regions of the world are involved in sex trafficking in some way—the industry is indeed global.

Regional Volume: Some Examples

Women are trafficked for or are currently working abroad in prostitution throughout the world. Examples include

- 100,000 to 200,000 Thai women in prostitution in other countries[7]
- 5,000 Thai women in prostitution in Berlin alone[8]

- 50,000 women from the Dominican Republic in prostitution abroad[9]
- 14,000 Albanian women in prostitution in various European countries[10]
- 35,000 women trafficked for sexual exploitation out of Colombia every year[11]
- 25,000 women trafficked for sexual exploitation out of Bangladesh each year[12]

Destination sites flourish across regions as well. Examples include

- 200,000 Bangladeshi women trafficked for prostitution into Pakistan over the last 10 years, and now brought into Pakistan at a rate of 200 to 400 per month[13]
- 150,000 foreign women in prostitution in Japan,[14] about 90,000 of whom are from Thailand or the Philippines[15]
- 75,000 Brazilian women in prostitution in the European Union countries[16]
- 35,000 former Soviet and Eastern and Central European women in prostitution in Italy[17]
- 1,000 to 2,000 women from the former Soviet states trafficked for prostitution into Israel each year[18]

Regional Growth

Although there is a lack of good, early baseline data (prior to the 1990s) to compare with the present, most researchers agree that human trafficking is the fastest-growing of the trafficking businesses in general, and that sex trafficking is one of the most, if not the most, rapidly growing forms of human trafficking.[19]

Regional data on *increases* in the number of women trafficked from or to particular areas or countries, or working in prostitution in a foreign country, provide evidence of growth and changes in the distribution of the trade:

- The number of Albanian women and girls working as prostitutes in Italy went from 8,000 in 1998 to 20,000 in 2000.[20]
- There was a tenfold increase in the number of Thai women trafficked for prostitution to South Africa between 1997 and 2000.[21]
- An estimated 25,000 women were working in the sex industry in the Dominican Republic in 1986; by 1996, that number had doubled to 50,000.[22]

- According to the International Organization for Migration, the number of women from the Balkans working illegally as prostitutes in other countries "has tripled or quadrupled in the last three to four years" [1996–2000].[23]

Many Western destination countries have experienced increases in the proportion, as well as changes in the source, of foreign prostitutes. Until the 1970s, for example, prostitutes in the Netherlands were largely local women. Since the 1970s, the number of prostitutes in the Netherlands has increased dramatically,[24] sparked in part by a rise in the number of foreign prostitutes. Initially, foreign prostitutes in the Netherlands were mainly from the Philippines, Thailand, Colombia, Brazil, and several African countries. In the 1990s, however, there was an influx of women from the former Soviet republics and other Eastern as well as Central European countries. By the mid-1990s there were an estimated 4,500 prostitutes from this latter region, accounting for 20% of the estimated total of 25,000 prostitutes working in the Netherlands.[25]

The number of women trafficked to the United States for prostitution has also risen throughout the 1990s, and women trafficked for prostitution are thought to account for half or more of the at least 50,000 persons trafficked into the United States annually. Traditionally, Southeast Asia and Latin America were the prominent source regions of foreign prostitutes in the United States. From the mid- to late 1990s, however, the proportion of women from the former Soviet states and other Eastern European countries steadily increased.[26]

Sex Industry Growth

Whereas Thailand probably has the best-known and most extensive sex industry, other countries also have sizable industries. One such country is Israel, where, by the end of 2000, there were some 250 brothels and escort agencies in Tel Aviv alone, up from 150 in 1999.[27] And, according to the Russian Ministry of Interior, there were by 1997 at least 200 sex-related businesses in Moscow.[28] In the United States, immigration officials have identified 250 brothels in 26 cities where known trafficking victims are working as prostitutes.[29] In fact, the sex industry has been expanding in all Western countries that serve as major destinations for foreign, trafficked women, including the United States, Canada, and some Western European nations.[30]

The sex industry is also thriving in many poor, developing countries. Consider the numbers in selected Asian countries:

- 1 to 2 million prostitutes in Nepal,[31] with some 5,000 prostitutes and 200 brothels in Kathmandu alone[32]
- 350,000 Nepalese and Bangladeshi women and girls in prostitution in India, with 60,000 Nepalese and 45,000 Bangladeshis in Bombay alone; 30,000 Bangladeshi women in Calcutta alone[33]
- 100,000 prostitutes in Bangladesh[34]
- 100,000 to 200,000 prostitutes in Vietnam[35]
- 50,000 to 55,000 prostitutes in Cambodia[36]

Even given the wide range in some of the estimates, the data strongly indicate that sex trafficking and the sex trade involve a substantial and continually increasing number of women. The data also suggest that the scope of sex trafficking is expansive, with women and children trafficked to or working in prostitution in distant regions as well as in areas closer to or even in their homelands.

The Personal and the Contextual

While the numbers documenting the size and scope of sex trafficking both from and to various countries are important, they say nothing about the vulnerability of trafficking recruits, or about the conditions under which women emerge as a supply for the trafficking market. The life experiences of women who have become trafficking victims are vividly conveyed through the stories of women such as Yelena, introduced at the beginning of this chapter, struggling to support herself and her daughter and in search of a better life. The conditions under which sex trafficking evolves and thrives are economic, political, and social. While some conditions are local, many are specific to the era of globalization.

Yelena's story reverberates in particular for many women from Ukraine, Russia, and other former Soviet republics. The rapid influx of women from these countries into the global sex trade has occurred during a period of major social change in the region (the 1990s and early 2000s), and the expansion of the traffic originating there is in part an outcome of these changes. Currently the most rapidly expanding source of sex-trafficked women, the region provides a good contextual example of the supply side of sex trafficking.

The Rise of Sex Trafficking from the Former Soviet States

The most recent estimates suggest that as many as 500,000 women from the former Soviet states may be sold into prostitution each year. An estimated 70% of these women are trafficked to Western European countries, and another 15% are sent to the Middle East and Southeast Asia. About 3%, or 5,000, go to the United States and Canada, and the rest are dispersed to Central or Eastern European countries.[37] While half a million women a year certainly qualifies as a sizable number, several human rights and other nongovernmental organizations believe the actual number is much higher.[38]

Clearly, many women from the former Soviet republics (now known as the Newly Independent States, or NIS)[39] are leaving their homelands, searching out employment or other opportunities for a better life in more affluent or stable places.[40] Most commonly, these emigrants exit on temporary visas, often for work identified as "performance" or "entertainment." And countries that are well-known destinations for women trafficked into the sex trade have been reporting increases in visa applications from the NIS region, as indicated in the examples below.

- Although the numbers vary, nongovernmental organizations consistently report that a rising number of Russian and Ukrainian women are trafficked into the United States for prostitution and entertainment jobs.[41] U.S. Immigration and Naturalization Service data show that visa applications from Russia, Ukraine, and Belarus jumped from 3,000 in 1988 to 129,500 in 1992.[42] And, in 1996, the United States granted visas to 124,000 citizens from Russia alone.[43] Some of the increase is accounted for by women coming in on temporary tourist, performer, or fiancée visas and then staying beyond the allotted time. It is through visa overstays that the majority of sex-trafficked women remain in the destination country. In the United States, at least half of illegal immigrants are on visa overstays.[44]
- Many Russian and Ukrainian women are trafficked to Japan on temporary visas and initially or ultimately funneled into the sex industry there. The Japanese Ministry of Justice reports that 22% (n = 22,060)

of the Russians who entered Japan in 1995 came in with entertainment visas—compared to only 2% (n = 17,513) of the Russians who entered Japan in 1989.[45]

- The number of Russian women entering Switzerland has risen consistently during the 1990s; many now enter on "dancer" visas. Switzerland's Federal Ministry of Foreigners reports that between December of 1991 and August of 1992, 5% of all dancer visas issued (n = 1,439) went to Russian citizens. Between August and December of 1995, Russians were issued 19% of all dancer visas (n = 1,613).[46]
- Officials on the German–Polish border report that, of the 681 people apprehended from January to May of 2001 for attempted illegal entry into Germany, 60% were women, primarily from Russia, Ukraine, and Moldova.[47]

Women from the NIS in Foreign Sex Industries: Size and Scope

Overall, women from the NIS have been trafficked into prostitution in at least 50 countries.[48] National estimates of prostitutes in a number of destination countries provide more specific evidence of the large flow of NIS women into foreign sex businesses:

- Over 120,000 Russian women are registered as prostitutes in Turkey.[49]
- According to one Ukrainian source, counting unregistered as well as registered prostitutes, some 6,000 Ukrainian women work as prostitutes in Turkey today.
- Another 3,000 Ukrainian women are in prostitution in Greece, and 1,000 more are in prostitution in the former Yugoslavia.[50]
- In a single case, in 1995, Philippine police arrested between 50 and 100 Russian women who had been trafficked temporarily to Philippine brothels, after which they were to be taken to their final destination in Japan.[51]
- Of the 400 women arrested in brothels in Israel in 2000 and eventually deported by the Israeli government, all but one were citizens of former Soviet countries—46% were from Ukraine, 28% from Russia, and 17% from Moldova.[52] Russian and Ukrainian prostitutes are so prevalent in Israel that prostitutes there are often simply referred to as "Natasha."[53]
- An estimated 15,000 women from the NIS and Eastern Europe work in the red-light, or brothel, districts of Germany.[54]

Again, the surge of sex trafficking from Russia, Ukraine, and other of the NIS has largely occurred since the breakup of the Soviet Union in 1991. This is not, many have argued, coincidental. Rather, there appears to be a strong association between the Soviet collapse, resultant conditions and changes in the former republics, and the growth in the sex trafficking of women from the region.

Collapse of the Soviet Union and Economic Transition

The sudden demise of the Soviet Union left more than a few cracks in the infrastructures of its republics. Economic decline has been massive. In Russia alone, at the end of the 1990s, the government owed its people "billions of dollars" in unpaid wages and salaries.[55] Without government subsidies, many businesses there have simply shut down, and from 1991 to 1995, Russia's Gross Domestic Product (GDP) declined by 34%.[56] As their state-run economies collapsed and their socialist governments toppled, the former Soviet republics began an uneven transition toward market economies, becoming increasingly dependent on capitalist subsidizers—global lending institutions such as the World Bank and the International Monetary Fund. The buildup of debt added to the sense of dependence and actual loss of self-sufficiency. In addition, an already active underground, criminal economy began to thrive. As researcher Donna Hughes points out, by 1995, the "shadow economy," consisting of "privatized, criminal businesses," made up 50% of the Ukrainian economy.[57] Among the more lucrative of these criminal businesses is sex trafficking.

Decline in the Status of Women and Vulnerability to Traffickers

Although there is some disagreement about the overall status of women in the Soviet Union, it is generally agreed that they have been an important part of the industrial, and even professional, labor market.[58] There is also considerable agreement that in the post-Soviet period, the status of women has worsened.[59] Author Rosalind Marsh argues that although there was legitimate "ambivalence" regarding gender equality during the Soviet period, by the mid-1990s, it had "become clear that the economic crisis, nationalist revival and desire for de-Sovietization [had] led in most of the new states to" a notably "conservative reaction against women."[60] In fact,

Marsh continues, in 1993 the official TASS News Agency reported the finding of a Supreme Soviet discussion group that the "position of women is deteriorating in all spheres of public life."[61]

Through the initial collapse and into the ongoing transitional period, women in the NIS have experienced economic decline. Of those in the NIS who lost their jobs in the first few years following the Soviet breakup, an estimated 80% were women.[62] In Russia, between 1990 and 1995, 7.6 million jobs held by women were eliminated, a loss of about 20%. During the same period, the number of male-held jobs declined by only 1.6%.[63] Women's share of unemployment in the NIS was also far greater than that of men. As of 1999, women accounted for 60% of the unemployed, and 90% of the newly unemployed, in Ukraine.[64] In Russia, by the late 1990s, women accounted for over 70% of the officially unemployed.[65] And, from 1985 to 1997, female employment dropped in the Baltic states—by 33% in Latvia, 31% in Estonia, and 24% in Lithuania.[66]

At the end of the 1980s, women's wages in the Soviet republics were some 20% to 30% below those of men. Wage differentials between women and men widened as the republics gained independence and adopted market economies, or at least privatized parts of their economies. In Russia, the widening was dramatic: women's wages went from 70% of men's in 1989 to 40% of men's in 1995.[67] The growing wage gap during the transition appears to be due in part to the greater retention of male-dominated industries, as well as to better job opportunities for men in the private, market economy.[68] One view is that the new market system has facilitated "the aggressive re-masculinization of post-Soviet Russia,"[69] a phenomenon that applies to other NIS as well.

In that context, consider that while the educational rates of women in Russia, Ukraine, and other NIS tend to be the same as or higher than those of men, education does not appear to benefit women in the job market, at least when compared to men. In Ukraine, for example, women account for 60% of workers with higher education, yet their average wage is 29% lower than that of men.[70]

Contributors to Sex Trafficking from a Region in Transition: Conclusions

The transition forced by the Soviet breakup contributed to the rise of the former Soviet republics as important source countries for the sex trade. The move to a market economy, subsidized by global funding entities, has created debt and obligation. Economic and general resource losses have devastated the countries generally, and women's status even more so. Increasing numbers of educated women are seeking work outside the country and, as such, are vulnerable to traffickers. The breakdown in governing infrastructures has provided an opportunity for organized crime groups to become more powerful and to expand their illegal businesses to include trafficking in humans—sex trafficking in particular.

The post-Soviet transition serves as an introduction to the ways in which local and global conditions intertwine to contribute to the rise in the potential supply for sex trafficking. Although conditions in the various source countries and regions vary, they virtually always include economic adversity and political instability, along with globalization policies that don't always work in the (source) countries' best interests and which sometimes actually encourage sex trafficking.

While the level and nature of involvement also vary, virtually all countries today participate in sex trafficking. Women and girls are trafficked daily in a plethora of directions—within countries, to and from neighboring countries, and across countries and regions. It is a money-making industry for traffickers, whose networks continue to expand, allowing more and more people to cash in on the trade.

Coming Up

This chapter began by noting the increasingly high volume and wide scope of the sex trafficking industry. Evidence was provided of a sizable and growing industry across regions, wherein women and children are trafficked into prostitution around the world, often being moved from poorer source or sending countries to better-off destination or receiving countries. The fastest-growing source region—the former Soviet states—served as an introductory, contextual example of the supply side of sex trafficking.

Chapter 2 begins with a look at profits in the sex trafficking industry and then describes how debt bondage, a system central to the global sex trade, helps maximize profits by cutting costs and reducing risks to the traffickers. Living and working conditions for women in enslaved prostitution under the debt bondage system are also discussed.

In Chapter 3, the spotlight is on the trafficking industry, including various trafficker roles and the networks through which the industry operates both locally and globally. Also investigated is the complicity in sex trafficking of "corrupt guardians" such as law enforcement officers and immigration officials, as well as legitimate private sector operators such as travel agents. Chapter 4 examines the involvement in sex trafficking of various organized criminal groups, ranging from established and newer mafias to loosely organized small groups. Connections among as well as differences between organized criminal groups across regions are also explored in this chapter.

Having looked at the system of sex trafficking and enslaved prostitution, along with the trafficking industry and criminal groups within it, Chapter 5 comes back to the analytical task, expanding the discussion of economic conditions introduced and illustrated in the case of the Soviet transition in Chapter 1, and providing context for the stories of trafficked women and girls. It examines in greater depth macrolevel factors that have contributed to the supply side of sex trafficking and shaped the roles that particular countries play in the sex trafficking industry. These factors include globalization trends and policies as well as local levels of human, economic, and gender development.

In Chapter 6, the demand side of the sex trade is explored, first with a look at the history and currency of rape and sexual enslavement during wars, as well as male socialization into the military that prepares men for and normalizes violence against women during wartime. The chapter also offers examples of patriarchal belief systems across cultures that rationalize and legitimate male domination of women and control of female sexuality.

Chapter 7 follows from Chapter 6, looking backward to the historical organization of recreational prostitution for military troops and ways in which militarized prostitution in modern wars—World War II, the Korean War, and the Vietnam War—contributed to sex industrialization and sex trafficking, especially in Southeast and East Asian countries. Finally, the chapter takes a look at what I call congregational prostitution: the building of a sex industry wherever large numbers of men congregate to work or accomplish particular tasks.

Chapter 8 lays out some of the consequences and complications for women and children trafficked into the sex industry. These include problems due to legal policies and laws (or the lack thereof); health risks and realities, most notably HIV/AIDS and other STDs; and the special perils for the increasing number of very young children trafficked into the sex industry. The final part of the chapter provides examples of strategies and programs aimed at curbing sex trafficking and offers recommendations for future actions to this end.

Notes

1. As reported by Dave Montgomery (2001), "Dreams of Better Life End in a Nightmare of Sexual Slavery," Knight Ridder/Tribune, January 3.
2. Donna M. Hughes (2000), "The 'Natasha' Trade: The Transnational Shadow Market of Trafficking in Women," *Journal of International Affairs*, Special Issue: "In the Shadows: Promoting Prosperity or Undermining Stability?" 53 (Spring), p. 626 (pp. 625–651). Also, for a discussion of definitional variations that reflect the framing of trafficking (e.g., moral problem, criminal problem, human rights problem, labor issue), see Foundation of Women's Forum/Stiftelsen Kvinnoforum (1998), *Trafficking in Women for the Purpose of Sexual Exploitation: Mapping the Situation and Existing Organisations Working in Belarus, Russia, the Baltic and Nordic States* (Stockholm: Swedish Ministry for Foreign Affairs).
3. There is an ongoing feminist controversy over whether sex work should be viewed as a job choice that some women freely make (advocates of the "choice" point of view refer to women in the sex trade as sex workers), or as violence against women (advocates of the "violence" point of view refer to women in the sex trade as prostituted women). For a discussion of the issues and a critique of the "prostitution as violence against women" perspective, see Jo Doezema (1998), "Forced to Choose: Beyond the Voluntary v. Forced Prostitution Dichotomy," pp. 34–50 in *Global Sex Workers: Rights, Resistance, and Redefinition*, ed. by J. Kempadoo and J. Doezema (New York: Routledge). For classic "prostitution and pornography as violence against women" points of view, see Andrea Dworkin (1987), *Intercourse* (New York: Free Press); Andrea Dworkin and Katharine MacKinnon (1988), *Pornography and Civil Rights: A New Day for Women's Equality* (Minneapolis, MN: Organizing Against Pornography); Kathleen Barry (1995), *The Prostitution of Sexuality: The Global Exploitation of Women* (New York: New York University Press).

   In this book, the terms "prostitute," "sex worker," and "worker in the sex industry" are used interchangeably, with all referring to someone who trades sex (intercourse or otherwise) for money, whether voluntarily or coerced.
4. International Organization for Migration (2001), "New IOM Figures on the Global Scale of Trafficking." *Trafficking in Migrants: Quarterly Bulletin* 23 (April) (Geneva), available at http://www.uri.edu.artsci.wms/hughes.htm; Hughes (2000), op. cit.; Amy O'Neill Richard (1999), *International Trafficking in Women to the United States: A Contemporary Manifestation of Slavery and Organized Crime* (November), DCI Exceptional Intelligence Analyst Program: An Intelligence Monograph (Cen-

ter for the Study of Intelligence); Gillian Caldwell, Steven Galster, and Nadia Steinzor (1997), "Crime and Servitude: An Exposé of the Traffic in Women for Prostitution from the Newly Independent States," report presented at conference on "The Trafficking of Women Abroad" (Washington D.C.: Global Survival Network).

5. Ji Hyun Lim (2002), "FBI Busts Korean American Sex Trafficking Ring," *Asian Week*, August 9, available at http://www.asianweek.com/2002_08_09/bay_sextrafficking.html (3 pp.); Richard (1999), op. cit.
6. Francis T. Miko, with assistance of Grace (Jea-Hyun) Park (2000), "Trafficking in Women and Children: The U.S. and International Response," Congressional Research Service Report 98-649 C (May 10), International Information Programs, U.S. Department of State, available at http://usinfo.state.gov/topical/global/traffic/crs0510.htm (11 pp.).
7. Lin Lean Lim (1998), *The Sex Sector: The Economic and Social Bases of Prostitution in Southeast Asia* (Geneva: International Labour Office).
8. Corie Hammers (2001), "International Trafficking in Women in the Asian Region in the Era of Globalization," unpublished master's thesis, Portland State University, Portland, OR.
9. International Organization for Migration (1996), "Trafficking in Women from the Dominican Republic for Sexual Exploitation" (June) (Budapest: Migration Information Programme).
10. "More than 14,000 Albanians Work as Prostitutes in Europe" (1998), Agence France Presse, July 18.
11. Timothy Pratt (2001), "Sex Slavery Racket a Growing Concern in Latin America," *The Christian Science Monitor*, January 11, available at http://www.csmonitor.com/durable/2001/01/11/p7s.htm.
12. Rokshana Yesmin (2001), "Rehabilitating Trafficked Women," *Independent Bangladesh*, September 7. [Cited in The Protection Project (2002), *Human Rights Report on Trafficking in Persons, Especially Women and Children: A Country-by-Country Report on a Contemporary Form of Slavery*, 2nd ed., "Bangladesh," p. 42 (The Paul H. Nitze School of Advanced International Studies, Johns Hopkins University).]
13. Ibid.; Indrani Sinha (retrieved November 5, 2002), paper on "Globalization and Human Rights," SANLAAP India, available at http://www.uri.edu/artsci/wms/hughest/pakistan.htm.
14. Miko (2000), op. cit.
15. Caldwell et al. (1997), op. cit.
16. Isabel Murray (2000), "Sex Slavery: One Woman's Story," BBC News, December 12, available at http://news.bbc.co.uk/hi/english/world/americas/newsid_1067000/0167533.stm.
17. Melanie Orhant (2001), "Sex Trade Enslaves East Europeans," *Stop-traffic*, available at http://fpmail.friends-partners.org/pipermail/stop-traffic.

18. Miko (2000), op. cit.
19. Orhant (2001), op. cit.; Miko (2000), op. cit.; Vanessa von Struensee (2000), "Globalized, Wired, Sex Trafficking in Women and Children," *Murdoch University Electronic Journal of Law* 7 (June), available at http://www.murdoch.edu.au/elaw/issues/v7n2/struensee72_text.html (14 pp.); Michael Specter (1998), "Traffickers' New Cargo: Naive Slavic Women," *The New York Times*, January 11, pp. 1, 6.
20. The Protection Project (2002), op. cit., "Albania," pp. 5–6.
21. "Thai Women Rescued from Abroad" (2000), *Nation* (Bangkok), November 30.
22. Kamala Kempadoo (1999), "Continuities and Change: Five Centuries of Prostitution in the Caribbean," pp. 3–33 in *Sun, Sex and Gold: Tourism and Sex Work in the Caribbean*, ed. by K. Kempadoo (Lanham, MD: Rowman & Littlefield).
23. Orhant (2001), op. cit.
24. Gerben J. N. Bruinsma and Guus Meershoek (1999), "Organized Crime and Trafficking in Women from Eastern Europe in the Netherlands," pp. 105–117 in *Illegal Immigration and Commercial Sex: The New Slave Trade*, ed. by Phil Williams (London/Portland, OR: Frank Cass).
25. Ibid.
26. Richard (1999), op. cit.
27. The Protection Project (2002), op. cit., "Israel," pp. 267–268.
28. Caldwell et al. (1997), op. cit.
29. Duncan Campbell (2000), "Young Girls Sold as Sex Slaves in US, CIA Says," *The Guardian*, April 3, available at http://www.guardian.co.uk/international/story/0,3604,178485,00.html (3 pp.).
30. Richard (1999), op. cit.
31. S. M. Tumbahamphe and B. Bhattarai (retrieved November 1, 2002), "Trafficking of Women in South Asia," ANNFSU-Asian Students Association, available at http://www.ecouncil.ac.cr/about/contrib/women/youth/english/traffic1.htm.
32. Ibid.
33. Coalition Against Trafficking in Women—Asia Pacific (retrieved October 31, 2002), "Trafficking in Women and Prostitution in the Asian Pacific," Available at http://www.catwinternational.org/fb/html.
34. Hammers (2001), op. cit.
35. "Japan Gives 3.6 Million Dollars to Fight AIDS in Vietnam" (2000), Agence France Press, June 27; Coalition Against Trafficking in Women—Asia Pacific (2002), op. cit.
36. Perla Aragon-Choudhury (2001), "Successful (Uphill) Battle Against Exploiting Women," *Business World* 28 (September). [Cited in The Protection Project (2002), op. cit., "Cambodia," p. 97.]

37. Margaret Coker (2001), "Russian Women Prime Cargo for International Trafficking Operations," Cox News Service, March 10; Miko (2000), op. cit.; Specter (1998), op. cit.; Caldwell et al. (1997), op. cit.
38. International Organization for Migration (2001), op. cit. Also, recognizing the typical undercounting of illegal migration and trafficking, some researchers feel quite certain that the numbers are higher than the official estimates, but few actually commit to a new estimated number.
39. The 15 former Soviet republics now referred to as the Newly Independent States (NIS) are Russia, Ukraine, Belarus, Moldova, Tajikistan, Kyrgyzstan, Uzbekistan, Turkmenistan, Kazakhstan, Azerbaijan, Armenia, Georgia, Latvia, Lithuania, and Estonia. The evolution of the NIS will be discussed in greater detail in Chapter 5.
40. The National Bureau of Statistics of Russia. [Cited in Elena Tiuriukanova (1997), "Women in Search of Jobs Abroad: Female Labour Migration from Russia," *Valday-96, Proceedings of the First Summer School on Women's and Gender Studies in Russia* (Moscow).]
41. Gillian Caldwell, Steve Galster, Jyothi Kanics, and Nadia Steinzor (1999), "Capitalizing on Transition Economies: The Role of the Russian Mafiya in Trafficking Women for Forced Prostitution," pp. 42–73 in *Illegal Immigration and Commercial Sex: The New Slave Trade*, ed. by Phil Williams (London/Portland, OR: Frank Cass).
42. Victoria Pope (1997), "Trafficking in Women: Procuring Russians for Sex Abroad—Even in America," *U.S. News and World Report*, April 7, available at http://www.globalsurvival.net/other/usnews/9704.html (5 pp.).
43. Caldwell et al. (1997), op. cit., p. 14.
44. Dutch Foundation Against Trafficking in Women (STV)/La Strada Program (1996), "One Year La Strada: Results of the First Central and East European Program on Prevention of Trafficking in Women" (September 13).
45. "Number of Russians Who Entered Japan 1989–1995" (1996), Japanese Ministry of Justice. [Cited in Caldwell et al. (1999), op. cit., p. 46.]
46. "Effectif des danseuses (artistes de variétés), par nationalite et cantoni" (1995), Federal Ministry for Foreigners, Switzerland (December). [Cited in Caldwell et al. (1999), op. cit., p. 45.]
47. Roger Cohen (2000), "The Oldest Profession Seeks New Market in Western Europe," *The New York Times*, September 19.
48. MiraMed Institute (1999), "Who is Trafficking CIS Women?" *Preliminary Report on Trafficking in the CIS* (June), Moscow.
49. International Organization for Migration (1995), "Trafficking and Prostitution: The Growing Exploitation of Migrant Women from Central and Eastern Europe" (May) (Geneva: Migration Information Programme).

50. "Ukraine Cracks Down on Sexual Slavery," Part II (1998), Newsline 2, April 14 (Prague, Czech Republic: Radio Free Europe/Radio Liberty).
51. "Ukrainian Woman Says Russian Prostitutes Working in Philippines" (1995), Deutsche Presse-Agentur (July).
52. "Trafficking in Persons for the Purpose of Prostitution in Israel" (2001), Hotline for Migrant Workers (June). [Cited in The Protection Project (2002), op. cit., "Israel," p. 268.]
53. Hughes (2000), op. cit.
54. Caldwell et al. (1997), op. cit.
55. Ibid.
56. Janet Guttman (1997), "Russian Economic Problems Remain After IMF Handout," Reuters, February 9.
57. Hughes (2000), op. cit.
58. Suzanne LaFont (1999), "Male Economies and the Status of Women in the Post-Communist Countries," available at http://geocities.com/suzannelafont/eewomen.htm (9 pp.).
59. Ibid.; Lynne Attwood (1996), "The Post-Soviet Woman in the Move to the Market: A Return to Domesticity and Dependence?" pp. 255–266 in *Women and Ukraine*, ed. by Rosalind Marsh (Cambridge: Cambridge University Press); Rosalind Marsh (1996), "Introduction: Women's Studies and Women's Issues in Russia, Ukraine and the Post-Soviet States," pp. 1–28 in *Women and Ukraine*, ed. by Rosalind Marsh (Cambridge: Cambridge University Press);
60. Marsh (1996), op. cit., p. 19.
61. Ibid., p. 19.
62. Human Rights Watch (1999), "Russia: Too Little, Too Late: State Response to Violence Against Women," Human Rights Watch Report 9; Caldwell et al. (1997), op. cit.
63. "Rossiya v Tsifrakh (Russia in Statistics)" (1995), Goskomstat, p. 44. [Cited in Human Rights Watch (1999), op. cit., p. 9.]
64. International Organization for Migration (1998), "Information Campaign Against Trafficking in Women from Ukraine," Project Report (July).
65. Marsh (1996), op. cit., p. 13; Sergei Strokan (1995), "Russia: NGOs Condemn Sexual Discrimination in the Moscow Workplace," Inter Press Service, November 3, p. 3.
66. Jennifer Hahn, Robert Sklar, and Lillian Awidi (contacts) (2000), "International Status Report: Women's Share of Paid Employment Increases in Most Regions of the World," UNIFEM—Progress of the World's Women Report (June 1), available at http://www.unifem.undp.org/progressww/pr_progress1.html.
67. Swanee Hunt (1998), "For East Bloc Women, A Dearth of Democracy," *International Herald Tribune*, July 7.

68. Ewa Ruminska (2002), "Gender Differences in Changes on the Labour Market in Transition Countries," Working Paper No. 3, Conference of European Statisticians, Statistical Commission and Economic Commission for Europe, Geneva, Switzerland, September 23–25.
69. Attwood (1996), op. cit.
70. Ukraine Report for UNICEF (2000). [Cited in Ruminska (2002), op. cit.] This is also true in the United States, where both high school and college graduation rates are higher for women than for men (see U.S. Census data, 2000).

2

Industry Profits and Debt Bondage, or How Traffickers Make Money from Modern-Day Slavery

The trafficking of women and girls into prostitution is profitable for many participants—criminal gangs and club owners can make a bundle; mid-level traffickers, such as recruiters, can make a good, steady income; desperately poor families may be able to stave off starvation for a short time with the small sum they receive for the sale of a daughter. Least likely to profit are the women and girls who are trafficked into the sex trade. The trafficking system relies heavily for its profits on excessive charges that become the trafficked woman's "debt," a sum that often takes up a good portion, or even all, of the money she earns in the sex trade. In this chapter, we take a look at profits in sex trafficking, as well as the debt bondage system that helps ensure those profits. Just how profitable is this industry? And how are women and girls exploited for profit maximization?

Industry-Wide Profits and Safeguards

Human trafficking is now the third most profitable of the illegal trafficking industries, behind only that of drugs and arms. Both the U.N. and the International Organization for Migration report that human trafficking brings in at least $7 billion in profits annually.[1] Other groups believe that the yearly profit is much larger—at least $12 billion, and maybe more.[2]

At first glance, even the higher estimates pale next to the U.N. estimate of annual drug trafficking profits at $400 billion (equal to 8% of the world's trade),[3] or the estimated yearly $56 billion profits from international arms trafficking.[4] But several points are worth noting. To begin with, some believe that the U.N. estimate of the worth of the illegal drug trafficking industry is grossly exaggerated. One source, for example, suggests that yearly illegal drug profits are more likely around $150 billion—a value that is about half that of the pharmaceutical industry and less than that of either the alcohol industry (at $252 billion) or the tobacco industry (at $204 billion).[5] Others emphasize the potential of the expanding human trafficking industry, pointing out that sex trafficking is the most rapidly growing form of human trafficking, and that its profits may surpass those from other trafficking enterprises in the not too distant future.

Because of the positive cash flow in sex trafficking, criminal groups are depending more heavily on profits from it than on those from other illegal activities, including drug trafficking.[6] The potential in sex trafficking stems in part from the low cost and reusable nature of the commodity itself. As Phil Williams points out in his economic analysis of sex trafficking, there are "few other criminal activities in which the profit to cost ratio is so high."[7] Once brought into the trade (and often there is no initial purchase cost for traffickers), women are frequently resold several times, with each sale bringing in a new profit.

Additionally, the debt bondage system requires the woman to pay back the trafficker for her travel, job arrangements, and various other fees—all at highly inflated prices. The trafficked woman can also be used to bring in profits from activities related to prostitution. According to the Women's Information Center in Zurich, for example, women working as prostitutes or hostesses in bars and clubs there are expected to generate at least $10,000 per month in the sale of alcohol.[8] Or the woman can be used as payment-in-kind—for example, by requiring her to provide sex to corrupt immigration or law enforcement officials as a payoff for "looking the other way."

Another benefit is the remarkable stability of the sex market. Whether the economy is up or down, across regions, the sex market remains consistently strong. As Global Survival Network found, "Although total net earnings may not compare with profits from . . . [other] criminal activity, it [the sex trade] is a stable industry that endures through good and bad economic times."[9] Demand does not seem to decline, and customers appear to be willing to pay the going price, again regardless of the state of the economy. Also, the market is proliferating, expanding beyond club and brothel prostitution. Related businesses, such as those that provide mail-order brides, women for rent, and sex tours, have taken off around the world. The consumer market has expanded through exposure to the Internet, where photographs and profiles of literally thousands of women and a vast array of sex tourism sites can be viewed.[10]

The viability of sex trafficking is also enhanced by the fact that the risks to traffickers are so low.[11] The trafficked women—in a foreign country, often without documentation, unable to speak the language, unfamiliar with the culture, and at risk of being arrested—are at the mercy of the traffickers.[12] And should they try to rebel, their captor uses his or her greater power, including violence or the threat of violence, to keep them in place.

Laws against sex trafficking in most countries tend to be uneven (some, but not all, parts of the sex trade are conditionally legal), vague, or nonexistent.[13] When cases are pursued and arrests are actually made, convictions are often difficult to obtain, and for those traffickers who are convicted, sentences are minimal. As a British police officer put it:

> If you get caught smuggling cocaine, you're looking at 20 years. If you smuggle women, the profits can be just as high and if you get caught the only thing you're looking at is living off immoral earnings. If you're a criminal, the choice about which to go for is pretty simple.[14]

Furthermore, trafficking cases are often complex, requiring law enforcement or court resources that may not be available, even in affluent countries. In fact, in a recent report, the CIA pointed out that the "low penalties and the long, complicated and resource-intensive nature of trafficking cases tends to make them unattractive to many United States attorneys."[15]

Finally, unlike the illegal trafficking of other products, most notably drugs, the trafficking of women and girls has garnered little public attention. Law enforcement officials in some cities or states recognize the problem, but feel they are simply ill-equipped to deal with it. Other law enforcement bodies see sex trafficking, if they see it at all, as a low-priority problem.[16] The U.S. government continues to fight a war on drugs with a relatively large budget, along with presidential authority to place economic sanctions on the largely poor countries perceived as unresponsive to its antidrug policies. The focus in the U.S. war on drugs is largely on the supply, in spite of the fact that the United States itself is the biggest consumer of illegal drugs. What little the United States may be doing to curb sex trafficking is also focused on the supply rather than the demand. However, an aggressive war to reduce either the supply or the demand for sex trafficking, or to try to disable the industry in any substantial way, has not been forthcoming.

Regional Profits

For many countries, the sex trade is a critical part of the national economy. Consider these figures:

- The International Labour Organization estimates that the sex trade now accounts for somewhere between 2% and 14% of the GDP in Indonesia, Malaysia, the Philippines, and Thailand.[17]
- Annual profits from the sex trade in Cambodia are reportedly about $511 million;[18] in Japan, the estimate is $400 million,[19] and in Israel it is $450 million.[20]
- According to a Thai economist, even using conservative figures, Thai sex workers in Japan produce at least $3.3 billion annual gross income, a very small part of which actually goes to the sex workers themselves.[21]

In cases investigated in the United States, sex traffickers have made between $1 and $8 million in time periods ranging from 1 to 8 years.[22] In one such operation, the Cadena gang, a family group of Mexican sex traffickers, made about $2.5 million in a 2-year period in the mid-1990s from the prostitution of 25 to 40 Latina women they trafficked to the United States and put up in brothels in Florida and neighboring states. According to Lou DeBaca, a prosecuting attorney for the U.S. Justice Department, the men who ran the business "tapped into the American dream and perverted it."[23] The four Cadena brothers grew up in poverty in Mexican villages like those from which many of their victims came. The brothers were joined by other family members, and together they created a thriving trafficking and prostitution business in the United States. As word of their success as "businessmen" spread, they were able to persuade some families that they could help their daughters earn quick money from legitimate jobs in the United States. Immediately after being brought into the United States, the young women were enslaved in one or another of the brothels owned by the Cadena family. Eventually, several women escaped and alerted the police. Between November of 1997 and February of 1998, raids by the U.S. Border Patrol resulted in the closure of three Cadena brothels; another three had been abandoned by the time the Border Patrol arrived. Rogerio Cadena, the bothers' uncle, was arrested in 1998 in Florida (while mowing the lawn at one of the family brothels!). Rogerio was ultimately convicted and sentenced to 15 years in prison, but most family members have not been prosecuted and continue to prosper, investing their prostitution money in real estate and other ventures.[24]

Also in the United States, a group of Thai traffickers took in $1.5 million in a little over a year from a brothel in New York, where they prostituted Thai women. And one Thai broker reported to investigators that he made about $215,000 over a 2-year period by selling women to brothel owners for anywhere from $700 to $1,500 apiece.[25]

In Israel, a big destination site for Russian and Ukrainian women, Israeli police say the problem of sex trafficking is out of control because of the money to be made from it. Yitzhak Tyler, the chief of undercover law enforcement in the port town of Haifa, laments, "We've got a hell of a problem on our hands." Haifa has become a favorite point of entry for bringing women into Israel for prostitution. Tyler says that sex trafficking is "a sophisticated, global operation," and although he views it as "evil," he recognizes that "it's successful because the money is so good. . . . Do you understand what I am telling you? They will buy these women and make a fortune out of them."[26] The Haifa undercover unit estimates that even small brothels make over $200,000 a month, and a single person sometimes owns four or five of these businesses. Tyler adds: "No taxes, no real overhead. It's a factory with slave labor. And we've got them all over Israel."[27] There appears to be a never-ending flow of customers in Israel; in addition to Israeli citizens, the country has about 250,000 foreign male workers, the great majority of whom are single or are living and working in Israel without their wives and families. Israeli police estimate that there are about 25,000 paid sexual transactions in the country every day.[28]

Sex trafficking is very profitable for traffickers from high-volume source countries as well as brothel owners in destination sites. Mikhail Lebed, the chief of criminal investigations for the Ukrainian Interior Ministry, also expressed concern: "We have a very serious problem here and we are simply not equipped to solve it by ourselves. . . . It is a human tragedy, but also, frankly, a national crisis. Gangsters make more from [trafficking] these women in a week than we have in our law enforcement budget for the whole year. To be honest, unless we get some help we are not going to stop it."[29]

Net profit per woman can vary substantially. According to one study, a Russian or Ukrainian woman earns for her pimp between $50,000 and $100,000 a year in Israel.[30] Brothel owners in Cambodia report earning less, an average of about $40,000 a year for each prostituted woman.[31] At the high end, a Kosovar pimp testified that he was making $9,000 per night from three young Kosovar girls he was prostituting in Switzerland.[32] And police in the Netherlands found that one criminal organization trafficking women from Ukraine to the Netherlands earned about $144,000 a year per woman, with profits split between several high-level members.[33]

Profits in the sex trafficking industry depend heavily on the debt bondage system, which has many women working with little or no pay under what they often see as an inescapable contract—albeit one they may never have actually seen, let alone signed.

The Debt Bondage System

An estimated 27 million people around the world today are living under some form of slavery, and the great majority, including most women trafficked for prostitution, are victims of debt bondage (or contract) slavery.[34] Prohibited under international law, debt bondage involves "a situation in which debtors pledge their personal services against a debt they owe, but the person to whom they owe it fails to deduct the value of their services from the debt, or the length and nature of those services are not respectively limited and defined."[35]

Debt bondage in sex trafficking most commonly develops as follows: A woman hears (through word of mouth, or from a particular individual) or reads (e.g., in a newspaper advertisement or an employment agency brochure) about job opportunities abroad for young women. Typically, the jobs call for "nannies" or domestic workers, restaurant workers, dancers, or entertainers. The recruiter convinces the potential recruit that the job is legitimate and may even offer her a contract. (S)he will also help her get a passport or visa and take care of her travel arrangements.

The great majority of recruits do not know that they are actually being trafficked for prostitution, and virtually none of them are aware of the enslaved conditions under which they will live and work.[36] In their interviews with Nepali girls who had been trafficked into prostitution in India, for example, Human Rights Watch–Asia found that in all cases, the girls had expected legitimate jobs, but upon arrival had been told by their brothel bosses that they would have to work as prostitutes in order to pay off their debts.[37] Across the world in Brazil, according to one study, 95% of the women trafficked out of the country for prostitution had been deceived about the nature of the job that awaited them and about the living and working conditions at their destination.[38] And, according to prominent sex trafficking researcher Donna Hughes, most—at least three-fourths—of women trafficked out of the Newly Independent States (NIS) into the sex trade have not known that they would be forced to work as prostitutes.[39]

"Neela's" situation is typical of that of many young Nepali girls who believe they are being taken to a legitimate job. Neela was only 14 in 1989 when she went from her village to Kathmandu, where a friend of her stepfather had gotten her a job in a carpet factory. When she had been working in the factory for several months, she was introduced to a male factory worker, who, she was told, was her cousin. This "cousin" convinced Neela that there were better, more lucrative jobs in a town just across the Indian border. With her stepfather's agreement, she went with the "cousin," who took her to Bombay (instead of the border town) and left her in a house with two women; from there she was moved by someone else to another house, where 16 to 18 other young girls were living. She was told that she had been sold to a brothel owner for $500 and that she would be working as a prostitute to pay off her debt. All the money she earned went to the brothel owner, and she was never told how long she would have to work in order to repay her debt. She worked in the brothel for about a year, until she was arrested in a police raid. At the shelter for children to which she was subsequently taken, she tested positive for HIV.[40]

Many of the youngest girls from the poorest countries are told almost nothing about the terms of their debt. The first and last they may hear is the alleged price for which they were purchased. "Sita," another Nepali girl trafficked to India, was told upon her arrival that she owed the brothel owner her purchase price of $666, and would have to work as a prostitute to pay it off. She was kept in the same brothel for 10 years, and never was told that she had satisfied her debt.[41] Similarly, upon escaping from the brothel in Guatemala City to which she had been trafficked, a young Nicaraguan girl told the Nicaraguan police that when the girls in her brothel asked about their debt and earnings, the owner "never told us anything. He never said 'this is how much is left, this is yours, you earned this' or anything."[42]

"Santhi," yet another Nepali girl trafficked into prostitution in India, was not told her purchase price, but each of several times she was resold, she was told it was for more money, and thus her debt increased at each new establishment. Santhi had heard somewhere that the brothel could keep a girl there for only 3 years, after which she would be paid Rs 20,000 (about $666), along with gold and clothing items. But she was kept in brothels for 9 years, surviving mainly on tips, before the brothel owner told her she could leave. When she left, she was paid Rs 5,000 (about $166), which she gave to her father who came to take her home.[43]

Debt Amounts

Debt amounts tend to be far above the actual costs incurred by the traffickers. The debt typically includes not only transportation fares, but also various trafficking costs, such as a job finding fee, a broker payment, or a travel escort payment. Also incorporated into the woman's debt, or taken separately from her earnings, are room and board costs, and sometimes medical insurance or a "protection" fee (many brothels employ guards, ostensibly to protect the women from the police and abusive customers). Fines for violation of a host of rules also deplete her wages. If she is given a contract, it is usually incomplete or misleading. Sometimes, the recruit is told in advance that she will be charged for her travel costs. She may be asked for money up front, or she may be told that she can pay for her travel after she arrives at her destination. If she is told she can pay later, the estimated amount is often understated.

Southeast Asian women trafficked to Japan, the United States, and Canada tend to have particularly high debts. Almost all (95%) of a sample of 171 Thai women who had been trafficked to Japan had acquired debts of over $24,000. In most cases, the women had been misled about the amount of money they would owe or about the terms of the payoff. One of the women, Phan, was told prior to the trip that she would owe a debt of about $4,000 for her travel and job arrangements, and that it would take her only a couple of months to pay it off. Phan said: "I saw so many other girls going to Japan, so I agreed." After she was settled in Japan, she was told that her debt was almost $30,000. Another interviewee was misled by recruiters about currency values, and although she was told beforehand that she would have a debt upon arriving in Japan, her understanding was that it would be about $1,200, instead of the actual $26,000. None of the women "had fully understood the economics of the situation they were entering, nor had any clear idea of the kind of conditions they would face."[44]

In another study of Asian women trafficked into the sex trade in Japan, the average debt was $35,000, but women had accumulated debts as high as $300,000.[45]

Thai women trafficked to the United States for sex work have been burdened with debts of up to $40,000.[46] In a trafficking and prostitution ring case in Atlanta, Georgia, women from South Korea were found to owe debts from $30,000 to $40,000.[47] Debts of Russian women trafficked into the sex trade in the United States have, on average, been found to be lower, typically around $15,000.[48] Still, even with the lower debt amounts, specific charges were clearly inflated. In one case, Russian women trafficked to the United States together were charged by a travel agency about $1,800 apiece, a service fee for arranging their trip.[49]

Debts for travel within regions are generally, although not always, much less. One study, for example, found that among Russian women trafficked to Germany, debts ranged from $6,000 to $18,000, to be paid back with interest.[50] For most, this meant handing over 50% to 60% of their monthly earnings to the holder of their debt, usually the club or brothel owner.

Although the women had been told that they would have to pay for their travel costs once they arrived at their destination site, they had been given much lower estimated sums. With the high cost of living in Germany, the women found that they were able to save very little, if any, money. Most of the women in the study had entered Germany on a 3-month visa; at the end of a 3-month stay, brothel owners, on average, had netted about $21,000 from the work of each prostitute.[51] In fact, an official from the German Organized Crime Bureau has concluded that, on average, foreign prostitutes in Germany earn about $300 a day, but may net, after expenses, only about $12.[52]

Debt amounts within poorer regions tend to be even less, but the customers' fee for prostitution services is typically quite low as well—$1 to $3 in some brothels. Included in the debts of women trafficked from the Himalayan region to India are the amount the brothel owner says (s)he paid for the woman, a protection fee, and sometimes a fee for medical services. One study found that Nepali girls trafficked to India were typically sold to brothel owners in India for somewhere between $500 and $1,000.[53] The girls' debt amount was, on average, around $1,800.[54] However, often they were neither paid nor told how much they had actually earned, and were expected to live on tips. The researchers reported that every "Nepali girl or woman with whom [they] spoke said that the brothel owner or manager forced her to work by invoking her indebtedness," and that the "supposed debt, and the threats and beatings that accompanied it, were the major obstacles between her and the possibility of freedom."[55] That is, the debt bondage system was ubiquitous and effective.

Debts of African women trafficked within Africa tend to be similar to those of women trafficked within other poor regions, but when African women are trafficked to Western Europe, they are sometimes saddled with very high debt amounts. In one study, for example, Nigerian women trafficked into prostitution in Western Europe were found to have debts of up to $50,000.[56]

It should be noted that while *young* girls trafficked to the *poorest* countries are often kept for many years in debt bondage (as in the cases of Nepali girls in India discussed above), more often, debts are paid off within 2 to 3 years.[57]

Living Expenses and Earnings

Most women trafficked into the sex trade report that they learned only after they arrived at their "job" site of a number of unexpected and inflated charges that worked against their making much money. Sometimes they were not told what the money they had to pay out of their earnings covered. The following examples are illustrative:

- One Thai woman, trafficked to Japan in 1993, said that she was charged $900 for monthly expenses; of that amount, she was told that $270 was for rent, but she was never told what the remainder covered.[58] Another, who arrived in Japan in 1999, had monthly charges of $430 for rent, $260 for food, and $430 for protection from customer and police harassment.[59]
- Women who had been trafficked from Eastern Europe to the Netherlands for prostitution were promised 25% of their earnings, but after they began working, they learned that a debt payment and rent charge were deducted from that 25%. Moreover, local prostitutes working in similar brothels in the Netherlands at that time were typically getting 50% of their earnings, and of course, they had no travel debt to pay off.[60]
- Although Lola, a young Russian woman, had a relatively small debt of several thousand dollars, paying it off was not so easy. She had to give a percentage of her earnings to her Yugoslav pimp (who paid for her apartment), as well as something to the Russian trafficker who had paid for her trip to Germany. After paying the pimp and the trafficker, she got about $36 per customer, but from that amount she had to pay for all her own food, clothing, transportation, and miscellaneous items.[61]
- A sample of women trafficked from the NIS to Geneva, Switzerland, where they worked as dancers, did somewhat better. They were paid $90, on average, for each day they worked. One of the women reported that she, like most others, earned about $1,733 a month; half of this sum was deducted for her apartment, and another 12% of it went to the repayment of her debt. From the remainder, she had to pay for her food, protection, medical costs, and any other incidentals.[62]
- In the United States, women working at the "Russian Touch Massage" in Maryland were charged $150 per week for housing and were not paid any salary (they thought, but were not sure, that it was going toward their debt). One woman reported that she had earned $150 in tips in the prior month, but that this had to cover all additional living expenses.[63]

Women who had been trafficked from the Dominican Republic for prostitution in Greece also found the pay and job conditions different from what they had been told. The Dominican women had initially signed contracts to work as dancers in Greece, but upon arrival, were also forced to have sex with customers to help pay down their debt. They were regularly rotated each week to a different club and were given one day off from work per week. The women worked for the first 3 months without pay, after which, they were told, they could keep from 25% to 30% of what they earned. Their debt payment, however, was taken from this 25% to 30%.[64]

Julia, a Russian woman trafficked to Japan and working in a sex club with 29 other women from the NIS, talked about her experience. A single mother with a 9-year-old daughter, Julia was one of many women displaced by a failing Russian economy. She had heard about club work in Japan from a friend, who put her in contact with a company arranging such trips. She signed a 3-month contract with the company (a joint Russian–Japanese venture) and entered Japan on an entertainment visa. When interviewed in 1996, Julia was living in a small apartment with eight other women; she was earning about $250 a week and was given 2 days off from work each month. Her debt payment was deducted from her earnings, and she had to cover all living and other expenses from what remained. In Julia's words, she was working in a "big system." "Russian mafiya, Japanese mafia, Russian promotion, Japanese promotion," she said. "My salary may be big, but Japanese take my money, and mafia take my money." [65]

Women trafficked from the poorest source countries to the poorer destination countries tend to be paid very little and to work under the most abysmal conditions. Many Indonesian women and girls working in brothels in Malaysia, for example, earn less than $5.00 a day—some as little as $1.50 a day.[66] Author Hnin Hnin Pyne tells the story of one young girl she interviewed who had been trafficked from Myanmar (Burma) to Thailand to work in enslaved prostitution in a brothel.

Aye Aye was only 14 when her family was approached by a woman who said that she could get Aye Aye and her sister good jobs working as maids in Bangkok. Needing the income, their parents allowed the two children to go to Thailand. Upon their arrival, they were given to a group of men, who sold them to a brothel owner in Bangkok. When Aye Aye was finally rescued in a raid on the brothel where she was working, she had been in Thailand for 3 years and had worked in two different brothels there. Pyne continues:

> When rescued, she [Aye Aye] was living on the fifth floor of the brothel, which had a pool hall and a bar on the first two floors. The building housed approximately one hundred women. From noon until two in the morning, Aye Aye, wearing a numbered button, would sit behind a glass partition, while men ogled her and the others from across the room. She would watch television while waiting for her number to be called.[67]

At the brothel, Aye Aye was paid $1 a day for servicing from 12 to 20 men on any given day. Each of the men paid a fee of $6.00 for a half hour with her.

Other Charges: Fines, Medical Costs, Passport Buybacks

In addition to board and room charges, the prostituted women are given a set of "house rules" by which they must abide; violations result in fines, beatings, and other punishments. Trying to escape, refusing to work, or turning down a particular customer are virtually always at the top of the list of forbidden behaviors. Among other behaviors for which women report being fined are leaving the premises without a guard, coming to work late (if they live off the premises), fighting with one another, giving out their telephone number, gaining weight, failing to do the laundry or keep the club clean, failing to be "animated" with the customer, failing to get the customer to buy drinks, failing to keep ice in the customer's drink, not wearing provocative clothing, not applauding during strip shows, and failing to please or giving bad service to the customer.[68]

Fines are sometimes substantial. One Thai woman trafficked to Japan for prostitution, for example, was fined $4,300 for giving the brothel phone number to her parents! Several other Thai interviewees said that their brothel manager fined the girls for gaining weight; in one case, the fine was $75 for each kilogram gained.[69]

Sometimes trafficked women have a "medical insurance" fee added to their monthly board and room charges. In other cases, women are under a fee-for-service system, except that the fee is set by the employer and is generally much higher than what would be charged by the health provider. Padded medical charges also serve to warn the women that staying healthy, and in particular avoiding STDs and pregnancies, while not exactly a rule, is certainly advised. For one young Thai woman who did get pregnant, the brothel manager arranged an abortion, but charged her $3,200 for it, and added this sum to her debt. At that time, abortions in Japan, even in a private hospital, cost somewhere between $650 and $750.[70]

The woman's passport or visa and any other identification papers are usually confiscated by her traffickers or employers. The papers will be held, she is told, until her debt is paid off. This practice secures the trafficker's investment in his commodity, who is less likely to take off without documentation of her identity.

Furthermore, there is often an additional financial gain for the traffickers from the confiscation of passports. What the woman is usually *not* told until she has paid off her debt is that she has to buy her passport back. If she is unable to come up with the money, then, still in debt to her pimp, she must keep working. Buyback costs, like everything else in this business, vary. Traffickers from the NIS and Eastern Europe operating in the United States typically charge the women they've brought in about $900 to get their passports back. For Asian women trafficked to the United States by Asian traffickers, the average fee is about twice that amount. And there are cases in which women have been charged much more.[71]

At least one crime group has found another way to benefit financially from document confiscation: Albanian crime groups trafficking women to Britain routinely take their newly arrived transports' papers and use them for the next group of women they bring in.[72]

The police often claim that there is not much they can do to help a person who has no documentation of her identity. Without this key piece of evidence, a woman who says she was brought to the country under false pretenses and then enslaved as a prostitute is unable to make much of a case to authorities. According to law officers in Queens, New York, who have been involved in raids on several establishments run by trafficking rings there, 99% of the women have no identity papers of any sort when they are arrested.[73]

Living and Working Conditions

When she was only 15 years old, Maria was entrusted to a family friend, who said he could find her a job as a restaurant worker or nanny in Miami, where she would be paid in a week more than what she could make in a year in her hometown of Santiago Tuxtla, in the state of Veracruz. What Maria and her family did not know was that the man was a recruiter for a multimillion-dollar sex trafficking ring, run by the infamous Cadena family (discussed earlier), with whom Maria's mother had grown up. When Maria and a dozen or so other young girls arrived in Miami, they were enslaved as indebted prostitutes and taken around southern Florida to service field hands and other working men. Maria reported that the traffickers made them work 6 days a week and that they were threatened or beaten if they did not obey. "There were up to 25 men, more, in a night," she continued. "I had to do what they said. I had to do what they wanted. They [the customers] paid $20 and we got $3." What's more, the $3 was applied to their debt. No matter how many men they serviced, the girls testified, their debt never seemed to go down. Sometimes it actually increased, as the girls were charged monthly for room and board and other fees.[74]

Said Rosa, another victim of the Cadena ring: "There seemed to be no end to my nightmare. My debt continued to grow." Only 14 at the time she was taken into the Cadena sex trade, Rosa reported that because she was a virgin, she was repeatedly raped by the brothel guards, as a way of introducing her to sex.[75]

One of the Cadena victims managed to escape and get in touch with the FBI. Testimony given to the authorities by girls who were eventually rescued from the Cadena brothels included the following:

> Forced abortions, beatings and threats were all part of their new life in America, the women said later in depositions given in Florida. They worked six days a week, having sex in 15-minute sessions with men who paid their bosses $20 or $25. Thirty men a day was not unusual, and after the brothels closed for the night, the men who guarded the girls took their turn.[76]

By the time the girls were rescued, Rosa had undergone an abortion (about which she had no say and for which she was charged, and after which she was immediately put back to work). Maria was pregnant. Back home and poor, Maria now struggles to support her young daughter, fathered by one of the many men with whom she was forced to have sex. As mentioned previously, many of the Cadena gang seem to be living with impunity, enjoying their illegally gained wealth. Indeed, Maria has said that she often sees several of the men who were her brothel guards in her hometown, where she once again lives.[77]

One FBI agent on the scene during the raids that led to Maria's and Rosa's freedom described the brothels as filthy—with broken or boarded-up windows, dirty mattresses on the floor, and garbage, including used condoms, everywhere. He said about the bathrooms: "I can't begin to tell you how bad they were. . . . We walked in there and we were covered up from head to toe and using gloves and trying to insulate ourselves from whatever was lurking inside those places."[78]

Expecting a regular job in the United States, Maria, Rosa, and other victims of the Cadena gang found themselves instead in enslaved prostitution, debt-bonded to a ruthless group of traffickers. Moreover, like many other trafficked women, Maria and Rosa were totally unprepared for the living and working conditions they would have to endure. Such conditions include unsanitary and crowded living and working quarters, long working hours, work overloads, physical and social isolation, excessive controls, and physical and psychological abuse.

Living Quarters

Tatana had been trafficked from the Czech Republic to New York City, where a group of Czech traffickers had several clubs. One of the clubs was called the Playpen; another, the Playground. She had expected a legitimate entertainment job (as a dancer or a hostess), but instead she was forced into prostitution and inhuman living conditions. A police officer participating in a raid on the business described the apartment in which Tatana and other Czech women lived as "unspeakable," infested with cockroaches, and completely empty except for "kitchen equipment, a table and a few chairs."[79]

Lola, the young Russian woman mentioned on page 29, had worked as a prostitute and escort in Austria before being convinced by a Russian trafficker that she could do better in Germany. When interviewed by Global Survival Network, she was working in a brothel in Berlin. Lola described the sex room and couches in the club where she worked as "filthy"; on an overhead television set, hardcore pornographic movies ran continuously. The customers were frequently "rough" and drunk. Lola continued: "For me, it's very difficult that I have to humiliate myself here. . . . Men come in here and begin to ask questions like 'Do you find me attractive, do you love me?' A normal person knows very well that in a place like this there can be no loving." She said, "The sooner I forget this German horror the better. I really want to go home."[80]

While living quarters tend to be substandard across regions, in the poorer destination countries, they are likely to be particularly bad. Describing the findings from several reports on brothel conditions in Cambodia, for example, Donna Hughes says that the "rooms the women and girls live in are narrow, dark, unhygienic and foul smelling."[81] The "squalid brothels" in India known as "pillow houses," in which many trafficked Nepali girls live and work, consist, according to another study, of "nothing more than dark, claustrophobic rooms with cloth dividers hung between the beds."[82]

Work

Efficiency

As it grows, the sex trade becomes an increasingly efficient industry. In many countries, steps have been taken to ensure that prostitution businesses runs smoothly—serving as many customers, using as little space, and getting as much work out of the women as possible. Israel provides a good example: high demand and a huge influx of women trafficked from Russia and Ukraine have fueled a bustling sex industry in parts of that country. To accommodate this trade, according to journalist Michael Specter, rigid but efficient systems have been devised. The women "are held in apartments, bars and makeshift brothels. . . . Often they sleep in shifts, four to a bed."[83] Specter described the working conditions in one of the brothels in Tel Aviv—the Tropicana:

> There are 12 cubicles at the Tropicana where 20 women work in shifts, 8 during the daytime, 12 at night. Business is always booming, and not just with foreign workers. Israeli soldiers, with rifles on their shoulders, frequent the place, as do business executives and tourists.[84]

"Israelis love Russian girls," the owner of the Tropicana and several other Tel Aviv brothels told Specter. "They are blond and good-looking and different from us," he continued. "And they are desperate. They are ready to do anything for money."[85] Traffickers have responded to the high demand for Russian and Ukrainian women in Israel by delivering increasingly large numbers of women from the NIS region to club and brothel owners there. The owners have, in turn, devised efficient systems for handling this large supply and maximizing their profit from it.

The system in brothels in India where young Nepali girls work has also been described as organized and orderly. In the Indian brothels, according to one observation, the girls "stood or sat in a row," and customers selected from the line. The girls "were expected to stand or sit in line the entire time, whether or not there were customers. They were given no time off."[86]

Long Hours

Generally, the expectation is that women and girls working in clubs and brothels will work long hours, with few, if any, days off. In one U.S. case, trafficked Thai women were forced to work 20-hour days, with very few days off.[87] And at one of the Indian brothels described above, girls worked from 8:00 a.m. until late into the evening; at another, the workday went from 4:00 p.m. until 2:00 a.m.[88]

Not uncommonly, bar and brothel women who start their sex work in the afternoon or evening have other chores, such as housecleaning and cooking, to fill the earlier hours. Almost all of the Thai women trafficked into prostitution in Japan who were interviewed by Human Rights Watch said that they were forced to work 7 days a week (even if they were ill or menstruating), and that their work included more than prostitution. One of these women, Nuch, described her work day as follows:

> she was woken up every morning at 9:00 a.m. to clean the house and the snack bar before lunch. After lunch, she and the other women from the snack

> bar had to work in a field behind the bar where the owners grew vegetables and rice. They worked there until dinner-time, and they were closely supervised to make sure they did not steal any produce; anything they wanted to eat from the fields had to be purchased with their tip money. After dinner, Nuch went to work in the snack bar, serving clients from 6:00 p.m. to 3:00 a.m. as she struggled to repay her debt.[89]

A slightly different, but no less taxing, scenario was described by Vera to Global Survival Network interviewers. Vera was housed with five other Russian women in a small apartment in Japan. Her job duties were "to show up every night by 6:30 p.m., to be dressed in a sexy outfit, and to entertain her clients with a positive attitude until closing at 2:00 a.m. During her 'time off,' Vera was expected to telephone at least 20 Japanese men to invite them to the club." She and the other women she worked with had to give a "telephone log" to the manager of the club each day when they arrived for work. Vera also reported that she was under constant scrutiny by the club manager.[90]

Heavy Customer Loads

Women trafficked into debt-bonded prostitution often service 20 or more customers a day. In some instances, they are forced to do a high-volume business, and in other cases, the women themselves take on heavy workloads in order to pay off their debt, hoping that they can then start making and saving money, or that they can leave the brothel and return home. Evidence of heavy workloads has been found across regions:

- In the prostitution ring run by the Mexican Cadena family, the women were forced to service 25–30 men per night.[91]
- Women trafficked from the NIS and Eastern Europe into brothels in the Soho district of London were found in one study to service between 20 and 30 customers a day.[92]
- Ukrainian women trafficked to Brussels have reported that they were forced to provide sex for 20 men a day.[93]
- In the Tropicana in Tel Aviv, described earlier, women serviced up to 15 men a day.[94]
- Several studies of Cambodian brothels report that women receive up to 15 customers per day.[95]

Control Mechanisms: Creating Dependence

Control over the "commodity" is a central part of the "low cost, low risk" formula that has made sex trafficking such a profitable industry. Control mechanisms are intended to make the "commodity" dependent on pimps or traffickers and to deter individual acts of disobedience or rebelliousness. Irina, a young Ukrainian woman working in a brothel in Haifa, Israel, recalls her first recognition that she had lost her freedom. Responding to an ad in a Ukrainian newspaper, Irina expected to make big money as a dancer in Israel. For the first couple of weeks, she did work as a dancer and felt that she had made the right decision, but then one day her club manager drove her to a brothel, where he burned her passport in front of her. Irina recalls him telling her: "I own you. You are my property and you will work until you earn your way out. Don't try to leave. You have no papers and you don't speak Hebrew."[96] He then told her she would have to start working as a prostitute. She first refused, but was beaten and raped until she gave in. Irina's case includes all the major forms of control utilized by traffickers: social isolation and deprivation of agency, place and space restrictions, and violence or the threat of violence.

Social Isolation and Deprivation of Agency

Anyone who is moved from their familiar surroundings, on a journey that has been arranged by someone else, to a foreign country where they lack familiarity with the language, culture, and people is likely to experience feelings of social isolation. But under normal circumstances, these feelings decline as people become acclimated and increasingly integrated into the new community. The intent of traffickers, however, is to maintain dependence in the women they traffic or employ by keeping them from feeling that they are part of the local (outside the brothel) community and by taking away their sense of agency (i.e., their feeling that they can act on their own, that they have some control over their lives). Steps toward the goal of social isolation include the taking away of the woman's identification papers, forcing her to live and work in the same place, and preventing her from having any contact with the outside world.[97] Agency is diminished as the employer sets her work hours and activities, regulates her living conditions, and punishes her if she is not submissive and obedient.

Young Nepali girls trafficked into Indian brothels have talked about being cut off from the outside world. Sita, for example, said that food, clothing, and other essentials were brought in from the outside, effectively keeping her and the other girls from contact with local shopkeepers. Additionally, she reported, the girls were not allowed to have any contact—including writing a letter—with their families. Moreover, as is common among women trafficked into prostitution elsewhere, the Nepali girls in India were not allowed to have a personal relationship with a customer. In some instances, having any conversation at all with customers was forbidden. Of course, long work hours with few or no days off reduced the likelihood that the girls would have been able to develop a personal relationship with anyone, even if it had not been specifically against the rules.[98]

Psychological abuse and generally poor treatment by the person or persons who have almost total control over the woman's day-to-day life break down her sense of agency, often resulting in the woman's belief that she can do nothing other than follow her employer's dictates. Describing her own state of mind as an enslaved prostitute, Lola, the Russian woman working in a Berlin brothel, said: "I'm like a machine now. I don't think anything anymore. I only work. There's no happiness in life. . . . I know what it is to live when you can't smile, or laugh, when you can't live freely."[99]

Personal agency is also diminished by requiring the women to accept and obey all customers. In many brothels, women cannot turn down a customer for any reason, and in most cases, they must perform whatever acts he demands. Burmese women working in brothels in Thailand reported that they were not allowed to turn down any customer and were beaten if they did not do what the customer wanted them to do. Many felt that their lives, over which they had little control, " had been ruined." Yet, some also felt ashamed of what they had gotten themselves into, and said that they felt that "they deserved whatever happened to them."[100]

Place and Space Restrictions

Research consistently indicates that place and space restrictions are virtually always used to control women in enslaved prostitution. In most cases, women are not allowed to leave the premises (a club, brothel, or massage parlor) where they work (and often live) without being accompanied by a guard, or at the least, without getting permission.[101] All of the 43 trafficked Burmese women (in four different brothels in Ranong, Thailand) who were interviewed in one study reported that they were forbidden to go anywhere unless in the company of the brothel manager, a brothel guard, or a taxi driver. They also said that all of their movements were monitored in order to prevent escapes.[102] Place confinement as a control mechanism has been documented in diverse regions and cultures, including, for example, Greece,[103] Japan,[104] Austria,[105] and India.[106]

Space is also restricted. As previously indicated, women are most often housed in crowded quarters, sometimes with several to a bed, in a way that makes it difficult for them to have personal or private spaces. Space restriction may carry over into work settings, where cubicles for sex may be cramped and crowded together, or, as is often the case, women must live and work in the same close quarters.

The description of work life by two Thai women trafficked into enslaved prostitution in Saudi Arabia provides an example of another kind of space restriction. The women had expected to be taken to Saudi Arabia for employment as restaurant workers, but such was not the case. When they arrived in Riyadh, they were housed in one tiny room with seven other young women. Each girl had to service four to ten customers daily. To accomplish this, they were "forced to travel in a tiny compartment below the truck's undercarriage . . . in the scorching sun, from one construction site to another," providing sex to construction workers.[107]

Violence and the Threat of Violence

Violence against trafficked women serves several purposes. There is "breaking-in violence," in which a newly recruited woman or girl is subjected to repeated beatings, rapes (often gang rapes), and other torture upon her arrival at the destination. Breaking-in violence may be used to create or ensure submission among women or girls who, upon learning that they are expected to be prostitutes, try to resist. "Routine violence," in which women are regularly subjected to beatings and sexual assaults, is used to maintain their ongoing submission and obedience; to remind them that they cannot predict or control the abuse (deprivation of agency); or, as one report indicates, "purely for the gratification of the trafficker or pimp."[108] Finally, women are beaten or otherwise hurt as punishment for alleged misdeeds, or threatened with violence (to themselves or to their families) to ward off potential disobedience.

Most of the women trafficked into enslaved prostitution who have been interviewed or have given formal testimony report being physically abused—beaten and raped—by their traffickers or pimps. Many also describe cases they know of in which women have been murdered because they have attempted, or were thought to have attempted, to escape, to have withheld some of their earnings from their boss, or to have broken any of the myriad rules and regulations set by their owners. The women's stories of violence are so numerous and so compelling that it is difficult to choose which of them to tell.

Breaking-in Violence Mira was only 13 years old when her father agreed to let her go from their hometown in Nepal to Bombay, India, with a man who said he could find domestic work for her there. Instead, the man took her directly to a brothel in Bombay, where "tens of thousands of young women are displayed in row after row of zoo-like animal cages." When she refused to have sex, she was taken to a small, windowless room that was used to "break in" new girls and left there for several days without food or water. Next, one of the brothel "henchmen" came in and banged her head against the wall until she lost consciousness. When she came to, she was naked—a "rattan cane smeared with pureed red chili peppers shoved into her vagina." Later she was raped by the henchman. The breaking-in was "successful," as Mira from then on did as she was told. Although not all stories are as extreme as Mira's, most indicate that "breaking-in violence" is typically continued and intensified until the woman does what she is told—that is, until it is effective.[109]

Children are not protected by their young age from victimization—often, quite the contrary. Maya was 10 when she was sold by her aunt to a brothel in Bombay, India. When Maya refused to have sex with a customer, she was "locked in a room for two days, scared with snakes and beaten unconscious. When she came around she was raped by the client." Four years later, at age 14, Maya was still working as a prostitute in Bombay, but now had a 2-year old child, fathered by some customer, to care for.[110]

While rape is deemed a useful mechanism for breaking girls in, in the case of virgins, it may go against the financial interests of the trafficker or pimp. A virgin usually brings a much higher price from the customer. For virgins, then, psychological abuse, along with threats of physical abuse, may be used with particular intensity and intentionality.[111]

Jane Osagie, coordinator of a Nigerian research group, who has worked with Nigerian girls trafficked into prostitution, reported on one case in which food was withheld for days from two young trafficked Nigerian girls, 13 and 14, who had refused to work as prostitutes. These girls were eventually rescued, but Osagie, pointing out that the violence, including forced starvation, is sometimes lethal, says of the trafficked Nigerian children: "A lot of them die. A lot don't come back."[112]

Routine Violence Reports of routine violence are common among women trafficked into prostitution. In some cases, all the women at a particular club or under the control of a particular criminal group report continuous and severe physical abuse at the hands of their traffickers. This was true, for example, of the Mexican victims of the Cadena gang operating in Florida, discussed earlier.[113] Across the ocean, a report on conditions of women trafficked into prostitution in Western Europe identified numerous cases in which the women were regularly beaten, raped, and threatened.[114] In one case, a specific club in Austria was identified by women who had worked there as a place where the managers were particularly vicious and brutal, and often beat them for no apparent reason.[115]

A number of studies documenting the routine abuse of women trafficked into prostitution rely on samples of women and girls who have been rescued and repatriated, often by an international group or a local nongovernmental organization. In these studies the rate of reported violence at the hands of traffickers varies.[116]

- An International Organization for Migration (IOM) report on approximately 1,000 women trafficked from Tajikistan found that 89% of the women were sexually abused by their pimps, and that 27% were subjected to severe beatings.[117]
- The Coalition Against Trafficking in Women (CATW) found among their sample of women trafficked into the United States ($n = 37$) that 73% had been abused by their traffickers and/or pimps.[118]
- Among a sample of 200 trafficked Kosovar women who were repatriated by the IOM between 2001 and 2002, 56% reported beatings and 55% reported sexual abuse by their traffickers.[119]
- In another study, a third of 125 trafficked women repatriated to their homeland in Albania said that they were beaten or raped by their traffickers.[120]

Routine violence often results in feelings of helplessness and stress in its victims. As Alison Phinney wrote in her report on the effects of violence on women in enslaved prostitution: "Women's descriptions of the abuse and its effects bear similarities to battered women's descriptions of domestic violence, particularly the experience of living in a state of constant vigilance, trauma and fear."[121]

Violence as Punishment: Specific Deterrence Beatings and other assaults are commonly used by traffickers and pimps as punishment for a particular "offense." Again, at the top of the offense list is attempting to escape. Amy Richard reports on an interview with one Russian woman, trafficked to the United States to work, she thought, as a maid. When the woman arrived in the United States, she was forced into prostitution. She tried to escape, but was caught and beaten so badly by one of the Russian brothel guards that she needed medical care. She was allowed to go to the hospital, but was met there by another of the brothel guards, who warned her not to talk to the police "or else." That is, the beating was followed with a threat of further violence against her.[122] And again, young age confers no protections. The African human rights group Molo Songololo, for example, reported on 13 children kidnapped and trafficked within South Africa by South African gangs. When they were finally found and freed by law enforcement officials, some of the girls reported that they had tried to escape on various occasions, but had not been successful. As punishment for these attempts, they were beaten and gang-raped by their pimp–owners.[123]

Failure to please or to meet the demands of customers is another offense that frequently results in beatings and other assaults (most commonly by brothel owners and managers, but sometimes by customers). Beatings for such rule violations have been reported by, among others, Thai and Burmese women and girls trafficked into brothels in Japan,[124] women trafficked from the NIS and Eastern European countries to Western European countries and to the United States,[125] Asian women trafficked into Africa,[126] and Nepali and Burmese women trafficked into India.[127]

Victims have described a number of additional rule violations that have resulted in moderate to severe physical punishments. Following her rescue, a young Thai woman who had been trafficked into enslaved prostitution in Abidjan, the capital of Côte d'Ivoire, said that she and the three other Thai women working with her had to report to their pimp by 9 a.m. each morning (their working hours were from 7 p.m. until 2 a.m.). If they were not there by the designated time, they were tortured and fined. The women finally got word of their plight out to a friend, who helped put together a rescue plan. In the end, two of the four women were found and safely repatriated. The other two women have never been found.[128]

Sometimes the owner's belief that a woman has not been making enough money for him, or that she has withheld earnings from him, provokes his violence toward her. Tanya, a young Russian woman forced into debt-bonded prostitution and living in an apartment in Zurich, Switzerland, was kidnapped and assaulted by men associated with a Moscow-based ring allegedly involved in trafficking women from the NIS to Switzerland. Seriously injured in the attack, Tanya told the police that three Russian men had abducted her, informed her that she had not paid off her debt in time, and then driven her outside of the city, where they beat her with an iron rod and raped her for several hours before leaving her alongside the road. Although the police took her report, her case never went forward. One year later, however, another trafficked Russian woman working in Geneva went to the police and reported threats against her by a Russian group who claimed that she owed them money. The police were able to arrest the suspects, some of whom were the same men who had assaulted Tanya the previous year. Prosecuted on several charges, including extortion, kidnapping, and attempted rape, the men were either found not guilty or given suspended sentences "on the grounds that they were young and that their crime was a first offense."[129]

Severe violence—even murder—in response to escape attempts or other acts of disobedience occurs across regions. One study found that a number of Thai girls who tried to escape their enslaved prostitution in Japan had been killed by their owners.[130] There is also evidence that Polish, Albanian, and Russian crime groups have killed some women who have resisted efforts to force them into prostitution.[131] The actual number of women and girls murdered by their traffickers, however, is not known.

Physical violence followed by threats of even more severe violence is also common. Kyi Kyi's experience is illustrative. Trafficked from her home country of Myanmar to work in a brothel in Thailand, Kyi Kyi worked 7 days a week, servicing a minimum of four to five customers each day. If she rejected a customer or one of his sexual requests, she was beaten by the brothel owner. At one point she tried to run away, but the owner caught her and beat her with a thick stick. He told her that next time she tried to escape he would shoot her, demonstrating his threat by putting a pistol to her head and saying, "Like this."[132]

Traffickers and pimps may threaten not only the prostituted woman, but also her family. Thai girls who had been trafficked to Japan have testified that their traffickers told them that should they escape or fail to repay their debt, their families would be harmed.[133] In several instances, the girls had escaped, but returned on their own when they learned from their families that an agent had actually gone to their home and personally threatened their family.

Violence by Example: General Deterrence While violence against women and girls who work as prostitutes (trafficked or otherwise) is often not considered noteworthy or newsworthy, several murders of trafficked prostitutes have been prominently featured in the localities where they have occurred. News of these murders tends to spread to trafficked and enslaved women across localities, and can serve as a general deterrent (by example) to "misbehavior" among them. In such a case in the United States, a Russian woman who had been trafficked into the sex industry in Maryland was killed in what was described as a particularly "gruesome" murder, allegedly for not turning all of her earnings over to her boss.[134] A 12-year-old girl trafficked into prostitution in a mining town in Amazonia, Brazil, was decapitated for rejecting her twelfth customer of the night. Other bodies of trafficked children have been found there as well, washed up in a nearby river.[135]

Sometimes a murder is committed publicly—most likely as a warning to others. Two such murders involved Ukrainian women. In one, a Ukrainian woman who tried to escape her enslavement as a prostitute in Serbia was beheaded in a public place by her owners (or their hired killers).[136] And in the other, two Ukrainian women trafficked into prostitution in Istanbul were thrown off a balcony to their deaths, while six of their

Russian women friends watched.[137] None of the above examples of "general deterrent" murders (all of which took place in the 1990s) has been solved.

Other Lethal Violence Some women working in foreign prostitution have been killed in the midst of systemic violence—that is, violence that is inherent in criminal industries and occurs in the course of criminal exchanges.[138] Even an unwilling participant in a criminal enterprise, such as a woman who may be violating immigration and/or vice laws, is at risk of being involved in this endemic violence, as the following case illustrates.

In as yet unsolved multiple murders, four Ukrainian women who had entered Germany on visitors' visas were killed in 1994 at the Frankfurt brothel where they were working. In spite of a lack of direct evidence, many authorities there believe that the killers were part of the Russian mafia, which controls several clubs and brothels in the area. The murders were well publicized, and several women who had worked at the Frankfurt brothel reported to the police that they thought their co-workers had been killed because they had been witnesses to the prior murder of the club's Hungarian owner, Barbor Bartos, and his wife. Although the couple's murder was not solved, it was widely believed that Bartos had been killed by the Russian mafia for refusing to pay them off when he went to Russia to recruit women for his Frankfurt brothel. According to other women working in the brothel, Bartos himself was an abusive pimp, keeping his women enslaved and routinely beating them.[139]

Finally, some deaths of women trafficked into prostitution are thought to be murders committed by their traffickers or pimps, but the circumstances surrounding their deaths are not known, leaving their families in perpetual anguish. Such was the death of Simone Borges Felipe, trafficked from her native Colombia to Bilbao, Spain. In the Colombian town of Goiania, where she and her family lived, Simone was offered a job in Spain that was to pay her $2,000 a month. The job offer, made by two female acquaintances from her hometown, sounded legitimate. After her arrival in Bilbao, Simone called home and told her father that things were not as she had been led to believe. "We are all kept here like prisoners," she reported. "We work in a club, they have taken away our documents, we are forced to stand around in just a tiny thong bikini, and it's cold." "We are forced to work as prostitutes if we want to eat. And 35 women sleep in the same room." After 3 months, Simone called her parents to tell them that she was going to be able to come home. But shortly thereafter, her family was notified that Simone had died in Spain from tuberculosis. Eventually, Simone's family was able to retrieve her body, and an autopsy showed that she did not have tuberculosis. Her parents think that Simone was probably killed by her employers or other traffickers. Her employers were arrested, but then let go.[140]

Also suspicious, but never resolved, were the deaths of 67 Ethiopian women, many of whom were trafficked to countries in the Middle East for work as domestics there. In the late 1990s, the bodies of these women were returned to Ethiopia, with no information about the circumstances of their deaths.[141]

Conditions Vary

The focus of this book is on the very large number of women who are recruited for trafficking through coercion or deception (usually regarding the nature of work opportunities or a specific job) and who are not fully aware of the travel, working, or living conditions in which they will find themselves. Most of these women are subjected to the control mechanisms described in this chapter, including repeated and often severe violence. Unlike the murdered victims described above, most women survive their trafficking experience. The overwhelming majority, however, live under the debt bondage system and endure its deprivations and cruelties.

Of course, some women who migrate to other countries to work in the sex industry go voluntarily, and even arrange the trip themselves or with nontrafficker friends.[142] Furthermore, some women who migrate to a foreign country for sex work are able to make and save money, and find that even a short stay abroad for sex work yields a far better income than anything they might be able to earn in their home country.

In their research on the influx of women from the NIS into the sex trade in North (Turkish) Cyprus, for example, Rodriguez, Guven-Lisaniler, and Uoural found that most of the women came voluntarily and knowing that they would be doing sex work; they tended to stay and work as prostitutes on 3-month visas, then return to their home country (and sometimes return again to Cyprus for another 3-month stay). The authors note that the North Cyprus government currently regulates and monitors inmigration for sex work, and that policies are in place to provide some protections for women coming and going. However, as they also point out, while the women are working, the conditions of their lives and labor are largely under the control of their employers. These women typically work under the debt bondage system, but with a bit more recourse should they decide to leave. [143]

In another study, Eastern European women trafficked into prostitution in Austria reported that they did not feel they were enslaved, and said that their working and living conditions were generally okay. They further stated that their activities were not constantly monitored, and that they had some freedom of movement. However, many worked 7 days a week, and so had little time to develop relationships outside of work. Although they were not permitted to reject customers, they often found ways to get around this rule with impunity, such as charging an exorbitant price or claiming illness.[144]

The likelihood of a negative versus a tolerable experience in the global sex trade varies with conditions in the country of origin; immigration and prostitution policies in the destination country; the power and ruthlessness of the particular criminal trafficking group or employer; and the recruitment situation. To the extent that women are deceived (or sold by family, or, as in some cases, kidnapped) and forced into prostitution when they arrive at their destination, the likelihood of a very bad experience for them increases. Also, there is some indication that the youngest girls, and girls trafficked from the poorest source countries to the poorest destination countries, are most likely to be paid poorly and to live and work under cruel, unsanitary conditions. Although there is some variation in conditions, it should be remembered that debt bondage is in and of itself a system of enslavement, and as such violates numerous international and national codes. It is pervasive in the sex trafficking industry—not surprisingly, in that it allows traffickers to capitalize on their business venture and maximize profits.

In the next chapter, we turn to the trafficking industry, examining the various roles that traffickers play as well as the overall structure of the industry in which they work. Also addressed is the complex mix of criminal and legitimate forces that shape and contribute to the success of sex trafficking.

Notes

1. See, for example, Pino Arlacchi (2000), "Opening Address," International Seminar on Trafficking in Human Beings, Brasilia, November 28–29, available at http://www.undep.org/odccp/speech_2000-11-28_1.html; Amy O'Neil Richard (1999), *International Trafficking in Women to the United States: A Contemporary Manifestation of Slavery and Organized Crime* (November), DCI Exceptional Intelligence Analyst Program: An Intelligence Monograph (Center for the Study of Intelligence); Victoria Pope (1997), "Trafficking in Women: Procuring Russians for Sex Abroad—Even in America," *U.S. News and World Re-*

port, April 7, p. 43. Unless otherwise stated, all dollar figures in this chapter refer to U.S. dollars.

2. "Government Plans to Fight Trafficking of Women" (2001), *Frankfurter Allgemeine Zeitung,* August 20; Melanie Orhant (2001), "Sex Trade Enslaves East Europeans," *Stop-traffic,* available at http://fpmail.friends-partners.org/pipermail/stop-traffic; Donna M. Hughes (2000), "The 'Natasha' Trade: The Transnational Shadow Market of Trafficking in Women," *Journal of International Affairs,* Special Issue: "In the Shadows: Promoting Prosperity or Undermining Stability?" 53 (Spring), pp. 625–651.
3. Pino Arlacchi (2000), "Opening Statement," Tenth United Nations Congress on the Prevention of Crime and the Treatment of Offenders, United Nations Office for Drug Control and Crime Prevention, Vienna, April 10–17; Mark Porubcansky (1997), "Drug Trafficking Equals 8 Percent of All World Trade, the U.N. Reports," *Philadelphia Inquirer,* June 27, A7.
4. Vladimir Lyaschenko (2000), "Russia on the International Arms Market: Vying for a Place in the Sun," *Military Parade* (November), available at http://www.milparade.com/2000/42/01_02.shtml.
5. Frances Cairncross (2001), "Stumbling in the Dark," *The Economist,* July 28, p. 84.
6. Sarah Shannon (1999), "Prostitution and the Mafia: The Involvement of Organized Crime in the Global Sex Market," pp. 119–144 in *Illegal Immigration and Commercial Sex: The New Slave Trade,* ed. by Phil Williams (London/Portland, OR: Frank Cass); International Organization for Migration (1997/1998), "Trafficking in Migrants," *Quarterly Bulletin of the International Organization for Migration* 17, p. 1.
7. Phil Williams (1999), "Trafficking in Women and Children: A Market Perspective," pp. 145–170 in *Illegal Immigration and Commercial Sex: The New Slave Trade,* ed. by Phil Williams (London/Portland, OR: Frank Cass), p. 153.
8. Gillian Caldwell, Steve Galster, Jyothi Kanics, and Nadia Steinzor (1999), "Capitalizing on Transition Economies: The Role of the Russian Mafiya in Trafficking Women for Forced Prostitution," pp. 42–73 in *Illegal Immigration and Commercial Sex: The New Slave Trade,* ed. by Phil Williams (London/Portland OR. Frank Cass).
9. Ibid., p. 53.
10. *Violence Against Women on the Internet* (retrieved April 12, 2003), available at http://eon.law.harvard.edu/vaw02/mod3-lb.htm.
11. This point is made by most researchers and authors who have written about the costs and benefits of sex trafficking as an industry. See, for example, Hughes (2000), "The 'Natasha' Trade"; Francis T. Miko,

with assistance of Grace (Jea-Hyun) Park (2000), "Trafficking in Women and Children: The U.S. and International Response," Congressional Research Service Report 98-649C, International Information Programs, May 10, available at http://usinfo.state.gov/topical/global/traffic/crs0510.htm; Williams (1999), op. cit.; Gillian Caldwell, Steve Galster, and Nadia Steinzor (1997), "Crime and Servitude: An Exposé of the Traffic in Women for Prostitution from the Newly Independent States," report presented at conference on "The Trafficking of Women Abroad" (Washington D.C.: Global Survival Network).

12. Traffickers or brothel owners typically confiscate the woman's passport or visa, leaving her unable to prove her identity, let alone her immigration status. Passport confiscation is a part of the debt bondage system, discussed later in this chapter.
13. Trafficking in persons generally, and for prostitution specifically, violates a number of international human rights conventions and treaties, but international law is often difficult to enforce. In 2000, the United States passed the Trafficking Victims Protection Act, which addresses both international and internal trafficking. Laws on prostitution and compelling prostitution (pimping) vary greatly by country and within countries, making it particularly difficult to prosecute cases that cross international boundaries.
14. Orhant (2001), op. cit.
15. Reported in Duncan Campbell (2000), "Young Girls Sold as Sex Slaves in US, CIA Says," *The Guardian*, April 3, available at http://www.guardian.co.uk/international/story/0,3604,178485,00.html (3 pp).
16. This point is made by many researchers and authors who have written about law enforcement and sex trafficking. See, for example, Anthony M. Destefano (2001), "Policing Prostitution—Cops: Trafficking of Immigrants Difficult to Investigate," Newsday.com, March 14, available at http://www.newsday.com/news/local/newyork/ny-smuggled-police,0,2129745.story (3 pp.); Richard (1999), op. cit.; International Organization for Migration (1996), "Trafficking in Women to Austria for Sexual Exploitation" (June) (Budapest: Migration Information Programme).
17. Alex Perry and Mae Sai (2002), "How I Bought Two Slaves, to Free Them," *Time*, March 11, p. 7; "WHO Notes Lucrative Asian Sex Trade" (2001), *Business World*, August 31.
18. Emma Poole (2001), "Illegal Sex Trade Valued at $511 Million," *Calgary Herald*, August 23.
19. Velisarios Kattoulas (2001), "Slaves of Tokyo," *Times* (London), January 27.
20. Pope (1997), op. cit.

21. Human Rights Watch (2000), "Owed Justice: Thai Women Trafficked into Debt Bondage in Japan" (September), available at http://www.hrw.org/reports/2000/japan.
22. Richard (1999), op. cit.
23. Sean Gardiner and Geoffrey Mohan (2001), "The Sex Slaves from Mexico: Teen-agers Tell of Forced Prostitution," Newsday.com, March 12, available at http://www.newsday.com/news/local/newyork/ny-smuggled-mexico.story (7 pp.).
24. Ibid.
25. Richard (1999), op. cit.
26. Michael Specter (1998), "Traffickers' New Cargo: Naive Slavic Women," *The New York Times*, January 11, pp. 1, 6.
27. Ibid.
28. Ibid.
29. Hughes (2000), "The 'Natasha' Trade," p. 9.
30. Ibid., p. 5.
31. Donna M. Hughes (2000), "Welcome to the Rape Camp: Sexual Exploitation and the Internet in Cambodia," *Journal of Sexual Aggression*, available at http://www.uri.edu/artsci/wms/hughes/rapecamp.htm (24 pp.).
32. Lori Montgomery (1999), "Some Female Kosovo Refugees Are Falling Prey to Criminal Gangs in Albania," *South Coast*, May 22, available at http://www.s-t.com/daily/05-99/05-22-99/c07/wn125.htm (4 pp.).
33. Gerben J. N. Bruinsma and Guus Meershoek (1999), "Organized Crime and Trafficking in Women from Eastern Europe in the Netherlands," pp. 105–117 in *Illegal Immigration and Commercial Sex: The New Slave Trade*, ed. by Phil Williams (London/Portland, OR: Frank Cass).
34. Pino Arlacchi (2000), "Opening Statement."
35. Human Rights Watch–Asia (1995), "Rape for Profit: Trafficking of Nepali Girls and Women to India's Brothels" (October), available at http://www.hrw.org/reports/1995/India.htm (p. 16 of 41). As such, debt bondage is prohibited through the Supplementary Convention on the Abolition of Slavery, the Slave Trade and Institutions and Practices. Debt bondage also constitutes forced labor, which is defined by the International Labor Organization as "all work or service which is exacted from any person under the menace of any penalty and for which the said person has not offered himself [sic] voluntarily." Along with slavery, forced labor is prohibited under international law.
36. This point is made by many researchers and authors who have written about women recruited for and trafficked into prostitution. See, for example, Allison Dunfield (2002), "Trafficking in Women from Baltic States to Nordic Countries Increases Sharply," *The New York*

Times, February 26, available at http://www.walnet.org/csis/news/world_2002/sanomat-020226.html; Caldwell et al. (1999), op. cit.; Piotr Bazylko (1998), "Poland, Ukraine to Fight Sex Slave Industry," Reuters, July 16; Hnin Hnin Pyne (1995), "AIDS and Gender Violence: The Enslavement of Burmese Women in the Thai Sex Industry," pp. 215–223 in *Women's Rights, Human Rights: International Feminist Perspectives*, ed. by Julie Peters and Andrea Wolper (New York: Routledge).

37. Human Rights Watch–Asia (1995), op. cit.
38. Maria Osava (2000), "International Trafficking in Humans: A $7.0 Billion-Dollar Business," *IPS*, available at http://www.commondreams.org/headlines/113000-02.htm.
39. Hughes (2000), "The 'Natasha' Trade."
40. Human Rights Watch–Asia (1995), op. cit.
41. Ibid.
42. DePaul University International Human Rights Law Institute (2002), *In Modern Bondage: Sex Trafficking in the Americas*, available at http://www.law/depaul.edu/opportunities/institutes_centers/ihrli/trafficking_women_children.
43. Human Rights Watch–Asia (1995), op. cit.
44. Human Rights Watch (2000), op. cit., p. 5.
45. Caldwell et al. (1999), op. cit.
46. Edward Hegstrom (2000), "Feds Bust Alleged Smuggling Scheme," *Houston Chronicle*, June 6.
47. David France (2000), "Slavery's New Face," *Newsweek*, December 11.
48. "U.S. Urges Ukraine on Prostitutes" (1998), Associated Press, May 15; "Female Migrants from Former Soviet Union Become Hookers" (1998), TASS News Agency, March 20.
49. Caldwell et al. (1997), op. cit.
50. Ibid.
51. Ibid.
52. Ibid.
53. Human Rights Watch–Asia (1995), op. cit.
54. Robert I. Friedman (1996), "India's Shame: Sexual Slavery and Political Corruption Are Leading to an AIDS Catastrophe," *The Nation* 262 (April 8), p. 10.
55. Human Rights Watch–Asia (1995), op. cit., p. 16.
56. Ian Pannell (2001), "Trafficking Nightmare for Nigerian Children," BBC News, January 10, available at http://news.bbc.co.uk/2/hi/world/africa/841928.stm.
57. Ibid. [on Nigerian women trafficked to Western Europe]; Human Rights Watch (2000), op. cit. [on Thai women trafficked to Japan]; Caldwell et al. (1997), op. cit. [on NIS women trafficked to Western Europe].

58. Human Rights Watch (2000), op. cit.
59. Ibid.
60. Bruinsma and Meershoek (1999), op. cit.
61. Caldwell et al. (1997), op. cit.
62. Ibid.
63. Ibid.
64. International Organization for Migration (1996), "Trafficking in Women from the Dominican Republic for Sexual Exploitation" (June) (Budapest: Migration Information Programme).
65. Caldwell et al. (1997), op. cit., p. 46.
66. "Police Arrest 722 Illegals at Work Site of Government Seat" (1998), Associated Press, April 23.
67. Pyne (1995), op. cit.
68. Fees for violation of numerous behavioral and attitudinal rules are commonplace across regions. See, for example, Hughes (2000), "The 'Natasha' Trade"; Human Rights Watch (2000), op. cit.; Anucha Charoenpo (1998), "Gang Members Stay in Pratunam Area," *Bangkok Post*, August 24, available at http://www.globalmarch.org/worstforms-report/world/links/thai-girls.htm; Gillian Caldwell et al. (1997), op. cit.; Human Rights Watch–Asia (1995), op. cit.
69. Human Rights Watch (2000), op. cit.
70. Ibid.
71. For examples, see Human Rights Watch (2000), op. cit.; Richard (1999), op. cit.
72. Dominic Kennedy, Stewart Tendler, and John Philipps (2002), "Times: Albanian Gangs Corner Britain's Sex Trade," *Reality Macedonia*, July 6, available at http://www.realitymacedonia.org.mk/web/news_page.asp?nid=1899 (3 pp.).
73. Destefano (2001), op. cit.
74. Gardiner and Mohan (2001), op. cit., p. 1.
75. Ibid., p. 5.
76. Ibid., p. 2.
77. Ibid.
78. Ibid., p. 5.
79. Graham Rayman (2001), "Stripped of Their Dignity: Czech Women Lured to Work at NYC Sex Clubs," Newsday.com, March 16, available at http://www.newsday.com/local/newyork/ny-smuggled-easteurope,0,4558166.story (6 pp.).
80. Caldwell et al. (1997), op. cit., pp. 26, 27.
81. Intradevi Association (2000), "HIV/AIDS/STDs Information, Counseling Assistance and STD Treatment and Substance Abuse Prevention and Education" (January). [Cited in Hughes (2000), "Welcome to the Rape Camp."]

82. Human Rights Watch (2000), op. cit.
83. Specter (1998), op. cit., pp. 1, 6.
84. Ibid., p. 6.
85. Ibid., p. 6.
86. Human Rights Watch–Asia (1995), op. cit., p. 19.
87. Campbell (2000), op. cit.
88. Human Rights Watch–Asia (1995), op. cit.
89. Human Rights Watch (2000), op. cit., p. 22. Snack bars [or "snacks"], as described in this report by HRW, are places where "many Japanese go for relaxation and conversation." There are various kinds of snack bars. "A *baishun*—or prostitution—snack bar is one which involves sexual exchanges and is almost exclusively patronized by men." *Baishun* snacks also take different forms, based on the nature of the arrangements for sexual exchanges. In some, for example, customers can take women outside of the bar for sex (see pp. 14–15).
90. Caldwell et al. (1997), op. cit., p. 43.
91. Gardiner and Mohan (2001), op. cit.
92. Kennedy et al. (2002), op. cit.
93. Lily Hyde (1998), "Ukraine: Film Warns of Forcible Prostitution Abroad," Radio Free Europe/Radio Liberty, July 8.
94. Specter (1998), op. cit.
95. Intradevi Association (2000), op. cit.
96. Specter (1998), op. cit., p. 1.
97. Many researchers and authors who have written about the conditions under which trafficked women live and work describe these social isolation mechanisms used by traffickers to maintain control over the women. See, for example, Human Rights Watch (2000), op. cit.; Miko (2000), op. cit.; Caldwell et al. (1997), op. cit.
98. Human Rights Watch–Asia (1995), op. cit., p. 18.
99. Caldwell et al. (1997), op. cit., p. 47.
100. Pyne (1995), op. cit.
101. This finding has been documented in most of the research projects looking at working and living conditions for women trafficked into a foreign sex trade. See, for example, Alison Phinney (2002), "Trafficking of Women and Children for Sexual Exploitation in the Americas" (Washington D.C.: Pan American Health Organization/World Health Organization); Human Rights Watch (2000), op. cit.; Caldwell et al. (1999), op. cit.; Human Rights Watch–Asia (1995), op. cit.
102. Pyne (1995), op. cit.
103. International Organization for Migration (2001), "Trafficking of Migrant Women for Forced Prostitution into Greece" (July) (Migration Information Programme).
104. Human Rights Watch (2000), op. cit.

105. International Organization for Migration (1996), "Trafficking in Women to Austria."
106. Human Rights Watch–Asia (1995), op. cit.
107. Preecha Sa-Ardson (1998), "Saudi Woman Procurer Surrenders Before Police," *The Nation*, July 18, available at http://www.uri/edu/artsci/wms/hughes/saudi/htm.
108. Janet Raymond (1999), "Health Effects of Prostitution," in *Making the Harm Visible: Global Sexual Exploitation of Women and Girls*, ed. by Donna M. Hughes and Claire Roche (North Amherst, MA: Coalition Against Trafficking in Women).
109. Friedman (1996), op. cit.
110. Jon E. Rhode (1996), "Child Prostitution in India," *UNICEF Report*, available at www.jubileeaction.co.uk/reports/CHILD96.
111. Human Rights Watch–Asia (1995), op. cit., p. 16.
112. Pannell (2001), op. cit.
113. Jim Loney (1998), "US Indicts 16 in Mexican Prostitute Slavery Ring," Reuters. [Cited in *Factbook on Global Sexual Exploitation* (1999), ed. by Donna M. Hughes, Laura Joy Sporcic, Nadine Z. Mendelsohn, and Vanessa Chirgwin (Coalition Against Trafficking in Women), available at http://www.uri/edu/artsci/wmn/hughest/mexico.htm.]
114. Organization for Security and Co-operation in Europe (1999), "Trafficking in Human Beings: Implications for the OSCE," Review Conference (September), prepared under the auspices of the Office for Democratic Institutions and Human Rights of the Organization for Security and Co-operation in Europe.
115. International Organization for Migration (1996), "Trafficking in Women to Austria."
116. It certainly is possible that the rate of experienced violence is lower for women and girls who have been rescued and repatriated than for those who remain trafficking captives. This, however, is an empirical question that has not been answered up to this point.
117. International Organization for Migration (2001), "Deceived Migrants from Tajikistan—A Study of Trafficking in Women and Children" (July) (Dushanbe, Tajikistan).
118. Janet Raymond, Donna M. Hughes, and C. Gomez (2001), *Sex Trafficking of Women in the United States: International and Domestic Trends* (North Amherst, MA: Coalition Against Trafficking in Women).
119. International Organization for Migration (2001), "Kosovo Anti-Trafficking Report" [Press Release], *BRAMA*, September 25, available at http://www.brama.com/news/press/010905iom_trafficking.htm.
120. Claire Doole (2001), "Albania Blamed for Human Trafficking: Gangs Use Albania to Lure Women into Prostitution," BBC News, April 17, available at http://www.uri/edu/artsci/wms/hughes/ukraine/alblame.htm.

121. Phinney (2002), op. cit., p. 5.
122. Richard (1999), op. cit. "Specific deterrence" refers to something that is done to an individual in order to deter that individual from engaging in a particular behavior. Specific deterrence differs from "general deterrence" in that the latter refers to something that is done to an individual in order to deter *others* from engaging in the behavior of that individual.
123. Molo Songololo (2000), *The Traffic of Women into the South African Sex Industry.* [Cited in BBC News (2000), "S. Africa's Child Sex Trafficking Nightmare," November 23, available at http://news.bbc.co.uk/2/hi/world/africa/1027215.stm.]
124. Human Rights Watch (2000), op. cit.
125. Caldwell et al. (1997), op. cit.
126. Charoenpo (1998), op. cit.
127. Human Rights Watch–Asia (1995), op. cit.
128. Charoenpo (1998), op. cit.
129. Caldwell et al. (1997), op. cit., pp. 50, 59.
130. Human Rights Watch (2000), op. cit.
131. Richard (1999), op. cit.
132. Human Rights Watch (2002), "Forced Prostitution and HIV/AIDS" (November 26), available at http://www.hrw.org/about/projects/womenrep/General-137.htm (4 pp.).
133. Human Rights Watch (2000), op. cit.
134. Richard (1999), op. cit.
135. June Kane (1998), *Sold for Sex* (Brookfield, VT: Ashgate).
136. Specter (1998), op. cit.
137. Ibid.
138. Erich Goode (1999), *Drugs in American Society*, 5th ed. (Boston: McGraw Hill).
139. Caldwell et al. (1997), op. cit.
140. Isabel Murray (2000), "Sex Slavery: One Woman's Story," BBC News, December 12, available at http://news.bbc.co.uk/hi/english/world/americas/newsid_1067000/1067533.stm.
141. International Organization for Migration (1999/2000), "Ethiopian Women Trafficked to the Arab Countries," *Trafficking in Migrants: Quarterly Bulletin* 20 (December/January), p. 3.
142. However, it is difficult to migrate to another country, legally or illegally, to work in the sex trade there without some kind of help or special connection. Even where foreign prostitution is not against the law, to gain immigrant status, arrange for travel, and get work requires considerable knowledge and is quite an undertaking for an individual woman, or even a small group of women, on their own.

143. Leopoldo Rodriguez, Fatma Guven-Lisaniler, and Sevin Uoural (2001), "Foreign Sex Workers and State Regulations in North Cyprus," paper presented at the European Association for Evolutionary Political Economy, Siena, Italy.
144. International Organization for Migration (1996), "Trafficking in Women to Austria."

3

Criminal Networks and Corrupt Guardians: The Trafficking Industry

The international sex trade is notable for the variety and complexity of the trafficking networks that operate and sustain it. The sex trafficking industry is simultaneously collaborative and fragmented, ever adapting to changing social and market conditions that may affect its business. Its networks extend to every region and virtually every country in the world—it is a truly global industry. Within and across these networks, traffickers play a number of roles, including recruiting women and young girls in remote villages; escorting women on a plane trip overseas; owning or managing a travel agency, an employment agency, a bar, or a brothel; producing false identification papers; and serving as the head of a trafficking ring—that is, as the "general contractor."

With its potentially high profits and relatively low risks, the sex trafficking industry attracts many players, some of whom regularly engage in criminal activity, some whose criminal activity is sporadic, and others to whom criminal activity is new or rare. Criminal participants include organized crime syndicates, small groups or gangs, and unaffiliated individuals. In market terms, traffickers can be "individual entrepreneurs, small 'mom and pop' operations, or sophisticated, organized rings."[1]

Participants also vary in their professionalism, with the largest, best-established organized crime syndicates (also referred to interchangeably hereafter as mafias or organized crime groups) tending to be the most professional. However, as the industry grows, smaller professional groups are emerging. In their research on the sex trafficking industry in the Netherlands, for example, Bruinsma and Meershoek found, in addition to organized crime traffickers, "cliques" of professional traffickers, which they described as "consisting of two or three professionals in the field, mainly traditional pimps," who were involved in trafficking a relatively small number of women.[2] Whether organized syndicates or cliques, professional traffickers are often part of a network that includes individuals or partners who are new to and not very knowledgeable about the sex trade ("amateur traffickers," in one author's terms).[3] Because they often associate with professionals, amateurs can learn about "doing criminal business," or at least about their part of the business, rather quickly. Initially, amateurs are likely to provide only one service, or to be involved only sporadically in the industry, but as they gain expertise, their involvement often becomes more expansive and regularized.

While many participants, most notably those who are members of criminal groups, operate under a criminal status, some persons participate in trafficking through a legitimate position of trust that provides them special access to trafficking crime (e.g., a police officer or an immigration official) or a legitimate entrepreneurial position that allows them to capitalize on trafficking business (e.g., a travel agent or a banker). Boundaries of legitimacy, however, can be fuzzy. A legitimate travel agent, for example, may find a perfectly legal way to arrange a trip, including getting a visa, for a woman that he or she only thinks *might* be a trafficking victim. Or an individual may allow others to use his or her legitimate business site—say, a club or restaurant—to arrange illicit transactions. Still others may hold a legitimate post and only occasionally use it for illegal purposes, such as a taxi driver who from time to time transports a trafficked woman to a designated brothel for a special fee.

In their discussion of transnational crime, Ho-Lin Chin and colleagues note that it is hard for authorities to get a clear understanding of the organized crime subculture precisely because it includes so many who "have no prior criminal record, no affiliation with an identifiable organization," and "no rigid structure, or clearly defined deviant norms and values"—for example, "import-export businessmen, community leaders, restaurant owners, workers, gamblers, housewives, and the unemployed." Moreover, the fact that the criminal activity of many participants is "sporadic rather than continuous" makes ongoing investigations more difficult.[4] Similarly, in her description of the variety of sex traffickers, Amy Richard, a research analyst with the U.S. State Department, says that globally, "the full spectrum of criminal organizations and shady businesses—from major criminal syndicates to gangs to smuggling rings to loosely associated networks"—participate in sex trafficking, "making detection and crackdowns difficult for law enforcement as targets are much more amorphous."[5]

In this chapter, we take a closer look at the sex traffickers and the industry in which they work. How is the industry organized, and how does it operate? What are the various trafficker roles? And how do corrupt officials, who are supposed to help curb crime, or at least to keep public order, facilitate the sex trade?

Key Structural Components of the Sex Trafficking Industry

In spite of its size and global span, the sex trafficking industry is not a singular, centrally organized entity. Business is typically carried out through numerous *small-group exchanges*, some planned in advance and some negotiated on the spot. Exchanges are formed and re-formed, based in great part on current needs and opportunities.

However, having connections one can count on and the right contacts for particular tasks are critical for maximizing profits and minimizing costs or risks. The most successful industry players recognize the importance of fostering *local ties* in countries where transactions are taking place, and they usually have people in their network who are familiar not only with national but also with village cultures in a particular locale.[6] At the other end, having contacts around the world is also important. Traffickers need to be ready to take advantage of a "deal" in another country; such deals vary with time and circumstance, and the ability to make a quick connection with someone in another part of the world is advantageous.[7]

Additionally, the sex trafficking industry relies more on *cooperative* than on competitive exchanges with other traffickers.[8] Keeping down costs and risks (and thus increasing profits) is managed primarily through exploitation of the exchange commodity—the trafficked women—and secondarily through identification of and marketing to consumers. To these exploitative ends, traffickers are likely to cooperate with one another. Both supply and demand are prolific—there is plenty of each for traffickers, and there is little reason to expect that this situation will change any time soon. This is not to say that the business is never competitive or conflictual, nor that it is without systemic violence. Indeed, many trafficking crime groups are known for their ruthlessness; and almost certainly, disloyalty or betrayal of one trafficker by another will result in swift and harsh retaliation. The sex trafficking industry does operate in a criminal environment—disputes and conflicts occur and can easily erupt in violence.

Finally, unlike other global industries, the sex trafficking industry is for the most part *nonhierarchical*. While hierarchy has been a feature of long-standing organized criminal syndicates, these groups do not always hold the position of power in sex industry exchanges.[9] Moreover, as an organizational form, hierarchy is not always conducive to efficient and effective exchange, particularly in a global marketplace. As one researcher points out:

> Traditional models of criminal organizations that emphasize hierarchical or pyramidal structures are not particularly appropriate to transnational criminal organizations or transnational markets. Indeed the key to understanding transnational criminal organizations and the markets they inhabit is through criminal networks that are active in criminal markets that are also populated by a myriad of other actors.[10]

Traditional organized crime groups heavily involved in global sex trafficking today—most notably the Russian mafia, the Japanese Yakuza (mafia), and the Chinese Triads—often rely on business partners outside of their organizations, valued for their expertise or their local connections. Additionally, the larger and more institutionalized the criminal group, the greater the likelihood that sex trafficking is just one of its trafficking and other illegal businesses. Diversification characterizes the business activity of organized crime groups involved in sex trafficking.[11]

Networks and Transnational Crime

The sex trafficking industry is often described as consisting of *"loosely organized" networks*.[12] But what exactly does that mean? Most definitely, "loose organization" does *not* mean disorganization. Phil Williams, an expert on transnational crime, suggests that networks, "which are far superior to traditional hierarchies in terms of organizational effectiveness, especially when it comes to innovation and teamwork," are increasingly relied on by criminal organizations and industries. Williams suggests that among law enforcement authorities as well as academic researchers, there has been a tendency "to treat centralized hierarchies as synonymous with organized crime and to treat networks as disorganized crime." This, he warns, "is a mistake," as a network is actually a "highly sophisticated organizational form."[13]

Williams's description of networks highlights their ability to transcend borders and their elusiveness, characteristics that make them relatively resistant to law enforcement and effective for global transactions. According to Williams:

> A network can be understood as a series of connected nodes. The nodes can be individuals, organizations, firms, or even computers, but the critical element is that there are significant linkages among them. Networks can vary

> in size, shape, membership, cohesion, and purpose. They can be large or small, local or global, cohesive or diffuse. . . . Networks are at once pervasive and intangible, everywhere and nowhere. [Moreover, the] pattern of authority and direction in these networks is not always evident, the balance between competing and cooperating networks is not readily discernible, and the nature of information flows through them is often elusive. [And] networks display a remarkable capacity to flow around physical barriers and across legal or geographical boundaries. They in effect transcend borders, and are the perfect means of conducting business in a globalizing world.[14]

Trafficking operations vary in size, level of professionalism, and criminal status, but the networks in which they are embedded operate across such differences. This loosely organized mix contributes, somewhat ironically, to industry stability. In fact, the sex trafficking industry works in great part because of its flexibility and adaptability.[15]

Networks, according to Williams, are particularly good for "managing risk and limiting damage to the criminal enterprise" in that if the network is threatened, it can "alter its shape" and still operate. Alteration of its shape is facilitated by the fact that network organization includes the compartmentalization of activities, the dissemination of knowledge on a "need-to-know basis,"[16] and the separation of various roles. However, flexibility also characterizes the organization of roles in a network; that is, although there is role specialization, roles are unlikely to be so specialized that "substitutes cannot readily be found."[17] This "loose organization" or, in another's words, "loose coupling,"[18] also helps in the management of emergent or unexpected problems.

To illustrate some of these principles, the network of "Gayla," a recruiter and individual entrepreneur (with a partner for certain transactions), is described below—as she herself described it in an interview with Global Survival Network.

One Recruiter's Trafficking Network

In 1994, Gayla was working in Moscow as a photo model promoter, trying to find overseas modeling jobs for Russian women. In the course of her work, Gayla found a much greater demand overseas for Russian prostitutes than for models. By the time she was interviewed by Global Survival Network a year or so later, Gayla had changed jobs, and was recruiting Russian women for prostitution abroad. That is, Gayla was up and running as an individual trafficking entrepreneur. She specialized at the time in the recruitment of Russian women for prostitution in Australia, where, through her modeling contacts, she had eventually found a partner. In Moscow, Gayla ran ads in newspapers and on television that read, "Agency invites girls to work abroad for escort services." She pointed out that some advertising outlets would not run the ad with the phrase "for escort services," and for these outlets she substituted the phrase "for highly paid work." Gayla's partner was an employee of the immigration service in Australia. The partner recruited customers in Australia, provided them with a book of photographs of available Russian women, and then sent "invitations" to Gayla for the chosen women. Through his job in the immigration service, the partner was also able to arrange the paperwork for the women's travel to Australia. For her part, Gayla was paid $24,000 by her partner (who might have been financed in part by an organized crime group for which he was doing "contract" labor)[19] for every 3-month period that one of her recruits worked in prostitution in Australia. She was paid half of this amount in advance by "someone who comes to me from Australia." This person then paid for the recruit's travel fees, and when the woman's work contract had been fulfilled, he returned to pay Gayla the remainder of her sum.

When Global Survival Network asked her about trafficking to the United States, Gayla told them that it was particularly important in trafficking women to the United States to complete all the paperwork, including obtaining a visa, prior to paying travel fees or other costs. In Gayla's words: "If the documents are officially prepared, then there shouldn't be any problems." Gayla indicated that her network included persons who could arrange for such papers in Moscow. The preference for trafficking to the United States, she continued, was to get the women a job *training* visa rather than an employment visa, as the latter required the U.S. contingent of the network to pay taxes on money earned by the trafficked woman. Paying the taxes would most likely have a ripple effect throughout the network, cutting into several people's share of the profits. Gayla was also asked about trouble that might come from the Russian government in regard to the trafficking of Russian women for prostitution. There are, she said, "no obstacles with the Russian government." The interviewers probed: "So, the Russian government doesn't care if [you] are lying about the real purpose?" "No," Gayla replied.[20]

Although Gayla was an individual entrepreneur with a well-established Australian network, she maintained connections with other sex traffickers inside and outside of Russia. While Australia was the focal destination for her recruits, her knowledge of business elsewhere suggests that she could (and probably did) send Russian women to other destinations as well. She was familiar with and knew how to manage potential local problems for her business, and implied that by allowing her trafficking enterprise to operate with impunity, the Russian government was at least passively complicit.

While Gayla's primary trafficking role was that of recruiter, running her own business required her to take on additional tasks, such as putting together the book of photographs and other promotional materials and making sure that there would be no problems with officials regarding identification papers. In the industry overall, some recruiters are employees (rather than entrepreneurs) who may have less expansive, but not necessarily less difficult, roles. Recruiter—whether entrepreneur or employee—is only the first of a number of trafficker roles essential to the movement of the "commodity" into the market and the exploitation of its value there. These roles and their place in the sex trade are explored in the following section.

Trafficker Roles

Most trafficker roles can be played by individuals, small cliques, or organized mafias. In mafias involved in sex trafficking, there tends to be greater specialization in the assignment of criminal roles, but here again this varies by situation and need. In some instances, an entire gang or criminal group specializes in a particular sex trafficking role. Some Chinese street gangs in the United States, for example, specialize in providing protection (from other criminal groups or from police raids) to brothels and clubs; others scout out new trafficking opportunities that they can recommend to an affiliated group.[21]

Several sources list and describe sex trafficker roles.[22] While there are some variations in terminology and some role behaviors that are specific to particular countries or cities, for the most part, there is agreement that the sex trafficking roles described in Table 1 are found around the world.

All but two of these roles are usually filled by persons doing crime *outside of* a legitimate job position.[23] That is, these persons do not participate in trafficking *through* their legitimate job position. The two exceptions are employment/travel agent and document thief/forger. In the former case, the agent may own a legitimate employment or travel business but may also allow his or her business to be used for trafficking purposes; or someone may work for an employment or travel agency and use his or her position (without the owner's knowledge) to handle trafficking cases. The document thief/forger may be someone who uses his or her job position (e.g., immigration officer, lawyer) to obtain false identification papers for the women being trafficked. Both of these roles, however, may also be played by people outside of a legitimate work setting. A travel agency, for

Table 3.1

Sex Trafficker Roles

Recruiter Finds and brings women into the industry, usually by deception, but sometimes by force. Recruiters sell their recruits to brokers or directly to employers, such as brothel or bar owners or managers.

Broker (agent) A go-between or middleman. Brokers typically buy women from a recruiter and then sell them to an employer. There may be more than one go-between (e.g., a broker may buy from a recruiter and then sell to another broker, who then sells to the employer).

Contractor Organizes and oversees an entire trafficking transaction, or more typically, a set of transactions. This role is usually played by a relatively professional criminal organization or group.*

Employment/travel agent Arranges for the trip and its alleged purpose (e.g., job, job training, tourism). An employment agent arranges for a "legitimate" job and job description; a travel agent arranges for a "legitimate" trip. Employment and travel agents may serve as "fronts" for the criminal trafficking activity. Sometimes employment or travel agents arrange for the travelers' visas, passports, and other identification papers.

Document thief/forger Arranges for and obtains "legitimate" documentation for travel to another country. Document specialists may steal or otherwise illegally obtain legitimate documentation, or they may create false documentation.

Transporter (escort, "jockey") Accompanies women on the trip—by airplane, train, bus, car, or on foot—to their destination. Transporters may take the women through one or more transit cities or countries. They usually deliver the women to a broker at a border or inside a destination country, but sometimes the delivery is directly to an employer.

Employer (procurer) Purchases and then sells the "commodity" to the customer, and provides a place of business for sex. Employers provide the women with a place to live and work; set up and tell them about the conditions of their work, living arrangements, and lifestyle; and inform them that they must work in the sex trade while they pay off their debt. Employers are most commonly bar, club, or brothel owners or managers; a small number of employers are street pimps and have no business establishment, and thus the sex transaction may occur in a public place.

Enforcer (guard, "roof") Provides protection for the place of business, and to a lesser extent, the trafficked women. Enforcers protect the business from other criminal gangs, from extortionists, and from police or immigration raids; they see that women follow the house rules, and in particular, that they do not escape. The enforcer may also make sure that the customer pays what he owes and otherwise abides by the house rules. Enforcers—particularly if they are members of organized crime groups—may also be **extorters**; that is, on behalf of their crime group, they extort or demand money from brothels or bars, and if the owners don't pay, the crime group retaliates (e.g., burns down the business, murders the manager, arranges for a police raid on the business). Extortion may be either a specialized enforcer role or one of several tasks of an enforcer; the line between extortion and payment for enforcement services is thin.

"Contractor" is the term for this role, which is comparable to that of a "general contractor" in legitimate business—a project overseer who contracts out some of the labor for the project.

example, may simply be a front for a trafficking ring, and the document forger may work entirely on his or her own.

Documents are often obtained through cross-country networks involving a mix of criminal and (otherwise) noncriminal actors. For example, Sergey, a Moscow-based trafficking entrepreneur, told Global Survival Network staff (posing as potential U.S. business partners) that he had contacts in other countries who could provide new identities for virtually anyone—often by stealing the identities of people who had died, or just disappeared. A Serbian contact, he went on, could provide him with Serbian passports, most likely using a "disappeared person's" identity. And, Sergey added, he was in contact with a Moscow-based company that did business with law firms abroad and that could provide him with South African passports, which would be registered in Russia's Interpol system, for about $25,000 each.[24]

There are myriad others whose involvement in sex trafficking is exclusively *through* their legitimate, public-sector work role. Such participants, hereafter referred to as "corrupt guardians," include law enforcement officers (police and border patrols), immigration agents, embassy staff, and other government employees holding positions that are intended to protect the public good. Finally, in the private sector there are a number of businessmen—from taxi drivers to bankers—who knowingly facilitate trafficking by providing a variety of services for a fee.[25]

One last point before we take a closer look at trafficker roles—and that has to do with the terms "trafficker" and "pimp." One view is that traffickers are *only* those persons involved in finding women and delivering them to their destination. This definition excludes employers and enforcers, who work with trafficked women but usually are not involved in the movement of women from the recruitment site to the destination. This narrower definition of "trafficker" also excludes the businessmen who facilitate the sex trade but, again, do not participate in finding, transporting, and delivering women for prostitution. A broader definition of "trafficker" includes all who allow or facilitate the trafficking of women and children, even the customer. While it is tempting to use the broader definition in order to make the point that any facilitation of trafficking makes a person, in effect, a trafficker, it is theoretically useful to distinguish between those who find and deliver the "commodity" and those who profit from it once it gets to the market. From here on, I will use the narrower definition, referring to those involved in the actual trafficking process as traffickers, and referring to other participants by their particular roles (such as enforcer) or positions (such as police officer).

The term "pimp" generally refers to a person who profits from sex transactions between a prostitute under his control and customers he has had a hand in soliciting for her.[26] In that sense, the term "pimp" is most applicable to the employer, or procurer, role. On the other hand, as with the term "trafficking," it can be argued that the term "pimp" applies to anyone who profits from the labor of a prostitute, and so includes all traffickers. Here again, I will use the narrower definition, using the term "pimp" to refer to trafficked women's employers. Most employers of trafficked women (at least those on whom the research has focused) are in establishments, but there are also some pimps who work "their" women on the street.

Recruitment and Transport

Almost anyone who knows anyone involved in sex trafficking can become a recruiter. All that is necessary is (1) to have a story to persuade, or the power to force, a recruit to go along with him or her; (2) to know where or to whom to sell the recruit; and sometimes (3) to have money to pay a family who will sell their daughter (often for a very small sum). Of course, the most successful recruiters are likely to be part of a well-developed trafficking network and to recruit on a more or less full-time basis. Recruitment can be face-to-face (with the potential recruit or her family or friends) or through advertising in a media outlet, such as a newspaper or the Internet. Recruiters may work alone, be part of a small group, or be members of a mafia. They may specialize—that is, participate in trafficking only as a recruiter—or they may play several trafficker roles (e.g., travel agent, document provider, broker, transporter).

In fact, many recruiters are also transporters, and this dual role can help ensure that the woman will not back out. Any last-minute anxiety on the part of the recruit may be quelled by contact with the person who has offered her the job or other opportunity—that is, the person she has come to trust. Recruiters are more likely to accompany the recruit on the way, or part of the way, to her destination when travel is by car, bus, or train. In one study, for example, women trafficked from Eastern and Central Europe to Austria were found to have been recruited largely by someone close to them—a husband, boyfriend, or girlfriend—and in most cases, the recruiter was the person who took them to Austria.[27]

When the trip is overseas and requires air travel and/or when the trafficking operation is run by an organized crime group (in the role of contractor), the transporter is more likely to be a professional in this one specific role. Organized Thai traffickers, for example, hire "jockeys" to accompany their recruits from Thailand to the United States. The Thai jockeys serve as the women's English-speaking translators and are responsible for getting them through customs and U.S. Immigration and Naturalization Services (INS) inspections. Once in the United States, the jockey's final task is to hand over the woman to a broker, whose job is to place her in a club or brothel. The Thai jockey's fee for each trip is around $1,000 per woman.[28]

Recruiters may transfer the woman to another trafficker—a travel or employment agent, transporter, or broker—prior to her being trafficked out of the country, or they may facilitate the woman's trip, arranging for her identification papers and setting up her travel plans. Recruiters working in a very poor country often sell their recruits to a broker within the country for a relatively low price, but one that may be "big money" to them. Local recruiters in Nepal, for example, buy village girls from their families for as little as $4 and then take them on foot to the Indian border, where they sell them to brokers for between $20 and $250, depending on the girl's age and physical assets.[29]

Individual or partnered entrepreneurs who are better off financially and well connected in the trafficking industry are more likely to play multiple trafficker roles, including the recruiter role. Such entrepreneurs may own several businesses and any number of prostitutes. In 1994, Simla Tamang, a well-known public figure in Bombay, was convicted, along with her nephew, of recruiting and trafficking women into prostitution in Bombay. Simla owned about 500 prostitutes, and the nephew's wife owned another 400 women. Tamang and her relatives placed the women in brothels they owned in Bombay.[30]

A popular practice in some regions is for trafficking groups or brothel owners to send formerly trafficked women back to their hometowns to recruit other young women. These recruiters may be offered a considerable discount on their debt, or even given their freedom, in exchange for successful recruitment. Some women trafficked from very poor villages in developing countries—from Nepal to India, for example—are enslaved for many years, and eventually work their way up in the business. Believing that they can get no other kind of work and that they will not be accepted back home, they may become recruiters, then mid-level managers. A small number eventually set up their own independent prostitution businesses.[31]

There are also re-recruiters, whose job is to seek out women who have just escaped or been released from debt-bonded prostitution and offer to help them find a "legitimate" job or provide them with some other service, with the ultimate purpose of bringing them back into the business. Once he or she has the woman's trust, the re-recruiter takes her to a new employer or employment agent, who again turns out to be a brothel or bar owner or a broker. The re-recruiter is paid a fee, and the woman is told that she has (again) been sold. It may seem naive on her part to be duped a second or even a third time, but many of these women are desperate, and, believing that they have nowhere else to turn, they may be too quick to accept what seems like a genuine offer of help. Re-recruiters can be likened to skilled salespersons—they are often very good at their job, which is, after all, how they make their living.

Recruitment is done by persuasion or by force. Persuasive strategies most often involve false promises of a legitimate job, but there are other lures, such as false promises of marriage, of lucrative and safe work in the sex industry, or of job training or educational opportunities.[32] Recruitment by force usually involves abduction, but it may also be done by incapacitating a woman (drugging her, knocking her out) or by threatening her or her family.

Recruitment by Persuasion: Illustrations

Recruiters who offer women and girls "good jobs" overseas usually work in developing countries or unstable, transitional countries, where women and girls (and their families) are particularly vulnerable to promises of lucrative jobs outside of or in another part of their country. Young girls from rural areas or remote villages are targeted because they are often more desperate for a job, more easily controlled, and more likely to be virgins, thus bringing a higher price for the traffickers and the eventual employers. Whether in a small village or a larger town, persuasion is enhanced by using recruiters with some connection to the community where the recruit pool resides. Often, even when the woman or girl desperately needs a job, there is some hesitation on her part or that of her family. Structural closeness (e.g., the recruiter lives in or grew up in the town; the recruiter is a family member, or a friend, or a friend of a friend) helps the woman overcome her doubts.

The Cadena family from Mexico, referred to in Chapter 2, capitalized on their local connections to recruit young Mexican women for prostitution in Florida. Recruits and their families thought of the Cadena brothers as much like themselves, growing up poor and living in their village or one nearby. One Cadena victim, Maria, whom we met in Chapter 2, tells a familiar story.[33] Although Maria's parents were reluctant, she finally convinced them that she should go to Florida with a man she thought to be her benefactor. Maria, 15 years old when she was recruited in 1996, recalled: "They told me I was going to work in Beto's [one of the Cadena brothers] house." "I told my mom. I said, 'they are going to pay me 1,000 pesos (about $125) a week.' She wouldn't let me go. . . . My father neither. They said no. But later I convinced them to let me go, so I could buy a little bit of land." With their permission, Maria left with Beto for Florida, where, for 2 months, she *did* work as a nanny for his children. Then, without warning,

Beto changed. He assaulted and raped Maria, and then told her that she would be working as a prostitute for the family organization from then on. Beto and his brother took Maria to a brothel and told her that "she had to work there." "I told them no," Maria said, "I cried. I kept saying no, that I didn't want to work there. Beto threatened me with the pistol again."[34]

Erika Maria, recruited at age 14, also lived in the same area as the Cadena family. One of the Cadena brothers told her and her parents that many young girls from the community, including his niece and his cousin, were going with him to Florida. Said the mother: "A lot of girls were going, to take care of children, wash dishes. So, she [her daughter] got excited. The truth is, we wouldn't let her go, but she got excited and said, 'Mama, I'm going, so I can pull us up.' How did we know they were going to trick her? With so many other girls going from here? And them saying their niece and cousin were going?" When they were interviewed, Erika Maria's parents had not heard from her for a year and a half.[35]

In their interviews with Thai women trafficked into the sex market in Japan, Human Rights Watch found that most had been recruited by a family member, neighbor, friend, or acquaintance. Rei, for example, said that she was approached by a Thai man who lived in her neighborhood and who was known to have gotten jobs in Japan for a number of women. Nam's friend convinced her to go to Japan for work, as "I could not find a job in Thailand and I saw that many women in the village had gone to Japan."[36]

The balance tips in favor of successful recruitment to the extent that the recruiter can establish rapport and win a potential recruit's confidence. Establishment of rapport is given a boost when the recruiter's credibility is verified by a friend, or even a friend of a friend, of the potential recruit. Girls and young women also seem to be more comfortable if a friend decides to go with them. When she was 16, Marina and her friends went to a dance in their hometown in Ukraine. Marina said that at the dance there "were a lot of young people and some boys from Kyiv [Kiev]. The boy from my school came up to me and said that one of the Kyivites wanted to speak to me. His name was Rostik. He offered me a job to work in Germany as a nurse. When my friend Nadja learned about this work she was also very interested in it." After the dance, however, Rostik disappeared, then resurfaced in the town some 6 months later. This time he said that he wanted to take Marina and her friend to Germany immediately. "He persuaded my friend and me that everything would be good. But Nadja's parents didn't allow her to go. I also started to hesitate but he persuaded me. Rostik promised that one woman who also wanted to work in Germany would go with me. I considered him a reliable and thoughtful person. So I agreed to go and promised to my grandmother to be back in a month."[37]

For Marina, like many whose trafficking does not require air travel, there were several stops along the way. Previously unknown persons entered and exited as they traveled by land and water. In Marina's words:

> Rostik asked me whether I had a foreign passport. But I hadn't even a Ukrainian passport. Then he said he would see to the affair by himself. . . . We went by car. There was a woman in the car, but she disappeared somewhere during the trip. I didn't notice that we crossed the Polish border. In Poland we stopped for a night in the house of one of Rostik's friends. He helped us to cross a river at night and we got to Germany. . . . We continued our trip by car. Some men brought me to a house. They told me that the owner was waiting for me inside and that I had to set the affair by myself. I left all my things in the car and came in. The owner was a middle-aged man. He told me some words in bad Russian and pushed me in a room and locked me there. I couldn't understand what had happened to me.[38]

Later, a Polish woman brought food to the room and asked Marina if she knew that she was to work as a prostitute. Marina "began to cry." But Marina was luckier than most. When, some days later, the Polish woman discovered that Marina, still locked in the room, was only 16, she helped her escape. With money and the woman's counsel, Marina got to Holland, contacted the police there, and, with the help of a nongovernmental group, was able to return to Ukraine. However, she felt that she could not go back to her small town to live, as the traffickers would find her there. In Marina's words, "the pimps are looking for me. They are very angry that I escaped. They said to my neighbors that I was a prostitute in Germany." Most likely, they were going to try to collect on their investment.[39]

While the specific circumstances vary, recruitment and transport experiences around the world have much in common. Women who believe they are doing something that will improve their lives or those of their families take off with or without the help of a recruiter and end up in a foreign country in enslaved prostitution. Potential recruits' misgivings, especially when the trip is overseas to a geographically and culturally distant land, can be assuaged when local recruiters offer their own successful experiences as examples—another persuasive tactic.

In her native Colombia, Maria badly needed a job when she met a girl at a party who said she knew a wealthy local woman with overseas job connections who could probably help Maria out. Maria went with her "new friend" to visit the woman at her elegant house, which, the woman said, was purchased with money she earned working overseas. The woman was encouraging, telling Maria that she could arrange a job as a domestic for her in the Netherlands, but that Maria would have to pay for her travel up front. Maria worked for a year to save the money. "My mother implored me not to go. She thought it was all so dubious. But I turned a deaf ear." When she went through customs after arriving at the airport in Amsterdam, Maria was apprehended because she did not have the required amount of money for admittance to the country.[40] She was taken into a room where several other young women in the same situation were waiting—and they had the same prospective employer's phone number. The next day the employer picked them all up at the airport, paying the police the necessary admittance fees. That first night, the employer raped Maria, and the next day he told her she would be working as a prostitute in a club. She had no choice but to comply.[41]

The trafficking of a young woman from The Gambia to culturally distant Sweden occurred in much the same way as the trafficking of Maria, except that in this case the recruiter was a foreigner. Susan was 17 and working in a hotel in her native Gambia when she was approached by a Swedish man who told her that he was a successful hotelier, was opening a five-star hotel in Sweden, and would like her to work there for him. He told her that the pay was much higher than what she was then making; moreover, the hotel would pay all her travel costs. Like other parents, Susan's father was not comfortable with her traveling so far alone with a stranger, but she decided to go anyway. The recruiter sent her a plane ticket and picked her up at the airport when she arrived in Stockholm. After putting her up in a hotel for the night, he delivered her to a brothel and left. There, Susan found herself with a group of teenage girls, three of whom were also from The Gambia. The girls told her that, like them, she had been sold by the recruiter into prostitution.[42]

Promises of marriage (to the recruiter or to an unknown husband in a destination country) constitute another, although less frequent, strategy for persuading potential recruits. Take Manuel, a Colombian man, who successfully recruited several women from Colombia to go to Western Europe with a promise that he would marry them there. Marcia, originally from the Dominican Republic but working in Colombia, met Manuel in a disco club in Bogotá. As, she later learned, he had said to others, Manuel said he would marry her in the Netherlands. She went with him, first stopping in Belgium (where obtaining a visa was easier than in the Netherlands). Once in the Netherlands, Marcia was forced into enslaved prostitution with other women and lived in terror under a changed Manuel—now hostile and violent. She finally escaped with the help of a customer, who let her stay at his house temporarily. Soon after her own escape, Marcia helped free Ana, another woman Manuel had trafficked from Colombia to Europe. Ana remembered that Manuel had come to "a rendezvous house for women who were looking for a husband. I was divorced and wanted to start a new life," she said. "I fell for him instantly. He even introduced himself to my parents as their future son-in-law. Later on I realized that he only did this to find out my parents' address so he could threaten them" should she cause him any trouble. Once in Europe, Manuel told Ana that she would be working as a prostitute and that he would kill her if she did not comply. He reinforced this threat by "putting a flick knife to her throat several times" and by killing her pet.[43] Manuel first had Ana work in brothels in Spain, then in Italy, and eventually in the Netherlands, where she met Marcia.

In developing countries, severe poverty and the desire to see daughters marry well make some families particularly vulnerable to such recruitment promises. Based on its study of trafficking from Nepal, Human Rights Watch notes that "village girls and their families are often deceived by smartly dressed young men who arrive in the village claiming to have come from Kathmandu and offering marriage and all the comfort of modern urban life." In some cases, the new couple actually have a wedding ceremony in the village, then leave, "never to be seen again." The girls are almost always forced into enslaved prostitution, usually in India.[44]

A show of affluence in small, rural villages can overwhelm and intimidate the local residents and yield new recruits for the trafficker. Human Rights Watch describes the arrival of a recruiter by helicopter in a remote Himalayan village, as she "descended like a celestial fairy mother in the midst of these poor village folk, in all her resplendent finery, and doled out little gifts of baubles and cosmetics to the starry-eyed adolescent girls." On this one trip, the recruiter took seven young girls with her back to Kathmandu.[45]

Recruiters also lure poor, young girls from Nepal and other Himalayan countries to work in carpet factories in Kathmandu, either to be eventually enslaved in prostitution there or as a first stop toward trafficking them to India or Pakistan for sale into the sex industry. In fact, brothels operate underground in some carpet factories in Kathmandu and other towns in Nepal. Some girls may migrate on their own, get a legitimate job in a carpet or cigarette factory, but then be recruited by a co-worker who supplements his or her own work in the factory with trafficking work.[46] That was the fate of 15-year-old Sanu, who in 1991 was working in a carpet factory in Nepal to help support her family when she was persuaded by a co-worker to go with him to another factory where, he said, she would have a better, higher-paying job. There Sanu was forced into prostitution, but was rescued and sent home a year later.

Many women and girls are initially recruited through advertisements—in newspapers, on the Internet, through an employment or travel agency, or through some other venue. Journalist Michael Specter found this ad, typical in Kiev:

> Girls: Must be single and very pretty. Young and tall. We invite you for work as models, secretaries, dancers, choreographers, gymnasts. Housing is supplied. Foreign posts available. Must apply in person.

A Ukrainian woman who responded to this ad told Specter that she met with the "employment agents," who asked her if she would be willing to work in a strip bar. She said she decided, "Why not?" They told her that it was necessary for her to leave immediately, and again she agreed. They traveled by car from Ukraine to Slovakia, and there the traffickers confiscated her passport, threatening her when she complained. From Slovakia they drove to Vienna, and then into Turkey, where she was set up in a bar, told that she owed her traffickers $5,000 for travel costs, and told that she couldn't leave until she paid off her debt. But she was arrested in a police raid just 3 days after her arrival.[47] She did not know whether or not she would have been forced to provide customers with sex, but she understood clearly that she had been lied to about the conditions of her work. While arrest, for this woman and others, brings an end to one "nightmare," it is often followed by days or months of waiting in jail. The usual outcomes of arrest—prosecution on criminal charges, release with no identification or money to get back home, deportation—give no recognition to the woman's victimization.[48]

Specter has found that the recruitment ads that were typically distributed in major cities in Ukraine have become less visible because, he believes, people in urban areas have become wise to the scam. The same ads, however, are now found more frequently in small towns and rural areas, where they are pulling in new recruits.[49]

Sometimes the ads are for specific jobs. German recruiter "Peter R.," arrested in 1996 on 36 charges of trafficking in humans, pimping, and bribery, had placed ads in Polish newspapers for babysitter jobs in Germany. Police believed that he had recruited and trafficked to Germany as many as 500 women.[50] And in Bangladesh, 475 women responded to ads run by an "employment agency" for jobs as housekeepers in the United Arab Emirates (UAE), signed contracts to that effect, and then were trafficked into enslaved prostitution in the UAE.[51]

Other ads emphasize the pay without even mentioning the work. In Brighton Beach, New York City, where there is a large Russian community, Russian-language newspapers have run ads such as, "Want to make $6,000 a month? You need to be pretty, communicative."[52] With new immigrants coming regularly into the community, the pool of young, unemployed women facing the high cost of living in the United States keeps growing. The income emphasis is targeted toward this pool of potential recruits.

Recruitment by Force: Illustrations

While most women and girls who are trafficked into debt-bonded prostitution go willingly, albeit hesitantly, with the trafficker *on the first part of their journey*, others are taken by force from the very beginning. Where traffickers have become more brazen, certain sites have become known places for kidnapping women and girls and forcing them into prostitution.

Refugee camps are often seen as ideal sites from which to abduct girls and women for trafficking into the sex market. Refugee camps in the war-torn former Yugoslav republics, for example, have become popular sites for abductions by Albanian traffickers, who then take the kidnapped girls and women through Albania and sell them into prostitution in neighboring Italy.[53] While some male refugees, desperate for money, sell female family members to traffickers, many other men live in constant fear of the abduction of their female relatives. As one husband and father living in a refugee camp lamented, "I would like to go out and fight in Kosovo, but how can I leave my family here?"[54]

Civil wars also "create" sex industry customers, and providers come forth to meet the demand. Albanian criminal gangs have been involved in the provision of women to soldiers and peacekeeping troops in the Yugoslav region. The Albanian traffickers have met military demand in part by extending their recruitment-by-abduction efforts in the region, kidnapping women from Ukraine, Moldova, Bulgaria, Romania, and other economically disadvantaged countries in Eastern Europe.[55]

In some regions, "bride abductions," in which traffickers kidnap women and sell them to brokers or directly to men seeking a wife, appear to be on the increase. According to the Coalition Against Trafficking in Women, the kidnapping of women for marriage by criminal gangs as well as individual entrepreneurs is a tremendous growth industry in China today.[56] Law enforcement and other local authorities have often been unwilling to take much action against such abductions, as they sympathize with the plight of Chinese men who are unable to find a wife.[57] However, in 1999, police did embark on a rescue campaign, and over the next few years rescued some 10,000 abducted women.[58]

Young girls are also kidnapped off the street, from their own yards, and from schoolyards. Some are trafficked into the adult sex industry, and some into pedophile sex and child pornography markets.[59]

Traffickers who are subsequently charged with trafficking by force typically claim that the girl migrated voluntarily. In the traffickers' network, there are often trafficker–witnesses who will testify in court that the defendant's testimony is true. But the experiences of so many victims tell another story. When she was 17, Kamala left her village in Nepal to visit relatives in a town close to the Indian border. While there, she was drugged and trafficked into India by her stepuncle and his son. Kamala recalls drinking milk given to her by her uncle that "smelled bad." Her next recollection is waking up on a train, and possibly after that, being transported by a taxi. When more alert, she found herself in a hotel lobby with her uncle and cousin. They left her there, ostensibly for a brief errand; shortly thereafter, two men approached her and told her she had been sold to them. Kamala described herself as "terrified," and then "shocked" when the hotel owner told her that her uncle and cousin were regular recruiters who had brought other girls to the hotel to sell. Unlike many, Kamala escaped her captors through a window in the hotel bathroom, but she had neither money nor means to get back to Nepal. She finally found work as a debt-bonded domestic servant in India. It took Kamala 9 years to work off her debt and save enough money for her trip back to Nepal in 1993.[60]

In other situations, women are lured to an apartment, house, or club, then held there against their will. In the early 1990s, two Bulgarian friends, Tonia and Natalie, were on their way to Greece for a vacation. In a café in Budapest, the two women met two Greek men, who told them that they were also on vacation. The men, who were brothers, invited the women to go with them to Germany for a few days, and after talking it over, they decided to accept the offer. In Düsseldorf, the men took the women to an apartment, where they imprisoned them. There they were gang-raped by customer–friends of the brothers. After they had been "broken in," the brothers took them from Germany to Amsterdam, where they forced them to work as prostitutes. The women finally escaped with the help of one of their customers and contacted the police, who later did find and arrest the brothers. At the trial, a number of witnesses for the defense countered the women's testimony, portraying them as ordinary professional prostitutes. In the end, the brothers were released and were even successful in suing the government for damages! After the trial, one of the women bitterly noted that all of the traffickers know one another and are part of an extensive support system for those facing criminal trafficking charges.[61]

Another scam, uncovered in 1999, resulted in the arrest of six men for forcing women into prostitution in Hong Kong. The six men were reportedly among a larger group of recruiters who hung out in train stations in Hong Kong, looking for female Chinese migrant workers who were coming to Hong Kong hoping to find work. The men were taught to recognize and approach such potential recruits, offering to help them get jobs. Women who went with the men to an apartment expecting employment assistance were gang-raped and photographed in the process. The recruiters typically threatened to send the photographs to the families of women who resisted their enslavement.[62]

Once women are broken in, their continued obedience is typically enforced by hired guards, whose job is to protect the interests of the sex establishment. This enforcer role is critical to the smooth running of the brothel or club business.

Enforcement and Extortion

Most employers who have purchased trafficked women for debt-bonded prostitution in their establishment (e.g., brothel, club, bar, massage parlor) use some kind of guard service. Guards, commonly referred to as "enforcers" or "roofs," are expected to watch over the women, to make sure that they are doing their jobs as told—showing up on time, getting customers to buy drinks, not refusing a customer for prostitution, dressing provocatively. Another enforcement task is to keep an eye on customers, seeing that they pay what they owe and that their behavior doesn't get too disruptive. Most important, however, is the enforcer's responsibility for making sure that the women don't escape. This responsibility often requires guards to escort the women whenever they are off the business premises.

The guard or enforcer role is pervasive in the trafficking industry, found across cultures and geographic regions and in large and small operations. In a report on sex trafficking throughout the Americas, Alison Phinney notes that a commonality among many women survivors, held in different types of establishments and under different employers, is their experience of confinement under the watchful eye of a guard. And, in most cases, if they were allowed to go outside the work premises, they were accompanied by a guard.[63]

Interviews with Thai women who had been trafficked into prostitution in Japan revealed similar experiences. As one of the woman, Pong, reported: "I was watched and controlled all the time. When somebody went out to buy food, another woman had to go with her. Mama ordered the Yakuza to watch the women to prevent escape. Mama told us that if anybody escaped from here, she would be killed." Pong was allowed to write home, but she could not give out her address, and thus could receive no mail.[64]

The Japanese mafia are known to be particularly protective of their "investment," usually assigning a guard to monitor the women's whereabouts at all times.[65] Should a woman escape, the Yakuza often post pictures of her, along with a request that other mafia members be on the lookout for her and return her to her employer should they find her. Sometimes,

Japanese police officers have actually been the ones to find and return the woman to her owner, collecting a fee or payment-in-kind for this service.[66]

In another trafficking operation, Asian women taken to American Samoa for work and then enslaved there reported being terrorized by and terrified of the ever-present guards assigned to watch over them as they worked. One woman reported that their movement was "very restricted." "Everyone leaving the compounds," she said, was searched by the guards, who "groped all over their body." Protests by the women resulted in strip searches; and, for other violations, women were beaten by the guards. The employer, according to this woman, "used big American Samoan guards to terrorize us," and told the women that the guards would kill them upon his order. Two women workers who had been able to get a complaint through to local authorities had disappeared, making everyone at the compound "fearful."[67]

Trafficking survivors commonly report brutalization by enforcers. Testifying at an antitrafficking conference in Washington, D.C., Inez, trafficked to the United States by the Cadena gang, recalled that one of the girls who had run away and been caught was severely beaten and raped in front of her and the other girls. "All I could do is stand there and watch," she said.[68] Rosa, another Cadena victim, said that because she was a virgin, she was subjected to repeated rapes by guards as a way of "breaking her in."[69]

Thai women trafficked to Japan also told interviewers that they were beaten by enforcers as a punishment for disobedience, and that beatings for escape attempts were especially brutal. Khai told an interviewer that when she was working in a snack bar in Japan, she was beaten if a customer complained about her in any way. Interviewees often retold stories that they had heard about others who had tried to escape. One, Miew, said that one of her co-workers at a snack bar had told her that a woman who had tried to escape for a second time was killed. "My friend said," Miew continued, "that if a woman escapes, she is killed and thrown away in the forest or the ocean."[70]

In addition to hiring on-site guards whose main responsibility is the employees, brothels and clubs also often pay guards for protecting them against police or immigration raids, interference from other criminal groups, and other external threats. In many instances, such a fee is demanded by guard–extorters. Extortion may be one of several profit-making activities of larger organized crime groups, or it may be an area in which a particular gang specializes. An example of the former is the Russian mafia: one report estimates that 70% to 80% of all businesses in major Russian cities are forced to pay protection money to the Russian mafia, and that protection may cost as much as half of a company's profits.[71] An example of the latter is Chinese gangs in the United States, which are paid by prostitution businesses for protection of their establishments.[72]

Sex business owners may be able to negotiate the fee for protection, even when dealing with organized crime extortionists. In an interview, the owner of one of the most successful Tel Aviv brothels, who employed trafficked Ukrainian and Russian women as prostitutes, revealed that initially, Israeli mafia protection cost him from 5% to 6% of his net profit, but that as time went on, the mafia regularly raised its fee. Eventually, he was able to negotiate a partnership with them, saving himself a good deal of money in the long run.[73]

In addition to mafias and gangs, protection may be provided by private companies, or even by law enforcement authorities. In research discussed earlier, Global Survival Network staff, posing as potential U.S.-based business partners, interviewed Sergey, a Moscow-based pimp–entrepreneur who was well connected in Russia and beyond. Sergey introduced GSN staff to the director of a private security firm, who in turn offered them a variety of protection services, including bodyguards, investigative work, and a guarantee of safe transport for recruits. The director told GSN staff that they "collaborate very closely with the police . . . and therefore don't have any problems with criminal groups." The director also noted that they had additional services in which the American company might be interested. His company, for example, had business associations with a local travel agency that could arrange for Russian women to be trafficked as "travel agents" to the United States.[74]

While extortion and protection are roles that can be played by either criminal groups or legitimate public officials, some services to traffickers require a position of trust, and thus must be provided by an insider. Services provided by such "corrupt guardians" are considered next.

Corrupt Guardians

The police and other public authorities facilitate sex trafficking by their failure to react, as well as by their proactive participation in the industry. It is clear that some police officers, border guards, immigration personnel, and other officials intentionally do not interrupt trafficking activities, and may take a bribe to "look the other way." Traffickers, according to one source, see the police and other public authorities as "valuable collaborators."[75] "In fact," as Human Rights Watch points out, "many believe that the international phenomenon of trafficking in women for forced prostitution could not exist at any level without the involvement of such officials."[76]

Inaction by the police and other public officials—whether for economic gain (such as a bribe), avoidance of trouble, lack of concern, or some other reason—includes allowing recruitment to go on (sometimes in public view), permitting illegal border crossings to occur, not questioning faulty identification papers, failing to make arrests of suspicious persons along trafficking routes, and turning away trafficked women who come to them for help.[77]

Public officials may also actively facilitate sex trafficking, using their positions of authority individually, without agency knowledge, or as members of a corrupt agency. Active involvement is usually in return for a monetary payment or payment-in-kind, and includes extortion and protection; the making, altering, or illegal issuing of identification papers; and the actual trafficking of women.

Inaction for Payment

In his market analysis of the sex trafficking industry, Phil Williams identifies corrupt police, immigration, and other officials who take payoffs or bribes for "turning a blind eye" to sex trafficking as critical "market actors" in the industry.[78] By their inaction, Williams points out, they reduce traffickers' law enforcement risks and thus increase their profits. The taking of payments for inaction against sex traffickers by corrupt officials is pervasive, found not just in developing and transitional countries, where poverty and unemployment may make the taking of bribes more understandable, but also in affluent destination countries, such as the United States, Japan, and Western and Central European countries.[79]

In Nepal, where sex trafficking revenues are important to the country and to poorly paid police and border guards, bribes are a regular part of doing business. A Nepali villager told Human Rights Watch that if "a trafficker ends up in prison it means he or she hasn't paid off the police," and that at all border crossing points, "the police come if they suspect trafficking. But they don't try to arrest; they just take bribes. You can see them go down through the bus collecting money. It's very visible."[80]

The paying off of police may be a regular task assigned to particular persons or groups in sex trade businesses. In one example, the Director of the Bombay Municipal Health Clinic described the "harmonious" division of labor among Indian organized crime groups in control of the sex industry in Bombay, in which one crime group was in charge of paying off police and politicians.[81]

In the United States, where sex trafficking revenues are much less important to the country and where police and border guards are paid much better than in most developing and transitional countries, there is evidence of a "relatively high degree of collusion" between traffickers and public officials, including bribes paid to law enforcement officers, border officers, and immigration officials at airports.[82]

As indicated earlier, refugee camps, which contain mostly women and children, have become a site of increased recruitment efforts. And there is growing evidence that in some camps—for example, camps for refugees from Kosovo run by Albanian authorities—guards can be bribed to allow the recruitment or abduction of women and children. The result is that, as refugee camps swell, traffickers have access to increasing numbers of women and children for forced trafficking into prostitution.[83]

Police, prosecutors, and judges also take bribes for dropping charges against traffickers. In one of many examples, Global Survival Network found evidence of the Yakuza paying the Japanese police to drop charges for a number of illegal activities, including trafficking.[84] And in Russia, where the legal infrastructure is severely compromised, some judges and procurators (who supervise criminal investigations) routinely give in to bribes and threats by reducing or dismissing criminal trafficking-related charges.[85]

Inaction Without Payment

Investigation of trafficking and prostitution rings is often a low priority for law enforcement authorities.[86] As long as the activity is not too disruptive or too flagrant, it may be easier to let it continue. To begin with, traffickers and the women they have trafficked into prostitution are typically foreigners, complicating the legal process all the way from law enforcement through the courts. Furthermore, the women are usually breaking the law, in spite of their enslavement—that is, they are most likely illegal immigrants and, in many countries, they are in violation of laws against prostitution and related vice. So one dilemma, in some officials' minds, is whether to treat the women as victims of trafficking (which is difficult to prove) or as offenders (which is much easier to prove). Add to this the cultural norms that place prostitutes at the bottom of virtually any scale of female goodness—as well as public ambivalence, at best, about the morality of prostitution—and it makes even more sense that prostitute-as-offender might prevail over prostitute-as-victim. There *is* evidence that the police in some jurisdictions are more likely to arrest the prostitutes than the traffickers behind them.[87]

Moreover, the criminal network in a given trafficking case is often complex and far-reaching. There is little inducement, as Richard Brown, the district attorney in Queens, New York, has pointed out, for vice officers to take on the "more complex, large-scale operations aimed at breaking up prostitution rackets tied into human smuggling networks believed to be active in the city."[88]

There are other reasons why the police may be reluctant to be proactive in a fight against sex trafficking, and they vary by place and situation. Just as financial gain may motivate some police officers to actively facilitate sex trafficking, economic issues figure in the disinclination of the police and other officials to try to do much about trafficking at all. In major source countries, such as Nepal, Ukraine, and some Caribbean nations, the police and other government officials are clearly aware of the importance of the sex trade to the economic well-being of the country.[89] And, in some cases, police officers contribute to the country's coffers as regular sex consumers themselves.[90]

Others have suggested that the police often do not intervene in trafficking due to their fear of retaliation by organized crime groups—a fear that is not unjustified. International organized crime groups can and do carry out threats they make against those who get in the their way, including the police and other public officials.[91] Why, then, the reasoning goes, use valuable resources in a fight against an activity that benefits your community financially, which might prove difficult and dangerous as well?

Active Involvement for a Monetary Payment or Payment-in-Kind

There are myriad ways in which public officials may help out traffickers in a particular situation, but most prominent and patterned among them are, first, the provision, typically by immigration officials or diplomats, of identification papers for the women to be trafficked, and second, the provision of protection to brothels and clubs by police.

Provision of Identification Papers Corrupt guardians with immigration and embassy positions or connections are involved in the illegal provision of identification papers for trafficking recruits—including passports, visas, and drivers' licenses.[92] Papers are either drawn up in the applicant's name but illegally issued, or issued in a fake or stolen name, and thus illegally produced. Available evidence suggests that in most cases, identification papers are illegally provided by corrupt individuals or small groups within an agency, and that the practice is not systemic. While traffickers know whom to contact to get illegal identification papers, the way in which such documents are actually produced may be unknown to them.[93] Similarly, when authorities or journalists have uncovered such document fraud, they have often been unable to penetrate the system deeply enough to get the whole picture of the practice.

Thai newspapers have published a number of stories about Thai officials getting false identification papers for a fee; and a Thai government official working in Tokyo told Human Rights Watch that traffickers were able to get Japanese visas from Thai embassy staff for about $1,600 (in 1995) apiece.[94] However, little has been published about the way in which this fraud is perpetrated.

Women who have been recipients of such documents seem to have only a sketchy understanding of the process. Khai, for example, trafficked from Thailand to Japan, told how she went with a broker (who had purchased her from her recruiter) to apply for a Thai passport in another woman's name. The broker picked the passport up later. Next she was sent to the Japanese embassy to apply for a visa, where she was asked no questions at all. Other Thai women trafficked to Japan had similar experiences; several noted that their brokers had connections with government officials, and thought that this accounted for the ease with which they were able to get passports and visas.[95] Yet another Thai woman trafficked to Japan told Human Rights Watch that her broker had given her a password to use when she went through immigration in Japan; she used it, and went through with no questions asked. This woman, age 21, carried a passport identifying her as a 51-year-old woman. Responding to these reports by trafficked women, a Metropolitan Division Deputy Commander in Bangkok said that it is "difficult to leave Thailand and enter Japan with a fake passport. Without assistance from the immigration authorities, it would be almost impossible for them to slip through the tight control [of immigration]."[96]

Reports from around the world indicate that in most source, transit, and destination countries, documentation and passage through immigration are facilitated by corrupt officials. In her report on sex trafficking to the United States, for example, Richard found evidence of corrupt American officials accepting bribes for passports, visas, and even citizenship papers.[97] The U.S. Immigration and Naturalization Service (INS) has admitted that traffickers have most likely "corrupted" some senior-level officials, along with officials in key positions, such as "immigration officials at airports" and "consular workers in U.S. embassies abroad."[98] Across the world, in Israel, the owner of a successful brothel in Tel Aviv told journalist Cynthia McFadden that he had contacts with corrupt officials in the Israeli Interior Ministry, from whom he could get false Israeli identification papers for $1,000 per person.[99]

Provision of Protection In some countries or cities, the police extort money from sex trafficking rings or prostitution businesses for protection from or warnings about investigations, raids, arrests, and other forms of harassment. Sometimes an entire police department is involved; in other cases, the extortion is done by a single officer or a small group of officers.

An example of the former is the reported involvement of police in the extortion of protection money from brothels in Delhi, India. According to one report, the protection racket there, at least in the mid-1990s, was complex and systemic. From each brothel, the police received 33 cents out of each standard customer fee of $1.83; from this income, money was paid out daily to police officers, with sums differing by officer rank.[100] The police also reportedly participated in a system of "registering" trafficked women, in which the brothel madam would notify them of and pay them a fee for each new arrival. The fee was figured as a percentage of the madam's purchase price for the woman, typically between about $166 and $833. If the new girl was a minor, the police were paid as usual, but the girl was held by them for a day, after which time she was taken in front of the local court with falsified identification containing a new (adult) age. Similar systems are said to operate in Bombay.[101]

Police agencies in Russia are also heavily involved in the extortion of money from sex businesses for protection. In fact, the police and the Russian mafia are often in competition for the provision of protection to brothels and other sex businesses. A former Moscow pimp reported, for example, that he had a choice between protection provided by the Russian mafia and by the Russian police, and said that he preferred to do business with the mafia because they were more effective and more trustworthy.[102] In some instances, however, there is a clear division of labor between the Russian mafia and the police. It is generally understood, for example, that the police "run" street prostitution in Russia, and that they are paid by pimps for protection.[103]

Individual police officers or small groups of officers, acting in opposition to agency norms, also extort money from and provide protection to traffickers and brothel owners. A 1998 raid on a Korean "massage parlor–health club" in Providence, Rhode Island, where six trafficked Korean women were working in enslaved prostitution, led to the finding that a local police officer had been extorting money from the club for protection. The officer was also paid by the club owners for finding women who had escaped, and in one case, he had actually gone to Hawaii to find and bring back a woman.[104]

Trafficking Women The police are also sometimes involved in the actual trafficking of women. A particularly egregious case occurred in Greece, where, following the 1998 filing of charges against police officers for their part in trafficking women into prostitution, an Internal Affairs Bureau was established to investigate police corruption. In the 1998 case, two police officers had been forced to resign due to charges against them for "procuring and forcing women into prostitution."[105] According to the press, these charges were among 16 issued against police officers for trafficking and for getting false residence and work permits for "foreign, illegal prostitutes working under appalling conditions as virtual sex slaves for Greek and Albanian gangs."[106]

In its first (2001) report, the Greek Internal Affairs Bureau recorded 146 charges against 74 police officers, about half of which were related to undocumented migrants, including such things as granting illegal resident and work permits, involvement in prostitution rings, and sex trafficking. Following the 2001 conviction and incarceration of one Greek police officer for trafficking in women, the Greek government acknowledged that some officers were involved "in networks which traffic illegal women" to Greece.[107]

Favors The police and other public officials sometimes exchange favors with traffickers and find that such cooperation works well, at least for a while, for both sides. In a 1996 case in Germany, the chief of the Special Commission on Organized Crime in Frankfurt an der Oder (on the German–Polish border) was arrested for his involvement in a prostitution ring in which women were trafficked into Germany from Eastern Europe. The chief was accused of exchanging favors with a local German sex procurer: the procurer gave the chief information about organized crime activities, and in turn, the chief told the procurer of planned raids on his own brothels. For this favor, the chief was paid a fee and also received payment-in-kind—free sex in the procurer's brothels.[108]

Another favor provided by police, either for a fee or in exchange for cooperation from traffickers, is the return to the employer of trafficked women who have escaped and gone to the police. Gillian Caldwell of Global Survival Network recalled the response to her effort to tell the police in Tokyo of GSN findings about police involvement in trafficking. "In Tokyo," she said, "a sympathetic senator arranged a meeting for us with senior police officials to discuss the growing prevalence of trafficking from Russia into Japan. The police insisted it wasn't a problem, and they didn't even want the concrete information we could have provided. That didn't surprise local relief agencies, who cited instances in which police had actually sold trafficked women back to the criminal networks which had enslaved them."[109]

Sri, a Thai woman trafficked into prostitution in Japan, described her contact with the police following a fire in the bar in which she was working. The police came to the building and asked the women if they wanted to go back home. She and two other women said "yes," and were taken by the police to the station house. Sri said: "We were separated at the police station and questioned by the police, but only about the fire. When the questioning was done the police released us the same day to our snack bar owner. The owner sold us to another snack in Ibaraki for $3,300."[110] Stating that there were many such cases, an attorney working with women's shelters in Tokyo referred to one in which a Filipina prostitute had been assaulted by a client at the bar at which she worked and had gone to the police, who subsequently returned her to the bar.[111] And in yet another Japanese case, two police officers were forced to resign (no criminal charges were filed) after turning two Thai women back to a known former Yakuza member, who was at the time reportedly involved in trafficking women.[112]

Traffickers also do business with politicians who will protect a trafficking ring or brothel, get a trafficker released from custody, or grant some other favor.[113] Research on trafficking in Nepal and India has revealed a close connection between politicians and the traffickers, in which traffickers routinely call on politicians to keep them out of the criminal justice system. At times, the police have released a trafficker as a favor to a politician.[114] In exchange, traffickers give politicians campaign contributions, votes, and "classified" information. For embassy officials in particular, information about sex trafficking may be of high political and diplomatic value.[115]

Concluding Comments

The trafficking industry is structurally organized as a collection of networks that are differentially called into play as needed for particular transactions. Although flexible, this structure includes a number of well-defined roles. Role specialization does occur, but there are also generalists who combine roles. The industry includes individual, small-group, and organized crime players. Networks link units at all levels (e.g., individuals with organized crime groups and organized crime groups with other organized crime groups). Corrupt guardians, in their positions of public service and authority, are an integral part of these networks. Donna Hughes applies Brunon Holyst's analysis of organized crime in Eastern Europe to sex trafficking specifically:

> As the influence of criminal networks deepens, the corruption goes beyond an act of occasionally ignoring illegal activity to providing protection by

> blocking legislation that would hinder the activities of the groups. As law enforcement personnel and government officials become more corrupt and members of the crime groups gain more influence, the line between the state and the criminal networks starts to blur.[116]

This has happened in particular, according to Hughes and others, in Russia and other Newly Independent States and Eastern European countries, where unstable transitions to a market economy have been fraught with income and employment decline and a breakdown in governmental infrastructure. The Russian mafia has gained control over, or at least influence in, much of the private and public sectors in Russia today. The next chapter examines the involvement in sex trafficking of the Russian mafia and other organized crime syndicates, including the Japanese Yakuza and Chinese Triads as well as other, newer groups.

Notes

1. James O. Finckenauer and Jennifer Schrock (retrieved February 18, 2003), "Human Trafficking: A Growing Criminal Market in the U.S.," National Institute of Justice International, available at http://www.ojp.usdoj/gov/nij/international/ht.html (8 pp.).
2. Gerben J. N. Bruinsma and Guus Meershoek (1999) "Organized Crime and Trafficking in Women from Eastern Europe in the Netherlands," pp. 105–117 in *Illegal Immigration and Commercial Sex: The New Slave Trade*, ed. by Phil Williams (London/Portland, OR: Frank Cass). The term "cliques of professionals" comes from H. Abadinsky (1983), *The Criminal Elite: Professional and Organized Crime* (Westport, CT: Greenwood Press) [cited in Bruinsma and Meershoek].
3. A. Graycar (2000), "Trafficking in Human Beings." *Australian Institute of Criminology* (July), available at http://www.aic.gov.au/conferences/other/trafficking.htm.
4. Ho-Lin Chin, Sheldon Zhang, and Robert J. Kelly (retrieved June 4, 2003), "Transnational Chinese Organized Crime Activities: Patterns and Emerging Trends," *Transnational Organized Crime*, Special Issue: "Combating Transnational Crime," ed. by Phil Williams and Dimitri Vlassis, available at http://www.frankcass.com/jnls/toc.htm.
5. Amy O'Neill Richard (1999), *International Trafficking in Women to the United States: A Contemporary Manifestation of Slavery and Organized Crime* (November), DCI Exceptional Intelligence Analyst Program: An Intelligence Monograph (Center for the Study of Intelligence).
6. S. M. Tumbahamphe and B. Bhattarai (retrieved November 1, 2002), "Trafficking of Women in South Asia," ANNFSU-Asian Students

Association, available at http://www.ecouncil.ac.cr/about/contrib/women/youth/english/traffic1.htm.

7. Susan Moran (1993), "New World Havens of Oldest Profession," *Insight on the News* 9 (June 21).
8. Sarah Shannon (1999), "Prostitution and the Mafia: The Involvement of Organized Crime in the Global Sex Trade," pp. 119–144 in *Illegal Immigration and Commercial Sex: The New Slave Trade*, ed. by Phil Williams (London/Portland, OR: Frank Cass).
9. Ibid., p. 124.
10. Phil Williams (retrieved June 4, 2003), "Organizing Transnational Crime: Networks, Markets and Hierarchies," *Transnational Organized Crime*, Special Issue: "Combating Transnational Crime," ed. by Phil Williams and Dimitri Vlassis, available at http://www.frankcass.com/jnls/toc.htm (p. 1 of 1).
11. Louise I. Shelley (1997), "The Price Tag of Russian Organized Crime," *Transition* (February), p 7.
12. Finckenauer and Schrock (2003), op. cit.; Richard (1999), op. cit.
13. Phil Williams (1998), "The Nature of Drug-Trafficking Networks," *Current History* 97, p. 154 (pp.154–159).
14. Ibid., p. 155.
15. Finckenauer and Schrock (2003), op. cit.; Graycar (2000), op. cit.; Phil Williams (1999), "Trafficking in Women and Children: A Market Perspective," pp. 145–170 in *Illegal Immigration and Commercial Sex: The New Slave Trade*, ed. by Phil Williams (London/Portland, OR: Frank Cass).
16. Phil Williams (1998), op. cit., p. 157. Williams argues that one way to keep others from understanding the network in its entirety is to provide members with only the information that they need to complete their particular task or to communicate with particular others in the network. This way, if an individual is arrested and prosecuted, he or she will not be able to describe and thus expose the network organization.
17. Ibid., p. 157.
18. Ibid., p. 157. Williams refers to Charles Perrow's 1984 book *Normal Accidents*, in which Perrow uses the term "loose coupling" to refer to flexible systems that offer "time, resources, and alternative paths" to manage threats to them. The opposite is tightly coupled systems, in which threats often result in a "chain reaction."
19. Information on sex trafficking operations is often incomplete, in great part because of the nature of trafficking networks, including the "need-to-know basis for knowledge" philosophy described in the narrative. That is, people involved in trafficking often do not know the whole

story, and some of what they report is hearsay. Also, trafficking networks are flexible and transcendent, making them difficult to follow. Finally, much of what is known about the experiences of trafficked women and girls comes from interviews or more formal testimony in which interviewees are asked about parts, but not all, of their experiences.

20. Gillian Caldwell, Steve Galster, and Nadia Steinzor (1997), "Crime and Servitude: An Exposé of the Traffic in Women for Prostitution from the Newly Independent States," report presented at conference on "The Trafficking of Women Abroad" (Washington, DC: Global Survival Network).
21. Moran (1993), op. cit.
22. Human Rights Watch (2000), "Owed Justice: Thai Women Trafficked into Debt Bondage in Japan" (September), available at http://www.hrw.org/reports/2000/japan; Richard (1999), op. cit.; Williams (1999), op. cit.
23. Also, as discussed in the upcoming section on "corrupt guardians," the police sometimes provide protection for and extort money from sex traffickers and sex businesses.
24. Caldwell et al. (1997), op. cit.
25. Chapter 5 discusses economic causes and benefits that motivate private sector participants in or facilitators of sex trafficking.
26. Because most persons trafficked for prostitution are women and girls and most customers are men, pimps in the sex trafficking industry are largely procurers for heterosexual transactions. More pimps are male than female. Female pimp–employers are usually found in brothels or clubs; most pimps who work women on the street are men.
27. International Organization for Migration (1996), "Trafficking in Women to Austria for Sexual Exploitation" (June) (Budapest: Migration Information Programme).
28. Amy O'Neill Richard (1999), "Appendix II: International Organized Crime and Its Involvement in Trafficking Women and Children Abroad," *International Trafficking in Women to the United States: A Contemporary Manifestation of Slavery and Organized Crime* (November), DCI Exceptional Intelligence Analyst Program: An Intelligence Monograph (Center for the Study of Intellience).
29. Human Rights Watch–Asia (1995), "Rape for Profit: Trafficking of Nepali Girls and Women into India's Brothels" (October), available at http://www.hrw.org/reports/1995/India.htm.
30. Ibid.
31. Ibid.
32. Virtually all researchers studying sex trafficking point out that the primary and most successful recruitment strategy is persuasion through

deception, and the lure is usually a false job promise. See, for example, Francis T. Miko, with assistance of Grace (Jea-Hyun) Park (2000), "Trafficking in Women and Children: The U.S. and International Response," Congressional Research Service Report 98-649C, May 10, International Information Programs, U.S. Department of State, available at http://usinfo.state.gov/topical/global/traffic/crs0510.htm; Richard (1999), op. cit.; Caldwell et al. (1997), op. cit.

33. Sean Gardiner and Geoffrey Mohan (2001), "The Sex Slaves from Mexico: Teen-agers Tell of Forced Prostitution," Newsday.com, March 12, available at http://www.newsday.com/news/local/newyork/ny-smuggled-mexico.story. Also, it should be noted that personal stories told by victims of sex trafficking largely come from interviews with or testimony of women who are no longer in trafficked prostitution. They have either been rescued, escaped on their own, or paid off their debt, and thus are, from one perspective, survivors of sex trafficking. Here again, they may have been asked specific questions, which would have guided the data collected in the interview and may have resulted in some information being left out, making their stories seem incomplete.
34. Ibid. (p. 3 of 7).
35. Ibid. (p. 4 of 7).
36. Human Rights Watch (2000), op. cit.
37. The Protection Project (2002), "Survivor Stories," *Human Rights Report on Trafficking in Persons, Especially Women and Children: A Country-by-Country Report on a Contemporary Form of Slavery*, 2nd ed. (The Paul H. Nitze School of Advanced International Studies, Johns Hopkins University).
38. Ibid.
39. Ibid.
40. Sietske Altink (1995), *Stolen Lives: Trading Women into Sex and Slavery* (London: Scarlett Press). Altink (p. 67) reports that in some destinations, foreigners are required to show immigration officers that they have a designated sum of money in order for them to stay in the country. Traffickers often lend women the sum, which they must give back once in the country.
41. Ibid.
42. Saihou Mballow (2000), *ECPAT News* (March), available at http://www.dreamwater.net/ecpatusa/enews1.html.
43. Altink (1995), op. cit.
44. Human Rights Watch–Asia (1995), op. cit., p. 10.
45. Ibid., p. 10.
46. Ibid.

47. Michael Specter (1998), "Traffickers' New Cargo: Naive Slavic Women," *The New York Times*, January 11, pp. 1, 6.
48. Ibid.
49. Ibid.
50. Caldwell et al. (1997), op. cit.
51. Farid Hossain (1995), "Bangladeshis in Persian Gulf Duped into Prostitution," Associated Press, September 7.
52. Victoria Pope (1997), "Trafficking in Women: Procuring Russians for Sex Abroad—Even in America," *U.S. News and World Report* (April 7), p. 43. Available at http://www.globalsurvival.net/other/usnews/9704.html.
53. Lori Montgomery (1991), "Some Female Kosovo Refugees Are Falling Prey to Criminal Gangs in Albania," *South Coast*, May 22, available at http://www.s-t.com/daily/05-99/05-22-99/c07/wn125.htm (4 pp.).
54. Ibid.
55. Hank Hyena (2000), "Albanian Gangsters Kidnapping Women and Girls to Service Troops," *Urge* [salon.com], February 9, available at http://archive.salon.com/health/sex/urge/world/2000/02/09/kosovo (3 pp.).
56. Coalition Against Trafficking in Women–Asia Pacific (retrieved October 31, 2002), "Trafficking in Women and Prostitution in the Asian Pacific," available at http://www.catwinternational.org/fb/html.
57. In China, the one-child-per-family population policy and a cultural preference for a male child has resulted in a shortage of women. With families limited to one child, the birth of a female is often negatively received, and the female infant may be abandoned, given up for adoption, hidden, or even killed, with the hope that a second child will be a boy.
58. Elisabeth Rosenthal (2001), "Harsh Chinese Reality Feeds a Black Market in Women," *The New York Times*, June 25.
59. Duncan Hewitt (2001), "China Targets Kidnappers," BBC News, April 1, available at http://news.bbc.co.uk/2/hi/world/asia-pacific/698145.stm; Human Rights Watch–Asia (1995), op. cit.; Casa Alianza (1999), Report by Guatemalan Human Rights Procurator, *Prensa Libre*, June 6; Shannon (1999), op. cit. Chapter 8 looks in greater depth at sex trafficking in children for pedophile and pornography markets.
60. Human Rights Watch–Asia (1995), op. cit.
61. Altink (1995), op. cit.
62. Feminist Majority Foundation (1999), "Hong Kong: Six Men Charged with Sex Trafficking," Feminist Daily News Wire, June 14.
63. Alison Phinney (2002), "Trafficking of Women and Children for Sexual Exploitation in the Americas" (Washington D.C.: Pan American Health Organization/World Health Organization).

64. Human Rights Watch (2000), op. cit., p. 21.
65. Center for the Study for Intelligence Report (2003), op. cit.
66. Ibid.
67. Ibid.
68. Gardiner and Mohan (2001), op. cit.
69. Ibid.
70. Human Rights Watch (2000), op. cit.
71. Annelise Anderson (1995), "The Red Mafia: A Legacy of Communism," p. 3 in *Economic Transition in Eastern Europe and Russia: Realities of Reform*, ed. by Edward P. Lazear (Stanford, CA: Hoover Institution Press).
72. Richard (1999), op. cit.
73. Shannon (1999), op. cit.
74. Gillian Caldwell, Steve Galster, Jyothi Kanics, and Nadia Steinzor (1999), "Capitalizing on Transition Economies: The Role of the Russian Mafiya in Trafficking Women for Forced Prostitution," pp. 42–73 in *Illegal Immigration and Commercial Sex: The New Slave Trade*, ed. by Phil Williams (London/Portland, OR: Frank Cass).
75. Martina Vandenberg (1997), "Trafficking of Women to Israel and Forced Prostitution: A Report by the Israel Women's Network" (November).
76. Human Rights Watch (2001), "Trafficking of Migrant Women for Forced Prostitution in Greece" (July).
77. Virtually all research examining connections between sex traffickers and law enforcement authorities has found evidence that the police occasionally or regularly allow sex trafficking to operate by "looking the other way."
78. Williams (1999), op. cit.
79. See, for example, Human Rights Watch (2001), op. cit. [on Greece]; Donna M. Hughes (2000), "The 'Natasha' Trade: The Transnational Shadow Market of Trafficking in Women," *Journal of International Affairs*, Special Issue: "In the Shadows: Promoting Prosperity or Undermining Stability?" 53 (Spring), pp. 625–651 [on the NIS and Japan]; Human Rights Watch (2000), op. cit. [on Japan]; Caldwell et al. (1999), op. cit. [on the NIS]; Richard (1999), op. cit. [on the United States]; Penelope Turnbull (1999), "The Fusion of Immigration and Crime in the European Union: Problems of Cooperation and the Fight Against the Trafficking in Women," pp. 189–213 in *Illegal Migration and Commercial Sex: The New Slave Trade*, ed. by Phil Williams (London/Portland, OR: Frank Cass) [on Poland].
80. Human Rights Watch–Asia (1995), op. cit.
81. Robert I. Friedman (1996), "India's Shame: Sexual Slavery and Political Corruption Are Leading to an AIDS Catastrophe," *The Nation* 262 (April 8), p. 10.

82. Finckenauer and Schrock (2003), op. cit., p. 4; Richard (1999), op. cit.
83. Montgomery (1999), op. cit.
84. Caldwell et al. (1999), op. cit.
85. Ibid.
86. Ibid.
87. Human Rights Watch–Asia (1995), op. cit.
88. Anthony M. Destefano (2001), "Policing Prostitution—Cops: Trafficking of Immigrants Difficult to Investigate," Newsday.com, March 14, available at http://www.newsday.com/news/local/newyork/ny-smuggled-police,0,2129745.story (3 pp.).
89. Human Rights Watch–Asia (1995), op. cit.
90. Ibid.
91. Miko (2000), op. cit. See Chapter 4 for a fuller discussion of organized crime groups' involvement in sex trafficking.
92. The illegal preparation and issuing of identification papers is another service that is also provided by otherwise legitimate businesses and entrepreneurs in the private sector.
93. Such lack of knowledge is consistent with the "knowledge on a need-to-know basis" practice in trafficking networks.
94. Human Rights Watch (2000), op. cit.
95. Ibid.
96. Ibid., p. 12.
97. Richard (1999), op. cit.
98. Finckenauer and Schrock (2003), op. cit.
99. Shannon (1999), op. cit.
100. Human Rights Watch–Asia (1995), op. cit., p. 20.
101. Ibid., pp. 20–21.
102. Caldwell et al. (1999), op. cit.
103. Ibid.
104. Kristen Lombardi (retrieved February 10, 2003), "Slave Labor: Trafficking in Women and Children," *The Phoenix*, Polaris Project: Combatting the Trafficking of Women and Children. Available at http://www.polarisproject.org/polarisproject/phoenix1.htm.
105. "Avalanche of Corruption Charges Blasts Police After Procurement Arrests," (1998), *Athens News*, November 11.
106. Ibid.
107. "Anti-Graft Office Has Its Work Cut Out" (2001), *Kathimerini*, February 16; "Editorial: Self-Cleanup" (2001), *Kathimerini*, February 16; "Probe into Huge Prostitution Racket" (2000), *Kathimerini*, June 12.
108. Caldwell et al. (1999), op. cit.
109. Michael Specter (1998), op. cit.
110. Human Rights Watch (2000), op. cit., p. 29
111. Ibid., p. 30.

112. Ibid.
113. Phil Williams (1999), op. cit.
114. Human Rights Watch–Asia (1995), op. cit.
115. Finckenauer and Schrock (2003), op. cit.; Graham Rayman (2001), "Stripped of Their Dignity: Czech Women Lured to Work at NYC Sex Clubs," Newsday.com, March 16, available at http://www.newsday.com/news/local/newyork/ny-smuggled-eastereurope,0,4558166.story (6 pp.).
116. Hughes (2000), op. cit. [paraphrasing Brunon Holyst (1999), "Organized Crime in Eastern Europe and Its Implications for the Security of the Western World," pp. 67–93 in *Organized Crime—Uncertainties and Dilemmas*, ed. by Stanley Einstein and Menachem Amir (Chicago: The Office of International Criminal Justice).]

4

Sex Trafficking and the Changing Face(s) of Organized Crime

In the summer of 1994, Russian police found the bodies of a young woman and a middle-aged man in a hotel in Vladivostok. The couple, who had been tortured prior to being shot, were later identified as 49-year-old Gary Alderice, a well-known Hong Kong lawyer and distant relative of the British royal family, and 20-year-old Natasha Samofalova, who had accompanied Alderice on several business trips to Hong Kong. Samofalova had been trafficked from Russia to Macau, where she was working in a club that had a business agreement with a Russian mafia group. Several months before she was murdered, Samofalova had left the club, flown to Vladivostok, and moved into an apartment there. The police learned that Alderice had been a customer of Samofalova's and had been instrumental in helping her escape from the club. According to friends of his, Alderice had planned to pay off her debt, thus securing her freedom. But to the Russian mafia, his actions constituted theft of their valuable merchandise—and for that the punishment was swift and severe.

Initially, the Russian police wrote the case off as a robbery "gone bad," bringing forth speculation that the police were working with, or at least deferring to, the mafia. Perhaps because of Alderice's prominence, however, pressure was put on the police for a more in-depth investigation. Eventually, they arrested a man by the name of Sergei Sukhanov for the murders. Prior to working in Macau, Samofalova had worked for Sukhanov at a travel agency that set up cruises for affluent Russians to go to Japan to buy cars. Sukhanov admitted that he had helped Samofalova find her apartment when she came to Vladivostok, but he denied any involvement in her murder. Within a few weeks, the police had released Sukhanov and had begun to investigate other possible suspects. Several good leads vanished when the suspects themselves turned up dead.[1] The case remains unresolved.

In their own investigation in 1996, Global Survival Network staff traveled to the Macau club where Samofalova had worked and found her employer, along with several other prostitutes with whom she had worked. None of them were willing to talk to GSN about the case, but they did indicate that since this murder, the sex trafficking of Russian women to Macau had slowed down. To the extent that this was true, it was short-lived, as by 1997 the number of Russian sex workers in Macau had begun to increase again.[2]

The Samofalova–Alderice case highlights the impunity with which powerful organized crime groups can retaliate against anyone who crosses them. Even in this very high-profile case, the police were at best disabled, and at worst, complicit. Organized crime groups today typically have multiple business partners within and across countries, making it difficult to track particular crimes in which they might have had a hand. And, as discussed in the last chapter, the dense and fluid network structures in which the trafficking industry operates protect those in high-level positions. Crime groups can use lower-level labor to carry out their work, leaving their top-level membership relatively immune from detection. Or, as organized crime expert Phil Williams puts it, the "core" is protected, while the "periphery" is more vulnerable.[3] When the police are able to make an arrest, it is often of someone at the periphery, as in the arrest of Sergei Sukhanov described above.

This chapter focuses on the positioning and participation of traditional and newer organized crime groups[4] in the global sex trafficking industry. Because of its profit potential, a number of well-established organized crime groups—most notably the Russian mafia, the Japanese Yakuza, and the Chinese Triads—have become heavily involved in sex trafficking. Newer organized crime groups, such as those in Albania, Ukraine, and Nigeria, have become active sex traffickers as well. Organized crime's role in sex trafficking has been growing in the last decade, in part because organized crime groups have adapted their ways of doing (criminal) business to fit new global market conditions.

Key Traditional and Adaptive Attributes of Organized Crime

Organized crime is today, as it always has been, an economic enterprise. Organized crime groups can be thought of as businesses, exploiting markets in order to maximize profits.[5] While organized crime groups may act politically to increase profits or lower risks, such groups have in and of themselves no political ideology or goals.[6]

Additionally, organized crime has always relied on violence or the threat of violence to accomplish its ends. As Fijnaut and colleagues point out, mafias "are *capable* of effectively shielding their activities, in particular by being *willing* to use physical violence or eliminate individuals by way of corruption" [italics mine].[7] In fact, organized crime's success is predicated on its ability to corrupt public officials and legitimate businessmen, whether by violence or other means.[8] In many places, but particularly in countries or regions with weakened infrastructures, the police and other public officials fear retaliation by organized crime groups should they interfere with their criminal enterprises.[9] Their fear is justified.

While retaining the above attributes, organized crime has also changed in several ways in recent decades. First, its geographic scope has clearly broadened. Whether well established or evolving, organized crime businesses today are transnational, and like legitimate businesses, they need global contacts to capture and exploit markets around the world. Second, organized crime today is more prolific and pervasive than ever. There are literally thousands—perhaps tens of thousands—of organized crime groups, and the number of contacts they have with other groups and individuals is staggering. This growth is not just in the number of groups and contacts, however. In recent years, as Phil Williams reports, the "scale, diversity and range of [economic] activities pursued by criminal organizations has broadened significantly."[10] As stated in the 1999 U.N. *Global Report on Crime and Justice:* "From the perspective of organized crime in the 1990s, Al Capone was a small-time hoodlum with restricted horizons, limited ambitions and merely a local fiefdom."[11]

In spite of considerable evidence that organized crime is heavily involved in sex trafficking, the exact nature of its involvement is not always clear to researchers and investigators. As Shannon notes, the "role of organized crime in the global sex trade is multifaceted; in many cases the exact functions performed by organized criminal associations remains unclear. In other cases, even when the nature of involvement is evident, the scale of such participation is vague."[12] A number of reasons for this lack of clarity have been offered. Some have to do with data collection (e.g., data are often anecdotal or collected from nonrandom samples of participants; there is no case follow-up).[13] Some experts say that the looser structure of the trafficking industry, and of organized crime more generally today, make uncovering organized crime's role in trafficking more difficult.[14] It may also be that older, stereotypical beliefs about a singular "Mafia" still reign. Findlay suggests that such "blinders" are particularly in place in the United States and that "by simplifying and generalising organized crime under the guise of the Mafia mystique, the true complexity and all-pervasive influence of capitalised criminal activity at all levels of American commercial and economic life is obfuscated."[15]

On the other hand, more is known about sex trafficking groups today than was known a decade ago. As the pervasiveness of such trafficking is exposed, data sources are improving, and there are now multiple sources that can be checked against one another for reliability. Progress toward understanding the role of organized crime in sex trafficking is being made. To begin with, it is quite clear that in addition to the involvement of traditional mafias in sex trafficking, there are numerous newer mafias that are taking advantage of the profit opportunities in sex trafficking. A number of characteristics of both the older and the newer crime groups facilitate their sex trafficking activity.

Characteristics of Established and Newer Organized Crime Groups as Sex Traffickers

Organized crime's involvement in sex trafficking has become increasingly prominent since the beginning of the 1990s, coinciding with the breakup of the former Soviet Union and its aftermath, and with the growing globalization of market economies.[16] Since the early 1990s, older mafias have added sex trafficking to their business repertoire, and newer mafias have emerged for the purpose of, or have grown stronger as a result of, participation in the sex trade. The older and the newer groups share some traits and differ in others; furthermore, there are some differences *within* both the older and the newer categories.

Older, well-established mafias, such as the Russian and Italian mafias, tend to have tight, hierarchical structures. But globalized sex trafficking today operates best, as has been noted, with a more lateral and looser network structure. While the older mafias have maintained hierarchies in one form or another, they have also accommodated a looser structure when business demands it.[17] Newer mafias are more likely to be laterally organized, although powerful leaders may emerge for a given transaction or set of transactions, in a specific region or town, or at a particular time.

Older mafias are more likely than newer mafias to have a diversified set of business activities. The older mafias have typically added sex trafficking to an already well-established set of business activities.[18] Moreover, as U.N. executive Pino Arlacchi points out, not only do large [traditional] criminal groups diversify with a "wide range of 'commodities'," but they also use "the same routes, networks and even corrupt officials to move people or goods."[19]

Newer mafias involved in sex trafficking are more likely to first proliferate and then diversify. Albanian crime groups, for example, first began to expand their sex trafficking territory, moving into neighboring countries, such as Italy, and then to more distant countries, such as the Netherlands. As the Albanian mafia proliferated, it also found opportunities to diversify. According to one account, the Albanians began to invest sex trafficking profits in the illegal drug industry, thus forming stronger connections with drug traffickers and the drug trafficking industry.[20]

The more established mafias involved in sex trafficking—Russian, Japanese, and Chinese—are much larger and have more resources than the newer ones. They have more members, more groups, more alliances with other organized crime groups, and a broader base of operations—across regions, commodities, and purposes. In addition, the best-established mafias are likely to have the deepest connections with the "upperworld" of police, other public officials, and businessmen.[21] Their greater resources allow them to provide services to newer, evolving trafficker groups or even individual traffickers. For example, they can loan money or provide security to other organized crime groups, club owners, or pimps. They have the freedom to work cooperatively on some ventures and independently on others.[22]

Although membership restrictions may be more rigid in traditional mafias, newer mafias tend to have some restrictions on membership as well. This feature is particularly important to protect the network core, which builds trust and loyalty from the bonding of members who share some primary trait, such as kinship, ethnicity, clan, common experience, or even criminal record.[23] Ethnicity, for example, has been an important criterion for membership in the Russian and Italian mafias. And Turkish criminal organizations are often formed around clans.[24]

Weak States and Recognition of Profitability: Entrees for Organized Crime

Organized crime has typically become involved in criminal enterprises in two ways: in the first, certain conditions precede and serve as an impetus for involvement; and in the second, involvement follows recognition of the profitability of a particular enterprise. Economic and political disruptions, along with the weakening of state authority, are conditions that have historically opened the door to organized crime. As Dickinson and Schaeffer note:

> Historically, organized criminal gangs emerged in periods of rapid economic and political change, particularly in regions where states are weak. Mafias in Sicily, triads in China and Yakuza in Japan all appeared first in the mid-nineteenth century, at a time when feudal economic relations and social obligations were dissolving and new capitalist relations were being introduced.[25]

The authors go on to point out that under such conditions, not uncommonly, "small groups of armed men [have] inserted themselves into economic life, extorting money" and providing "protection."[26] Eventually, the emerging organized crime groups take control of the local or regional vice industries. As their power grows, and with a vacuum in state authority, they are able to corrupt public officials and private businessmen.

The U.N.'s Pino Arlacchi points out that, in addition to countries with "ill-equipped police forces" and "uncertain market forces," organized crime groups are likely to gain a foothold in countries with "struggling democracies."[27] While they may be deficient in the ideal of "rule by the people," countries with strong, centralized governments have the authority to act quickly to stabilize infrastructures weakened by change and chaos.

In the second mode of involvement, organized crime groups move into a particular market when they become aware of its profitability. As Arlacchi notes, "just as legitimate companies move in to fill voids in the product market," newer organized crime groups emerge where and when profits are to be made. In fact, there still are opportunities for criminal groups to get into and make money from sex trafficking.[28] Demand remains high, and the commodity is readily available and cheap.

In the remainder of this chapter, the sex trafficking activity of organized crime groups in specific countries or regions is explored, beginning with a look at three established groups—the Russian mafia (and its offshoots or affiliates in other former Soviet republics), the Japanese Yakuza, and the Chinese Triads (and connected East Asian crime groups)—and ending with a focus on newer organized crime groups.

Established Mafias Active in Sex Trafficking

The Russian Mafia

As described in Chapter 1, the fall of the Soviet Union in 1991 created havoc in Russia and the other Soviet republics. Russia, by far the largest and most powerful of the republics, found itself with a seriously compromised infrastructure. It clearly fit the definition of what has been referred to as a "weak state," meaning that state authorities were not able "to govern legitimately, to enforce the law systematically, and to administer justice effectively throughout the national territory."[29] Even before the Soviet fall, however, the Russian mafia was institutionalized in Soviet society, so when the hard times arrived, it was able to capitalize on a "legacy of corruption and underground networks."[30] By the end of the 1990s, Russian organized crime had taken over large parts of the national economy and expanded its criminal undertakings. Organized crime businesses, which generated an estimated $10 billion annually, were thought to account for some 40% of the country's gross domestic product.

By 1996, according to one source, Russian organized crime groups controlled an estimated 40,000 Russian businesses, including 550 financial institutions and 500 joint ventures with foreign investors.[31] Moreover, the mafia itself opened a number of new banks, which it then reportedly used to carry out illegal transactions, most notably the laundering and investing of illegal profits. Its investments in criminal businesses generate return rates as high as 100%.[32] Extortion is an important profit-generating mafia business, both inside and outside of Russia. About 70% to 80% of all businesses in major Russian cities pay protection money to the mafia,[33] and the protection fee can be as much as half of a company's profits.[34]

Organized crime groups in Russia and in most (if not all) of the other former Soviet republics are involved in some way in the very profitable sex industry. By the mid-1990s, there were over 200 illegal sex businesses in Moscow alone, and most either were owned by the mafia or paid money to them for protection against police raids or harassment from other crime groups.[35] While mafia groups largely control prostitution in clubs and hotels, the police reportedly control and collect protection fees from street prostitutes. Escort businesses are the most independent, but generally they pay some percentage of their earnings to the mafia for protection.[36]

Cooperation and collaboration characterize at least part of the Russian mafia's relationships with the police and authorities in the Interior Ministry, the Federal Security Service, and the Ministry of Foreign Affairs.[37] In addition, many mafia members are former military men or national security agents (in the KGB).[38] Their backgrounds provide them with important contacts as well as knowledge about government business, making them "well-positioned to participate in domestic and international criminal activities."[39]

While the Russian mafia is often talked about in the singular, there are actually many Russian mafia groups. The U.N. reports that there are at least 200 Russian mafia groups, which have very dense, complex, and sophisticated networks with criminal operations in at least 50 countries.[40] But that is just the tip of the iceberg. Estimates of the overall number of Russian organized crime groups vary, but all are high. According to one report, in 2002 there were over 12,000 crime groups in Russia, three times as many as there were in 1992.[41] Another report put out by the Russian Ministry of International Affairs, states that as of 1993, there were at least 5,000 organized crime groups in Russia, with an estimated leadership of 18,000 and with 100,000 members; by 1994, the total number of groups had reached 8,000.[42] Some of the smaller mafias operate mainly in Russia or countries nearby. A sizable number, however, have global prominence. Operating in the United States alone, for example, are 15 known organized crime groups with Russian or other NIS (Newly Independent States) origins; and at least 200 organized crime groups in Russia have connections with crime groups in the United States.[43] A few of the larger, more powerful groups—such as Dolgopruadnanskaya, Izamilovskaya, Dagestantsy, Kazanskaya, and Solntsenskaya—have retained their hierarchical form, and many smaller ones have a single "boss," but virtually all are also part of more laterally structured networks.[44]

One key to the Russian mafia's economic success has been its diverse business activity. In addition to sex trafficking and money laundering, Russian mafias smuggle weapons, cars, fuel, cigarettes, and drugs. They also make money from bribing officials, forging documents, and racketeering.[45] To profit from these activities globally, Russian mafias have forged alliances with powerful organized crime and revolutionary groups in other countries, such as "U.S. crime syndicates, the Cali drug cartel, the Revolutionary Armed Forces of Colombia (FARC), the four main Italian organised crime groups . . . as well as Hungarian, Czech and Serbian crime groups, the Albanian fares [criminal clans], the Japanese Yakuza, Israeli and Turkish organised crime groups, and Chinese Triads."[46] Russian mafia investments in foreign countries soared during the 1990s. In just 7 years, for example, about 4 billion dollars of Russian organized crime money was invested in Israel—one of the biggest destination sites for trafficked Russian and Ukrainian women—in real estate, financial institutions, and other businesses.[47]

Today, according to most experts, the larger, higher-level Russian organized crime groups profit from the sex trade primarily through extortion, money laundering, club ownership, and other investments, while the mid- to lower-level mafia groups are most actively involved in setting up and carrying out sex trafficking from Russia and other NIS to foreign destinations.[48] The larger, more established mafia groups often provide newer, smaller trafficking groups with loans, network connections, investments, and money laundering services—all for a price, of course.

In one way or another, however, Russian criminal groups at all levels are involved in the transnational sex trade. They are known to work with Albanian, Turkish, and Yugoslav crime groups to traffic women from the NIS to Western Europe, and with the Japanese Yakuza and the Chinese Triads to traffic women to Japan and other East Asian destinations. From Russia's east, the mafia traffics women to brothels and clubs in places such as Hong Kong, Macau, and the Northern Mariana Islands. They also traffic women from Russia and other NIS to countries in the Middle East, such as Israel and the United Arab Emirates.[49] And their presence in trafficking and the sex industry in the United States, Latin America, and the Caribbean is continually expanding.[50] Additionally, they are known to be highly invested in prostitution—through ownership, management, extortion, or other financial arrangements—in Germany, Italy, Poland, Pakistan, Israel, and parts of the former Yugoslavia.[51] Transnational Russian organized crime's hand in the sex trade today is ubiquitous.

Other NIS Organized Crime

While the Russian mafia is by far the best established in the former Soviet republics, mafias in other NIS have moved into the profitable sex trade as well. The most sizable and formidable of these is the Ukrainian mafia, which dominates trafficking markets in Hungary and Austria and collaborates with the Albanian mafia to traffic women through Albania for prostitution in Italy. It also works with the Turkish mafia to traffic women to or through Turkey to other parts of Europe and the Middle East for prostitution.[52] Regional trafficking networks controlled by organized crime in

Kiev, the capital of Ukraine, also move women eastward to Asian countries such as Japan and Thailand.[53]

Like the Russian mafia, the Ukrainian mafia is diversifying and expanding its reach, including operations in the United States. In the summer of 1999, the FBI investigated a trafficking-related operation in the United States in which 10 billion dollars had been laundered over the previous year through one account at the Bank of New York. The account was that of Ukrainian-born Semion Mogilevich, the head of a Ukrainian organized crime network called the Red Mafia. The Red Mafia operated not only in Ukraine, but also in Hungary, the Czech Republic, and, as revealed in the Mogilevich case, the United States. In addition to money laundering, this mafia was involved in prostitution and sex trafficking, drugs and weapons smuggling, and "investment scams." Mogilevich himself oversaw a sizable prostitution ring in Europe, which trafficked women to work in clubs in cities such as Prague and Budapest.[54]

As in Russia, the Ukrainian mafia has taken advantage of the weak Ukrainian state and poor economy to co-opt and corrupt police and immigration officials.[55] According to the head of criminal investigations for the Ukrainian Interior Ministry, organized crime groups in Ukraine have a "huge monetary advantage" over the police and other public officials.[56]

Trafficking groups are evolving in other NIS. Georgian trafficking rings (with connections to the Russian mafia) reportedly specialize in setting up employment agencies as fronts for recruiting and trafficking Georgian and other NIS women. Organized crime has also surfaced in Moldova, the poorest of the NIS and one of the most popular recruitment sites in the region.[57]

Japanese Yakuza, Chinese Triads, and Other East Asian Crime Groups

Formalizing their concern about organized crime's involvement in the trafficking of humans—especially women and children—ministers from 18 Asian–Pacific countries issued a 1999 declaration calling on nations to pass laws and cooperate with one another to catch and punish traffickers.[58] Their concern is well founded, as Asian crime groups today, most notably the Japanese Yakuza and the Chinese Triads, continue to expand the size and scope of their human trafficking operations by building on alliances around the world. In Asia, the Yakuza and the Triads work with criminal groups from countries such as Thailand, Vietnam, and Korea to traffic women into prostitution in the region and elsewhere. Asian mafias also have connections with criminal elements in Europe, Africa, North America, and Latin America. Furthermore, they own, manage, or extort money from sex businesses in their own and other regions of the world. Although both the Yakuza and the Chinese Triads are heavily involved in sex trafficking, the nature of their current involvement, and the history that precedes it, are somewhat different.

The Japanese Yakuza

The Japanese mafia, known as the Yakuza, has a long history of involvement in the vice industries in Japan. Prostitution became particularly profitable for them following World War II, which produced in Japan first an occupied, and then a struggling, weak state, along with economic instability—conditions similar to the aftereffects of the breakup of the Soviet Union. Unemployment and poverty left many families vulnerable to recruiters who persuaded them to sell their daughters, and who convinced the daughters that they would get them good jobs in another city or country.[59] By the late 1960s, the Yakuza had built up a profitable prostitution industry, and then found another promising market. Travel agencies were beginning to capitalize on sex tours, booking Japanese men for such tours at largely East Asian destinations. The Yakuza was also there, leading as well as following the "tourists" to their nearby destinations, then expanding their reach by arranging sex tours in more and more distant sites. It was reportedly through this particular expansion that the Yakuza was introduced to and then became intertwined in the international sex trade.[60]

By the early 1980s, the Yakuza had also become involved in the trafficking of women, mainly from other Southeast Asian countries such as Thailand and the Philippines, into Japan.[61] Today, while its importation of women and girls from Southeast Asia remains strong, the Yakuza also facilitates sex traffic into Japan from Russia and other NIS and Eastern European countries, and on a lesser scale, from Africa, the United States and Canada, and Latin America.

Although accounts of the sex industry in Japan are more difficult to verify than those from Russia, many have implicated Japanese law enforcement as cooperative, in that informal policies promote inaction and noninterference in the sex trade business, at least in that controlled by the Yakuza. One brothel manager, for example, reported that her club, owned by a Yakuza company, never had any problems with the police, who allowed them to operate with impunity. A woman working in a club said that the "police don't do anything around here," noting that the police and the Yakuza had an agreement with each other.[62]

Thailand continues to be a major supplier of women for the sex industry in Japan. The trafficking of Thai women to Japan for prostitution is, in the words of one researcher, "well organized under the control of Japanese and Thai agents linked to the criminal underworlds of both countries."[63] Interestingly, the constellation of actors has changed over time. Earlier, Japanese men were typically the brokers, whereas the employers or bar managers were Taiwanese madams. In recent years, however, an increasingly larger number of the sex establishments in Japan are managed by Thai women who are married to Japanese owners, who in turn are often members of or affiliated with the Yakuza.[64] A letter written to her father by one Thai woman who had been trafficked to Japan reveals not only her despair, but also the intimidation and isolation tactics used by the Yakuza to control the women.

> I live without hope. What I do everyday is just have customers. I cannot go out. There are more than ten Yakuza here. This letter must be hidden from them. If they find it, I will be beaten. If I try to run away from here, I will be killed, and my body will be thrown to the sea. . . . I do not know where I am now. All of us do not speak. There are lots of Thais and Filipinas. I am prohibited to talk to them. . . . The Yakuza are always watching me carefully. I am forced to stay at the place where Yakuza live. . . . The Yakuza are threatening me. . . . Living here is like living in hell. Yakuza sometimes take us somewhere in order for us to get customers. They pack us into a truck without windows. I cannot look.[65]

After receiving this letter, the father traveled to Japan to look for his daughter. Although he was assisted by an international human rights group, he was never able to find her.[66]

The Yakuza's power in its home country is augmented by its international connections. It has strong alliances with organized crime groups in countries such as Russia, Mexico, and Colombia, and in Asia, with groups in Thailand, China, Hong Kong, Korea, and Taiwan.[67] There appear to be particularly strong ties between the Yakuza and ethnic Chinese organized crime groups operating in Thailand.[68] And, as a Manila nongovernmental organization reports, the Yakuza frequently come to the Philippines and work with local recruiters there to buy Filipina women to take back to Japan.[69] In the United States, they advertise for women in trade magazines—in San Francisco and Los Angeles, for example—using ads that call for models and entertainers to "try out" for jobs in Japan.[70]

Both in and out of Japan, the scope of Yakuza involvement in sex trafficking and the sex industry continues to widen. In some recent trafficking enterprises, notably the trafficking of Asian children to Canada and the United States, they have cooperated with another dominant Asian mafia force: the Chinese Triads.[71]

The Chinese Triads

From their beginnings in the mid-1600s as politically motivated secret societies, the Chinese Triads evolved over time into loosely organized criminal groups, eventually settling on smuggling and racketeering activities. The Triads remain organizationally fluid and flexible and relatively non-hierarchical in structure. They sometimes operate independently, and at other times collaborate with one another and with other Chinese groups—most often with youth gangs and with adult organizations known as tongs (some of which are crime groups, but many others of which are not).[72] Together the Triads and their Chinese partners constitute a powerful and globally active Chinese mafia. Their criminal businesses include alien smuggling, sex trafficking and prostitution, drug trafficking, money laundering, protection, and extortion.

Like the Yakuza, the Triads have alliances with virtually all other major transnational crime groups and are extensively involved in sex trafficking and prostitution around the world. They have, for example, worked with the Russian mafia on sex trafficking operations,[73] and they are involved in the trafficking of Asian women and children through Italy to the United States,[74] and from China through Spain to the United States, Canada, and Great Britain.[75] They buy young girls in Thailand, Malaysia, and the Philippines and then traffic them for prostitution in countries such as the United States, Australia, Japan, and Great Britain.[76] In fact, the American Embassy in London recently reported that, although there has been a rise in Russian and Eastern European traffickers there, the Chinese Triads are still major traffickers of women and girls from "Southeast Asia, South America, and Eastern Europe to Britain."[77]

Additionally, like other established organized crime groups, the Chinese groups have set up operations in other countries, where they profit from their ownership of bars, clubs, and brothels, or from providing protection for and extortion from sex establishments and other businesses. Malaysian police report, for example, that women trafficked into Malaysia are "fed into an extensive system of Chinese owned lounges, nightclubs, and brothels that exist throughout much of Asia."[78] While Asian crime groups own, manage, or are otherwise involved in sex businesses in many places in the United States, they are most concentrated in major cities in the West, such as Los Angeles, San Francisco, Sacramento, and Las Vegas.[79] Like the Yakuza, the Chinese mafia has also taken advantage of the successful sex tourism industry in the Northern Mariana Islands, where it profits from lending money at a high interest rate to women who have been sold into debt-bonded prostitution there.[80]

The Chinese Triads have a long history of involvement in the sex trade in the United States. When, in the early 1900s, the U.S. government brought in Chinese men to work on the railroads, the Triads followed—trafficking Chinese women to the United States to provide sexual services to the workers.[81] In another enterprise, the Triads reportedly paid U.S. soldiers in the Korean War from $5,000 to $10,000 to marry Korean prostitutes, thus providing them with legal entrance into the United States, where they were subsequently placed in brothels by the Triads.[82] And Korean women continued to be heavily targeted by the Triads for trafficking into the United States up until the 1980s. In the 1980s, the Triads began to traffic more Chinese women, as well as women from Vietnam, Laos, and the Philippines, to the United States.[83] Today, the FBI estimates that Chinese crime groups account for about 45% of all human trafficking into the United States. Of the remainder, about 29% involves Vietnamese groups and 7.3% Korean groups, with Japanese, Filipino, Cambodian, Thai, Laotian, and Polynesian groups accounting for the rest.[84] The FBI asserts that Chinese and other Asian organized crime groups involved in the sex trade in the United States operate "more like a loose confederation of organized criminal entrepreneurs as opposed to one large criminal syndicate controlling the trafficking process from beginning to end."[85]

Some Chinese youth gangs, often affiliated with the Chinese Triads, provide protection to brothels and extort money from other businesses in major western cities such as San Francisco and Los Angeles, as well as eastern cities such as New York, Philadelphia, and Chicago.[86] Often it is the Triad that directs the protection and other racketeering activities carried out by the younger gang members. Chinese gangs and Triads that have profited from prostitution in the United States for years are increasingly active in overseas recruitment and management of sex trafficking from China and other Asian sites to the United States. Chinese crime groups thought to be particularly active in this regard include the Sun Yee On Triad, 14K Triad, Wo Hop To Triad, the United Bamboo gang, and the Fuk Ching gang.[87]

While the Triads today operate out of several parts of China as well as in the United States, they first emerged as a major organized crime force in Hong Kong and are sometimes referred to in the literature as the "Hong Kong-based Triads." Today, Triads in Hong Kong traffic Asian women and girls into Hong Kong as well as to other countries.[88] In Hong Kong itself, there are an estimated 50 local organized crime groups that control prostitution and pornography businesses, illegal gambling casinos, and other places of entertainment.[89]

In recent years, Chinese organized crime has also participated in the kidnapping of young women and girls for marriage markets—a practice that has come to be known as "bride abductions." Due in part to a shortage of girls, an underground market for brides has swelled in China. Criminal "marriage brokers" search out and kidnap marriageable young women, particularly in rural areas, where local officials are reportedly disinclined to intervene due to their sympathy for Chinese men who are unable to find a wife. Between 1993 and 1995 in southern China alone, 3,000 women and children who had been abducted and sold, usually to prospective husbands, were rescued, mainly by human rights groups.[90]

Other Asian Crime Groups

In Taiwan, as in mainland China, organized crime groups purchase young girls from poor families in Thailand or China and then traffic them for prostitution to countries such as the United States, Australia, and Japan.[91] Taiwan is also a destination country, and Taiwanese crime groups actively recruit and receive women and girls for their own sex industry. In just such a case, in 1997, authorities broke up a Taiwanese-based international sex ring, known as "Lily," which had been recruiting and bringing women from Thailand, Malaysia, Singapore, China, Macau, and Hong Kong into Taiwan's sex industry. The police estimated that more than 120 women brought in by Lily were currently working in brothels in Taiwan.[92]

In addition to their involvement in the vast sex industry in Thailand, Thai crime groups traffic women for prostitution not only to Japan and other Asian destinations, but also to countries such as Great Britain, France, the United States, and Australia.[93] According to the American Embassy in Bangkok, Thai organized crime groups are sending, on average, 20 to 30 women a month to the United States and Canada alone.[94] There appear to be at least seven crime "families" in Bangkok that are recruiting, selling, and trafficking Asian women and girls into prostitution in destinations throughout the world.[95]

Vietnamese crime groups also profit from sex trafficking. In 2002, Vietnamese police cracked a criminal ring that was recruiting and trafficking Vietnamese women and girls to brothels in Malaysia. Expressing their concern about increased trafficking activity by Vietnamese crime groups, authorities reported that in the last 5 years, some 30,000 Vietnamese women had been trafficked for prostitution or marriage into China alone, and thousands more were sold to brokers in Cambodia.[96] Again, Vietnamese trafficking activities are not limited to Asia. In 1999, police in the United States prosecuted Vietnamese members of a transnational prostitution ring based in Atlanta, Georgia, that was responsible for trafficking an estimated 1,000 women and girls, some as young as 13, to the United States from Vietnam, Thailand, Laos, China, Malaysia, and South Korea.[97]

Like the Thai and Vietnamese groups, South Korean crime groups have trafficking operations in North America. In the United States, 12 members of a Korean trafficking ring based in San Francisco were arrested for trafficking Malaysian and Korean women into brothels in San Francisco and other California cities, as well as cities in Texas, Arizona, Minnesota, Louisiana, and New York—in all the ring was thought to be running brothels in at least 20 U.S. cities.[98] Korean criminal groups have also been implicated in trafficking women into Canada, sometimes directly and sometimes through the United States.[99]

Because these other Asian crime groups tend to be relatively small, scattered, and not consistently partnered, they are difficult to track. Information typically comes on a case-by-case basis, making it hard to come to any firm conclusions about the extent or scope of involvement in sex trafficking by these smaller mafia groups.

Newer Organized Crime Groups Active in Sex Trafficking

Eastern and Central European Crime Groups

Like the breakup of the Soviet Union, the 1990s breakup and continuing conflict in the former Yugoslavia has resulted in the weak states and economic devastation that open the door to organized crime.[100] Both collapses have contributed to the rise of organized crime groups in Eastern and Central Europe and, in particular, to their success in building up the sex trade in the region. Emerging in the 1990s as the most prominent and feared of the organized crime groups in the region was the Albanian mafia.

Albanian Crime Groups

Cataldo Motta, a well-known prosecutor in Italy, said about the influence of Albania's "dangerous mobsters" in the region: "Albanian organised crime has become a point reference for all criminal activity today . . . . Everything passes via the Albanians. The road for drugs and arms and people, meaning illegal immigrants destined for Europe, is in Albanian hands."[101] Motta should know. Albanian crime groups traffic thousands of women and girls into Italy for prostitution every year, and they are known for their ruthlessness and retaliation against anyone interfering with their trafficking business. Due to the risk of assassination by Albanian gangsters, Motta is accompanied by three bodyguards whenever he is out in public.[102]

The evolution and spread of Albanian organized crime in the 1990s was dramatic. According to one analyst, whereas Albanian criminal groups were, prior to the 1990s, "scattered and disorganised, and working for others," in the 1990s they "moved into independent operations, established a vast network of mules and troubleshooters throughout Western Europe, coordinated activity with supportive emigré communities, and managed to consolidate their operations on both sides of the Atlantic. Indeed, they appear to be growing and expanding their operations at an alarming rate."[103] However, this analyst continues, officials in both the United States and Europe "are at a loss as to the nature and extent of these groups and have succeeded in making only minor arrests."[104]

In other words, like many other network-embedded organized crime groups today, but perhaps even more so because of their meteoric rise, the Albanian mafia remains somewhat of a mystery. Some experts emphasize traditional elements of Albanian organized crime, including a hierarchical chain of command and clan- or family-based membership.[105] Others suggest that Albanian organized crime groups tend to be small-scale and quasi-independent, and do not appear to be part of a wider international network.[106] But there is evidence that, at the least, Albanian organized crime groups network with other regional mafias in countries such as Turkey, Poland, the Czech Republic, Hungary, Romania, and republics of the former Yugoslavia.[107] And, while there may be a hierarchy in the Albanian mafia, it seems to be decentralized and flexible. Actual trafficking activities are typically carried out by small groups, sometimes with an identifiable leader. Membership in at least some of the groups is clan- or ethnicity-based.[108]

Sex Trafficking into Italy While Albanian crime groups traffic women for prostitution all over the world, they traffic the largest number of women to (or through) Italy. Albanian groups typically bring women and girls from countries such as Moldova, Romania, Ukraine, Kosovo, Serbia, and Albania itself to the port town of Vlorë in Albania, and from there across the Adriatic Sea by boat into northern Italy. Vlorë is reportedly largely controlled by Albanian organized crime groups, which traffic not only women, but also drugs and other commodities, out of the coastal town with impunity. An estimated 10% of the population of Vlorë have business arrangements with the mafia there.[109] One journalist reported from Vlorë on a typical scenario, involving the trafficking of Kosovar refugees by an Albanian mafia group:

> After a 24-hour drive from the mountainous Kosovo border, two buses with more than 100 women, children and elderly refugees sputtered to a stop in a dusty speck of a village near the Albanian coast. Out of the evening murk, 50 armed men surrounded the buses. "You survived the Serbs; now we will do what we want with you: We are going to take the girls," a beefy Albanian man with a mobile phone and a Kalashnikov rifle called out.[110]

The above is not the only incidence of the "hijacking of entire buses" in order to abduct women for sex trafficking. In fact, abduction is not infrequently the Albanian mafia's method of recruitment; and in parts of Albania, fear of abduction has led families to keep their daughters out of school, a common site for such kidnappings.[111]

Albanian crime groups have a reputation for ruthlessness and brutality in their trafficking transactions. Italian authorities familiar with Albanian sex trafficking into Italy suggest that this reputation is deserved. According to Pier Luigi Vigna, Italy's national anti-Mafia prosecutor, Albanian gangs are particularly violent in their treatment of trafficking victims, and "uncooperative girls" have even been murdered by them. The Italian Interior Ministry reports that Albanian traffickers use "ferocious methods against young victims to induce them to submit to inhuman conditions and effective slavery."[112] In some cases, the traffickers have burned or otherwise tortured their trafficking victims for disobedience, and in one case girls were tattooed with the group's symbol.[113] An agent with the Organization for Security and Co-operation in Europe (OSCE) in Vlorë said about the Albanian mafia there: "These guys are constantly armed and they have a lot of money. . . . It's a bit dangerous to get in the way too much."[114]

Sex Trafficking in and from Kosovo, Bosnia–Herzegovina, and Other Parts of the Former Yugoslavia The debilitating conflict in the former Yugoslavia has been a boon to sex traffickers in several ways. For one, it has produced large numbers of refugees—a potential victim pool—as well as refugee or detention camps, which have become breeding grounds for Albanian and other traffickers in the area. For another, it has provided Albanian organized crime with partners of two types: local (Yugoslav) profit-oriented organized crime groups and revolutionary groups that are looking to fund their political cause.

Perhaps most affected by sex trafficking in the area have been women refugees, especially those who were living in Kosovo when the conflict erupted. Serbian dominance under Slobodan Milosevič in the former Yugoslavia in the late 1980s included a ruthless campaign against ethnic Albanians living in Kosovo. Anti–ethnic Albanian sentiment, which continued in the newly formed Bosnia–Herzegovina, resulted in the fleeing of Albanians in Kosovo back to Albania, where refugee camps began to swell. In these camps, women have been subjected to rapes and other assaults by Albanian camp guards, soldiers, and other refugees. The camps have also become major suppliers of women and girls for Albanian sex traffickers.[115]

In addition, ethnic Albanian rebel groups, most notably the Kosovo Liberation Army (KLA) and the National Liberation Army (NLA) in Macedonia, have found sex trafficking, either in partnership with criminal groups or independently, to be a profitable business that provides them with money for arms and other commodities.[116] Victims themselves have noted apparent partnerships between rebel groups and their employer–pimps in brothels or clubs in the former Yugoslavia. Tanya, a Ukrainian woman who had been forced into prostitution in Macedonia, said that at her club one night, she was awakened at about 3 a.m. when a group of armed NLA members broke through the door, demanding that her employer pay them money they said they were owed. When her employer said he would or could not pay, the men opened fire. In the ensuing chaos, Tanya was able to escape from the club for good.[117]

There are now thriving sex industries in Bosnia–Herzegovina, Macedonia, and other former Yugoslav states, fueled by the demand from soldiers, rebel groups, peacekeeping troops, and foreign businessmen. The demand is easily met with the large supply of poor, unemployed women in the former Yugoslavia and nearby refugee camps, as well as from countries such as Ukraine, Moldova, Bulgaria, and Romania.[118] In the northern corner of Bosnia–Herzegovina, near its borders with Croatia and the Federal Republic of Yugoslavia, sits the notorious "Arizona Market," a major center set up for illegal commerce. It is here that much of the buying and selling of women for prostitution in the region takes place, again with impunity.[119] The police are either unable or unwilling to intervene much; in fact, they are sometimes themselves complicit—by either facilitating the trafficking or being paying customers.[120]

While other local crime groups participate in and profit from the local sex trade, here again, the Albanians are at the center. According to one report, the Albanian mafia runs the brothels in Kosovo, and "in fact, some would say, runs the whole country."[121]

Other Sites The Albanian mafia's involvement in the sex industry is not limited to the former Yugoslavia region. Its rapid rise in the prostitution business in parts of London, for example, is noteworthy. In fact, one report indicates that in "less than two years, Albanians have taken over 70% of the brothels in Soho . . . becoming the majority of owners of a business worth at least 12 million [pounds] a year. The new vice kings are the criminal warlords of Albania, whose [sex trade] reach extends" to "the underworlds of most of Italy and parts of New York."[122] The Albanians are also profiting from their involvement in the sex trade in countries as diverse as Belgium, Turkey, Greece, and South Africa.[123]

Other Eastern and Central European Organized Crime Groups

Organized crime groups in many Eastern and Central European countries are involved in the sex trade, but discussions of these groups are often limited to their role in a particular case. For example, Romanian police cracked a Romanian ring that had trafficked some 300 women from Romania and Moldova for prostitution in Cyprus.[124] And in 1997, police discovered a joint Romanian and Hungarian ring that was running a sex trafficking enterprise in Belgium using women they had trafficked there from their respective home countries. In this case, five Hungarian and Romanian traffickers and three Belgian associates were eventually convicted of trafficking-related crimes.[125] In another transnational case, American and Czech police broke up a Czech trafficking and prostitution ring operating sex clubs in New York with Czech and Hungarian women they had trafficked there. This same ring was also thought to be associated with clubs in Florida and Texas.[126]

There are a growing number of Serbian prostitution rings, some of which recruit women from poor NIS countries such as Moldova. Others buy women from Eastern European traffickers, sometimes reselling them to Albanian traffickers.[127] Ravna Gora, a mafia group in the former Yugoslavia that has been known in the past mainly for weapons smuggling, is increasingly involved in the trafficking of women and children.[128] And the American Embassy in Warsaw reports that Polish criminal networks "recruit, transport, and deliver women from these [NIS] countries into the hands of organized prostitution rings in destination countries."[129] Turkish organized crime groups are also increasingly involved in sex trafficking[130] and, along with Russian and Yugoslavian mafias, have gained financial control of brothels and clubs in Germany.

These less-established Eastern European criminal groups tend to be small but well connected, and they are an important part of the overall transnational trafficking network. They are frequently headed by one or two ringleaders, who are responsible for overseeing trafficking transactions. A report by the U.S. Center for the Study of Intelligence gives an apt description of many of these Eastern European rings:

> Many trafficking and prostitution enterprises are conducted by small organized rings of five to six persons, with criminal contacts. In some cases, these

> small rings are operated on the side by bigger trafficking rings. Generally, traffickers in both the origin and destination country have links to professional criminal organizations, which provide protection for the traffickers and brothels, and are used to intimidate the women.[131]

A good example of such a ring is the Czech operation in the United States referred to above. The ring was headed by two Czech men, Ladislaw Ruc and Milan Lihanec, who were living in Queens, New York, at the time. Ruc and Lihanec picked up trafficked Eastern and Central European women as they arrived by airplane in New York or New Jersey, and put them to work in clubs or brothels in the area. Lihanec, well known to Czech police, had a criminal record in the Czech Republic for transporting stolen cars and for attempting to sell explosives stolen from military storage depots. The ring included Lihanec's brother Marek, who, with other members, set up a fake travel agency in the Czech Republic through which women were recruited for sex trafficking. Still other ring members, located in the United States, served as money smugglers, taking cash back to the Czech Republic to pay ring members there. In the U.S. clubs, the police eventually arrested 11 male traffickers and 18 women, all Czech and Hungarian nationals. They also searched the homes of Ruc and Lihanec, where they found guns, passports and airline tickets, and large amounts of cash. In 1998, Lihanec and Ruc were charged in federal court with fraud, human smuggling, and trafficking women for prostitution. Prior to trial, two of their associates—Edouard Slavik and Zdenek Padelek—attempted to bribe several trafficked women to keep them from testifying. These women were subsequently placed in a witness protection program. In court, Ruc and Lihanec pled guilty on the trafficking charges and were each sentenced to 5 years in prison in the United States. Slavik and Padelek were convicted in federal court on charges of witness tampering.[132]

Another example is a trafficking and prostitution ring in western Macedonia, headed by Dilaver Bojku, known in the business as "Leku." Bojku, an ethnic Albanian from Velesta, Macedonia, owns several clubs in the area, has a long criminal record for counterfeiting and contraband offenses, and is one of the sex trade's "Most Wanted" offenders. He had help trafficking women for prostitution in Macedonia and through Macedonia to Western Europe from a network that included, among others, Romanian transporters, ethnic Albanian rebels, and paid-off police officers and court officials. Early in 2003, in one of a series of raids, Bojku was arrested at one of his Macedonian clubs. Then, before being tried and while being transported from one prison to another, he escaped—and is still on the loose. With the help of his protective network, he may remain at large for some time.[133]

Although they are less notorious, or at least less well publicized outside of their local areas, organized trafficking rings like the ones just described in Eastern and Central Europe are found in other regions of the world as well. The next section briefly describes newer or lesser-known trafficking rings in South Asia, Africa, and Latin America.

Crime Groups and Rings in, from, and Around India

India, which is both a source country and a destination country, is home to powerful organized mafias that are heavily involved in the sex trade.[134] Of the several major Indian organized crime groups, the most feared is the Dawood Ibrahim group, based in Bombay, but with a network that has not just a nationwide, but a global reach. Its criminal enterprises include prostitution; weapons, drug, and sex trafficking; money laundering; extortion; and contract killings. It also has legitimate business holdings in India as well as in international centers such as Hong Kong and Dubai.[135] Dawood Ibrahim and several other organized crime groups reportedly run the thriving sex trade in Bombay.[136] Usually working in cooperation with one another, these crime groups have divided the labor among themselves (e.g., one is in charge of payoffs to the police and other officials, another heads recruitment, and another handles money laundering and other financial arrangements).[137] Social workers and health care employees who work with prostitutes in Bombay report that before they can even go into known prostitution areas, they must get permission from mafia heads, who then tell them what they are allowed and not allowed to do in these areas. The most powerful mafia head in Bombay, according to reports, is a man named Mehboob Thasildar, a prostitution procurer, who owns some 50 women and one of the biggest brothels in Bombay.[138]

In addition to these better-established mafias, there are numerous small, loosely organized Indian trafficking groups, some of which operate in the country and others that conduct business in foreign countries. One of the latter groups was located in Berkeley, California, and headed by Indian native Vijay Lakireddy. For 13 years, Lakireddy, his son, and other family members and friends had been trafficking girls from India to California for debt-bonded prostitution and other forced labor. Over time, Lakireddy bought rental properties and a restaurant with his trafficking profits and eventually came to be known as a wealthy Berkeley businessman. An investigation into the 1999 death of a young Indian woman, Sitha Vemireddy, who had been trafficked and was owned by Lakireddy at the time of her death (eventually ruled as accidental), led the police to Lakireddy. In 2001, the 64-year-old Lakireddy pled guilty to conspiracy to commit immigration fraud, transporting a minor in foreign commerce for illegal sexual activity, and subscribing to a false tax return. He was sentenced to 97 months in prison. Two of Lakireddy's relatives also pled guilty, but his codefendant sons await trial. Back in Velvadam, the Indian village in which he was born, Lakireddy is seen as a powerful and generous benefactor. He has paid for a number of improvements in the town, including two elementary schools, one high school, a new hospital wing, and the Lakireddy Bali Reddy College of Engineering.[139]

In source countries, such as Bangladesh and Nepal, both of which supply many women and girls for trafficking into debt-bonded prostitution in India, regional gangs recruit or kidnap women and take them to the border, where they then sell them to Indian agents. Such gangs typically gain the cooperation of some police and border guards by paying them off. In some villages near the border, hotel proprietors provide lodging for the traffickers as they wait to sell their women to agents, who then transport them across the border into India.[140] While these gangs tend to be well organized, even more powerful criminal syndicates seem to be moving more aggressively into the sex trade in the area. According to Shahidul Haque, the regional representative for the International Organization for Migration (IOM), well-known organized crime syndicates in South Asia are shifting their focus from drugs and weapons trafficking to the less risky human trafficking business.[141]

Nigerian, Other West African, and South African Networks

In the past decade, African criminal groups have also increased in number and scope. Perhaps best known internationally are the Nigerian and other West African groups that have been involved in drug trafficking and, more recently, transnational financial scams.[142] Now criminal groups in Nigeria (and to a lesser extent, other West African countries) are actively involved in trafficking women and girls from African countries for prostitution in Europe and the Middle East. As with other less-established mafias, there are inconsistencies in outsiders' views regarding the organization of Nigerian trafficking groups. The Nigerian traffickers are described by some observers as less complex and less well organized than other trafficking groups,[143] but by others, as well organized and sophisticated.[144]

Phil Williams's research indicates that there are actually three types of Nigerian criminal organizational structures: (1) a traditional, more hierarchical type, headed by "major organizers" or "crime barons" with transnational connections who are typically members of political and economic elites in the country; (2) a smaller, more flexible and loosely organized type of network based on family, tribal, or personal friendship relations, which often operates within a larger but still flexible network; and (3) a "self-contained cell," consisting of only a few people, that has a particular role or responsibility in some criminal enterprise, and which may serve as subcontractor to a larger, more organized group.[145] Williams believes that, across types, Nigerian crime groups and networks are well organized and very effective. He points out that they carefully plan and prepare for each criminal undertaking, that they adapt well to a "host society," and that they are found virtually everywhere around the world.[146] Like the Albanians, the Nigerians have moved from being employees and couriers to being employers and managers.

Nigerian sex trafficking groups are organized in keeping with certain African cultural traditions. Two culturally important roles in the trafficking operation are played by women. Both are known as "mama," sometimes called "madam" or "Mama Loa" ("the priestess"). One mama lives in Nigeria and serves as a "go-between," receiving girls from a recruiter, preparing them for their trip, and in some cases, making arrangements for transferring some of the girls' eventual earnings to their families. Often it is this mama who warns the girls that if they do not honor their "work contract," a curse will be placed on them and perhaps on other family members. Not uncommonly, there are initiation rites rooted in culturally significant voodoo practices that serve as powerful deterrents to "misbehaviors." A second mama (whose role is sometimes referred to as "mediator") lives in the destination country, where she receives new girls and oversees their lives and work under debt-bonded prostitution—that is, she "supervises, controls, and organizes" the girls (there are usually 10 to 15 in an arriving group) and "coordinates their activities and collects their profits."[147]

Nigerian groups traffic women and girls to many regions, but a large number of them are sent to Europe. In 2002, for example, French police broke up a Nigerian prostitution ring that was trafficking girls from Nigeria and Sierra Leone to France, where they were placed in brothels and clubs in Paris and other French cities.[148] Another Nigerian sex trafficking ring, operating in Brussels, was broken up by Belgian police in the late 1990s.[149] And research in the Netherlands on 1,350 prostitutes who had been trafficked into the country between 1997 and 2000 found that about half of the traffickers had been Dutch; the rest were largely Yugoslav, Turkish, and Nigerian.[150]

Nigerian criminal groups also traffic women into prostitution in Germany, Great Britain, Spain, and Italy.[151] In fact, several reports indicate a thriving Nigerian sex trade business in several Italian cities. The American consulate in Milan reports, for example, that there is a Nigerian "slave trade" in Genoa, in which Nigerian women and men facilitate illegal immigration into Italy, then force immigrating girls into debt-bonded prostitution.[152] And Italy's national anti-Mafia prosecutor states that the Camorra, an Italian organized crime group, works with Nigerian traffickers, renting streets to them where they can prostitute with impunity the women whom they have trafficked from Nigeria into Italy.[153]

While research has focused heavily on Nigerian organized crime groups, some point out that similar crime groups are evolving in other countries in West Africa, such as Ghana and Benin. In fact, says Phil Williams, law enforcers in Great Britain no longer talk about the Nigerian crime problem in Britain, but rather about the West African crime problem there. Williams goes on to point out that the Nigerian crime problem is on an "upward trajectory" and that other West African countries are following suit. Given the poverty and conflict in Nigeria, crime is becoming an "increasingly attractive career" for young and well-educated Nigerians, and most likely will become so for other young West Africans.[154]

Finally, organized crime groups are profiting from sex trafficking to South Africa, where there is a burgeoning sex industry.[155] From its 2002–2003 study, the IOM has concluded that transnational trafficking for prostitution in South Africa is far more "pervasive" than had been previously thought.[156] Women and girls are trafficked to South Africa from NIS and other Eastern European countries with facilitation by the Russian mafia, and from Asian countries with facilitation by the Yakuza.

While organized crime groups from outside are trafficking women into South Africa and investing in the sex industry there, organized trafficking groups within South Africa are also attuned to the profit potential in the local sex trade. The market for child prostitution is particularly robust in South Africa, and organized gangs traffic an increasing number of children there from countries such as Angola, Mozambique, Tanzania, Senegal, Zambia, Uganda, and Kenya.[157] In addition to trafficking by gangs peopled by native South Africans, some internal sex trafficking is organized by ethnically based "refugee syndicates," whose members are unemployed male refugees from other African countries. Fledgling individual sex trafficking entrepreneurs are often assisted by these refugee syndicates.[158]

As its popularity as a destination for sex tourism and child prostitution grows, South Africa's sex industry takes on a more important role in the nation's economy. Again, as elsewhere in Africa, there is every expectation that the "upward trend" in organized trafficking for prostitution in South Africa will continue.

Latin American Organized Crime Groups

In Mexico, Central America, and South America, alien smuggling and forced-labor trafficking have been much more visible than has the trafficking of women and girls for prostitution. Few doubt that organized crime has its hand in the sex trafficking of women and girls around and out of Latin America. But as a U.S. Intelligence report puts it: "In general, there is less information about the Latin American crime groups that traffic in women, though this does not necessarily mean that they are any less involved in [this form of] trafficking."[159]

Perhaps even more prominent than organized crime's participation in human smuggling in the region has been the involvement of large Latin American cartels and mid-sized crime groups in drug trafficking and, to a lesser extent, money laundering. While the once-powerful Cali and Medellín drug cartels based in Colombia have been defused, smaller, more decentralized crime groups have formed drug trafficking networks with alliances throughout the world.[160] There is evidence that Latin American organized crime groups specializing in drug trafficking and money laundering have become more involved in the sex trafficking of women and girls from the region to destinations in Europe, the United States, Canada, and Japan.[161] Connections with organized mafias in other regions have been facilitative. The Yakuza, for example, has strong ties with organized crime groups trafficking women from countries such as Colombia and Mexico to Japan.[162] And, inside several Latin American and Caribbean countries, the Russian mafia works with local criminal groups active in the sex trade.[163]

Organized crime groups use some of the same routes and methods for trafficking women and girls from Mexico and other Latin American countries into the United States for prostitution as they do for their drug and alien smuggling—including reliance on the complicity of police and border guards. In fact, according to an officer in Mexico's antitrafficking unit, sex traffickers buy the silence and support of several high-level government authorities in the state of Sonora with a weekly sum of $200,000.[164] While some Latin American drug trafficking groups have simply added sex trafficking to their business repertoire, other groups start out as sex trafficking businesses, prompted by an awareness of their access to a large, local pool of vulnerable women and girls and to a sizable, nearby market. The infamous Cadena gang, discussed in previous chapters, is an example of a family crime group's opportunistic rise to wealth and power through the trafficking of young Mexican girls into prostitution in Florida.[165]

Today, much of the sex trafficking in Mexico operates through "tightly organized associations" of traffickers typically "based on family hierarchies" and known as "Los Lenones." According to investigative journalist Peter Landesman, the father is the organizational head of the business, while younger male family members recruit or kidnap young women for the trade. Landesman reports that boys in trafficking families "leave school at 12 and are given one or two girls their age to rape and pimp out to begin their training, which emphasizes the arts of kidnapping and seduction."[166]

As in South Africa, the sex tourism and child prostitution markets have also expanded in Latin America, particularly in the Caribbean and some Central and South American resort areas. Here again, there are cooperative endeavors between organized crime groups bringing women into the region and the local receiving groups. Sex trafficking in the region goes both ways; that is, women are trafficked out of as well as into Latin American and Caribbean countries. The Dominican Republic, for example, has a long record of trafficking women to destinations in Europe and Asia, but it also feeds women into its own profitable sex industry.[167] The Directorate of Migration in the Dominican Republic has reported that there are about 400 trafficking and smuggling rings in the country.[168]

Summary Comments

Organized crime today has changed in some ways from its historical form. Although there are still crime groups that retain features—hierarchy, central authority, large size—of older mafias, many of the newer organized crime groups are small, loosely organized, and adaptable. The older mafias have usually added sex trafficking to their diverse criminal repertoire, whereas at least some of the newer ones come into being in order to serve the high-demand, high-supply sex market. As these newer groups become more established and broaden their constituency, they too tend to diversify. One of the most important developments in organized crime has been the formation of transnational networks, allowing organized criminal groups of all types and sizes to cooperate with one another to advance sex trafficking and maximize profits from it.

In the next chapter, we move to a discussion of economic and development policies in the global marketplace, how such policies are related to the economic and development standings of particular countries, and how both of the above factors shape the roles of particular countries in sex trafficking and the sex industry.

Notes

1. Gillian Caldwell, Steve Galster, Jyothi Kanics, and Nadia Steinzor (1999), "Capitalizing on Transition Economies: The Role of the Russian Mafiya in Trafficking Women for Forced Prostitution," pp. 42–73 in *Illegal Immigration and Commercial Sex: The New Slave Trade*, ed. by Phil Williams (London/Portland, OR: Frank Cass).
2. Ibid.
3. Phil Williams (retrieved August 3, 2003), "Transnational Criminal Networks," p. 73 (pp. 61–97) in *Networks and Netwars: The Future of Terror, Crime, and Militancy*, available at http://www.rand.org/publications/MR/MR1382/mr1382.Ch3.pdf. Phil Williams, an expert on organized and transnational crime, is the Director for International Security Studies at the University of Pittsburgh.
4. Organized crime (or criminal) groups are often referred to as mafias, sometimes as syndicates, and even at times as gangs or rings. Although the term "mafia" has traditionally been used for a type of crime group with certain characteristics (e.g., hierarchical and family-based), much of the literature today treats the terms "organized crime (or criminal) group" and "mafia" as interchangeable [Torry D. Dickinson and Robert K. Schaeffer (2001), *Fast Forward: Work, Gender, and Protest in a Changing World* (Lanham, MD: Rowman & Littlefield)]. And, by virtue of their network structure and transnationality, virtually all organized crime groups today could be said to be "syndicated." From this point on, then, I will use the terms "organized crime (or criminal) group," "mafia," and "organized crime syndicate" interchangeably, while recognizing that regardless of what they are called, organized crime groups do vary in form. The term "gang" is sometimes used in the literature to refer to a crime group that is loosely organized, is relatively low in professionalism, and has relatively young members. The meaning of "ring" is less clear, but as it is defined in one dictionary—"a group of persons cooperating for unethical, illicit, or illegal purposes" (*Webster's New Universal Unabridged Dictionary*, 2003)—it also seems to refer to a loosely organized and less formal crime group. While I will take the above into account, I may use these terms in some places simply because they were so used in the literature to which I am referring.
5. Caldwell et al. (1999), op. cit.
6. Richard Lindberg and Vesna Markovic (2000), "Organized Crime Outlook in the New Russia," Search International, available at http://www.search-international.com/Articles/crime/russiacrime.htm.

7. Cyrille J. C. F. Fijnaut, Frank Bovenkerk, Gerben Bruinsma, and Henk van de Bunt (1998), *Organized Crime in the Netherlands* (The Hague: Kluwer Law International), pp. 226–227 [Quoted in Gerben J. N. Bruinsma and Guus Meershoek (1999), "Organized Crime and Trafficking in Women from Eastern Europe in the Netherlands," p. 114 (pp. 105–117) in *Illegal Immigration and Commercial Sex: The New Slave Trade*, ed. by Phil Williams (London/Portland, OR: Frank Cass).]
8. Dickinson and Schaeffer (2001), op. cit.; Melanie Orhant (2001), "Sex Trade Enslaves East Europeans," *Stop-traffic*, available at http://fpmail.friends-partners.org/pipermail/stop-traffic.
9. Gustavo Capdevilla (2002), "Russian Women Trafficked for Sex Trade All Over the World" (July 6), available at http://www.oneworld.net/ips4/2002/07/-8-1/shtml; Dickinson and Schaeffer (2001), op. cit.
10. Williams (2003), "Transnational Criminal Networks."
11. United Nations (1999), *Global Report on Crime and Justice*. [Quoted in Pino Arlacchi (2000), "Fighting Transnational Organized Crime," VIC Guest Article, available at http://afa/at/globalview/042000/organized.html (p. 1 of 4).]
12. Sarah Shannon (1999), "Prostitution and the Mafia: The Involvement of Organized Crime in the Global Sex Trade," p. 140 (pp. 119–144) in *Illegal Immigration and Commercial Sex: The New Slave Trade*, ed. by Phil Williams (London/Portland, OR: Frank Cass).
13. Ibid.
14. Phil Williams (retrieved June 4, 2003), "Organizing Transnational Crime: Networks, Markets and Hierarchies," *Transnational Organized Crime*, Special Issue: "Combating Transnational Crime," ed. by Phil Williams and Dimitri Vlassis, available at http://www.frankcass.com/jnls/stoc.htm (p. 1 of 1). In addition, refer back to Chapter 3 for discussion of the loose structure of the trafficking industry.
15. Mark Findlay (1999), *The Globalisation of Crime* (Cambridge: Cambridge University Press).
16. This point was first made in Chapter 1. An in-depth discussion of market economies and globalization policies is included in Chapter 5.
17. Phil Williams (2003), "Organizing Transnational Crime." For a good discussion of the general organizational structure of the Russian mafia, see Lindberg and Markovic (2000), op. cit.
18. James O. Finckenauer and Jennifer Schrock (retrieved February 18, 2003), "Human Trafficking: A Growing Criminal Market in the U.S," National Institute of Justice International, available at http://www.ojp.usdoj.gov/nij/international/ht.html (8 pp.).
19. Pino Arlacchi (2000), op. cit.

20. International Organization for Migration (1996), "Trafficking in Women to Italy for Sexual Exploitation" (June) (Geneva: Migration Information Programme).
21. Williams (2003), "Organizing Transnational Crime."
22. Bruinsma and Meershoek (1999), op. cit.; Shannon (1999), op. cit.
23. Williams (2003), "Organizing Transnational Crime."
24. Ibid.; Lindberg and Markovic (2000), op. cit.
25. Dickinson and Schaeffer (2001), op. cit., p. 189.
26. Ibid., p. 189.
27. Pino Arlacchi (2000), op. cit.
28. BBC News Online (2002), "Crime Gangs Target Human Traffic," April 24, available at http://news/bbc/co/uk/2/low/uk_news/politics/1948407.stm (3 pp.).
29. Bruce Michael Bagley (2001), "Globalization and Transnational Organized Crime: The Russian Mafia in Latin America and the Caribbean," *Mamacoca: Globalization and Organized Crime*, October 31, available at http://www.mamacoca.org/feb2002/art_bagley_globalization_organized_crime_en.html (27 pp.).
30. Caldwell et al. (1999), op. cit., p. 51.
31. Stephen Handelman (1996), "Can Russia's New Mafia Be Broken?" *The New York Times*, November 9.
32. Caldwell et al. (1999), op. cit.
33. Brian Duffy and Jeff Trimble (1994), "The Wise Guys of Russia," *U.S. News and World Report*, March 7, p. 45.
34. Louise I. Shelley (1997), "The Price Tag of Russian Organized Crime," *Transition* (February), p. 7.
35. Phil Williams (1999), "Trafficking in Women and Children: A Market Perspective," pp. 145–170 in *Illegal Immigration and Commercial Sex: The New Slave Trade*, ed. by Phil Williams (London/Portland, OR: Frank Cass).
36. Caldwell et al. (1999), op. cit.
37. Vanessa von Struensee (2000), "Globalized, Wired, Sex Trafficking in Women and Children," *Murdoch University Electronic Journal of Law* 7 (June), available at http://www.murdoch.edu.au/elaw/v7n2/struensee72_text.html (14 pp.).
38. The KGB, the Soviet Union's national security agency, was replaced following the breakup of the Soviet Union by the FSB, the state intelligence bureau.
39. Williams (1999), op. cit., p. 51.
40. Center for Strategic and International Studies (1997), *Russian Organized Crime* (Washington D.C.), p. 10.

41. Walter Zalisko (2002), "Russian Organized Crime, Trafficking in Women, and Government's Response," available at http://www.monmouth.com/~wplz/Index1.htm (9 pp.).
42. United Nations (1995), "Crime: The World Ministerial Conference on Transnational Organized Crime," in *Crime Prevention and Criminal Justice Newsletter*, nos. 26–27 (November).
43. Daniel E. Lungren (1996), "Russian Organized Crime: California's Newest Threat," California Department of Justice (March), p. 9.
44. Zalisko (2002), op. cit.; Lindberg and Markovic (2000), op. cit.; Amy O'Neill Richard (1999), "VI. The Traffickers," *International Trafficking in Women to the United States: A Contemporary Manifestation of Slavery and Organized Crime* (November), DCI Exceptional Intelligence Analyst Program: An Intelligence Monograph (Center for the Study of Intelligence).
45. Bagley (2001), op. cit.; Shannon (1999), op. cit.; Williams (1999), op. cit.
46. Capdevilla (2002), op. cit.
47. Kevin Connolly (1998), "How Russia's Mafia Is Taking Over Israel's Underworld," BBC News, April 3. [Cited at http://www.northvegr.org/fow/001.html.]
48. Caldwell et al. (1999), op. cit.
49. Amy O'Neill Richard (1999), "Appendix II: International Organized Crime and Its Involvement in Trafficking Women and Children Abroad," *International Trafficking in Women to the United States: A Contemporary Manifestation of Slavery and Organized Crime* (November), DCI Exceptional Intelligence Analyst Program: An Intelligence Monograph (Center for the Study of Intelligence).
50. Bagley (2001), op. cit.; Amy O'Neill Richard (1999), *International Trafficking in Women to the United States: A Contemporary Manifestation of Slavery and Organized Crime* (November), DCI Exceptional Intelligence Analyst Program: An Intelligence Monograph (Center for the Study of Intelligence).
51. Caldwell et al. (1999), op. cit.; Richard (1999), "Appendix II."
52. Penelope Turnbull (1999), "The Fusion of Immigration and Crime in the European Union: Problems of Cooperation and the Fight against the Trafficking in Women," pp. 189–213 in *Illegal Immigration and Commercial Sex: The New Slave Trade*, ed. by Phil Williams (London/Portland, OR: Frank Cass); "Sources of Trafficked Women: Country Survey" (1998), *Fraud Digest* (August) (Bureau of Consular Affairs); Gillian Caldwell, Steve Galster, and Nadia Steinzor (1997), "Crime and Servitude: An Exposé of the Traffic in Women for Prostitution from the Newly Independent States," report presented at conference

on "The Trafficking of Women Abroad" (Washington D.C.: Global Survival Network).
53. Shannon (1999), op. cit.
54. Jaroslav Koshiw (1999), "A Native Son and the Bank of New York Scandal," *Kyiv Post,* August 26; "Les Nouvelles mafias d'Europe de l'Est" (1997), *Marianne en ligne,* December 5, available at http://www.marianne-en-ligne.fr/12-05-97/dessus-b.htm. [Both sources cited in Donna M. Hughes (2000), "The 'Natasha' Trade: The Transnational Shadow Market of Trafficking in Women," *Journal of International Affairs,* Special Issue: "In the Shadows: Promoting Prosperity or Undermining Stability?" 53 (Spring), pp. 625–651.]
55. "Sources of Trafficked Women: Country Survey" (1998), op. cit.
56. Shannon (1999), op. cit.
57. Richard (1999), "Appendix II"; The Protection Project (2002), *Human Rights Report on Trafficking in Persons, Especially Women and Children: A Country-by-Country Report on a Contemporary Form of Slavery,* 2nd ed. (The Paul H. Nitze School of Advanced International Studies, Johns Hopkins University).
58. Richard (1999), "Appendix II."
59. David E. Kaplan and Alec Dubro (1986), *Yakuza: The Explosive Account of Japan's Criminal Underworld* (Reading, PA: Addison Wesley). Kaplan and Dubro offer a comprehensive look at the history and organization of the Yakuza; their book is widely cited.
60. Shannon (1999), op. cit.
61. Pasuk Phongpaichit (1999), "Trafficking in People in Thailand," pp. 74–104 in *Illegal Immigration and Commercial Sex: The New Slave Trade,* ed. by Phil Williams (London/Portland, OR: Frank Cass); Pasuk Phongpaichit, Sungsidh Piriyarangsan, and Nualoni Treerat (1998), *Guns, Girls, Gambling, Ganja: Thailand's Illegal Economy and Public Policy* (Chiang Mai: Silkworm Books).
62. Caldwell et al. (1999), op. cit., p. 69.
63. Human Rights Watch (2000), "Owed Justice: Thai Women Trafficked into Debt Bondage in Japan" (September), available at http://www.hrw.org/reports/2000/japan; Phongpaichit (1999), op. cit.
64. Ibid.
65. Ibid., p. 21.
66. Ibid.
67. Gregory Gross (1996), "Mexican Women Forced to Be Sex Slaves: Taken to Japan, They Were Victimized by Organized Crime," *San Diego Union-Tribune,* May 3, A-1; Michael Vatikiotis, Sachiko Sakamaki, and Gary Silverman (1995), "On the Margin: Organized Crime Profits from the Flesh Trade," *Far East Economic Review,* December 14.

68. Chitraporn Vanaspong (1996), "A Multi-million Baht Business," *Bangkok Post,* August 18, p. 4; Vatikiotis et al. (1995), op. cit.
69. Caldwell et al. (1997), op. cit.
70. Susan Moran (1993), "New World Havens of Oldest Profession," *Insight on the News* 9, June 21, p. 2.
71. Kaplan and Dubro (1986), op. cit.
72. James O. Finckenauer (retrieved September 6, 2003), "Chinese Transnational Organized Crime: The Fuk Ching," International Center, National Institute of Justice, available at http://www.ojp.usdoj.gov/nij/international/chinese.html (6 pp.); Ko-lin Chin (1996), *Chinatown Gangs* (Oxford: Oxford University Press).
73. Richard (1999), "Appendix II."
74. Richard (1999), *International Trafficking in Women to the United States.*
75. International Organization for Migration (1997/1998), "Trafficking in Migrants," *Quarterly Bulletin of the International Organization for Migration* 17.
76. Melanie Orhant (2001), "Republic of Ireland: British Triads Turn to Lucrative Slave Trade," *Stop-traffic,* September 28, available at http://www.friends-partners/org/partners/stop-traffic/1999/0707.html; Moran (1993), op. cit.
77. Richard (1999), "Appendix II."
78. Ibid., p. 2.
79. Richard (1999), "VI. The Traffickers."
80. Ibid.
81. Moran (1993), op. cit.
82. Ibid.
83. Ibid.
84. Richard (1999), "VI. The Traffickers."
85. Richard (1999), *International Trafficking in Women to the United States,* p. 13.
86. Ibid.; Finckenauer (2003), op. cit.; Chin (1996), op. cit.
87. Richard (1999), "VI. The Traffickers."
88. Donna M. Hughes, Laura Joy Sporcic, Nadine Z. Mendelsohn, and Vanessa Chirgwin (1999, retrieved December 21, 2001), *Factbook on Global Sexual Exploitation,* "China and Hong Kong" (Coalition Against Trafficking in Women), available at http://www.uri.edu/artsci/wms/hughes/factbook.htm. Also see, for example, Paul Kahila (1991), "Imprisoned Prostitutes: The Gangs Run Lucrative Brothels," *Maclean's* 104, p. 24, for a discussion of how a Hong Kong gang trafficked young women into Canada.
89. Caldwell et al. (1999), op. cit.

90. Sophia Woodman and Stephania Ho (1995), "Trafficking of Women in China," *Voice of America* (September). [Cited in Hughes et al. (1999), op. cit., "China and Hong Kong."]
91. Shannon (1999), op. cit.
92. "Taiwan: 'Lily' International Sex Ring Disbands" (1997), Taiwan Central News Agency, December 22.
93. Human Rights Watch (2000), op. cit.
94. Richard (1999), *International Trafficking in Women to the United States.*
95. Richard (1999), "Appendix II."
96. "Vietnam Police Bust Gang Selling Women into Prostitution in Malaysia" (2002), Agence France Presse, September 17, available at http://www.walnet.org/csis/news/world_2002/afp-020917.html (2 pp.).
97. David France (2000), "Slavery's New Face," *Newsweek*, December 11; "Indictment: Group Smuggled Women" (1999), *St. Petersburg Times*, August 21.
98. Bill Wallace (2001), "19 Indicted in Area-wide Prostitution, Smuggling Ring—Allegedly Forced Asian Women in Brothels," *San Francisco Chronicle*, February 13.
99. "Korean Sex Slaves Nabbed at U.S. Borders" (1999), *Toronto Sun*, March 14.
100. David Binder and Preston Mendenhall (retrieved February 22, 2003), "Sex, Drugs and Guns in the Balkans," *MSNBC News*, available at http://www.msnbc.com/news/667790.asp (6 pp.).
101. Quoted in "Albanian Mafia Steps Up People Smuggling" (2000), BBC News, available at http://news.bbc/co/uk/2/hi/world/europe/863620 .stm.
102. Ibid.
103. Gus Xhudo (1996), "Men of Purpose: The Growth of Albanian Criminal Activity," *Transnational Organized Crime* 2 (Spring), pp. 1–20 (London: Frank Cass), available at http://www.kosovo.com/gus/html.
104. Ibid., p. 1.
105. Dominic Kennedy, Stewart Tendler, and John Philipps (2002), "Times: Albanian Gangs Corner Britain's Sex Trade," *Reality Macedonia*, July 6, available at http://www.realitymacedonia.org.mk/web/news_page .asp?nid=1899 (3 pp.); Richard (1999), "Appendix II"; Xhudo (1996), op. cit.
106. International Organization for Migration (1996), "Trafficking in Women to Italy"; Xhudo (1996), op. cit.
107. See, for example, Sebastian Junger (2002), "Slaves of the Brothel," *Vanity Fair* (July), pp.112–117, 161–166; Kennedy et al. (2002), op. cit.; The Protection Project (2002), op. cit.; Barry Wood (2002), "VOA:

Study Shows Organized Crime Pervasive in Balkans," *Reality Macedonia*, April 10, available at http://www.realitymacedonia.org.mk/web/news_page.asp?nid=1757 (3 pp.); "A Living Hell: Europe's Sex Trade Network," *F2 Network*, June 4, available at http://old/smh.com.au/news/0106/04/features/features1.html (7 pp.).

108. Xhudo (1996), op. cit. In some cases, membership is restricted to a particular clan or ethnic group. In the crime group's view and experience, such restriction better ensures loyalty and commitment.
109. International Organization for Migration (1996), "Trafficking in Women to Italy"; Richard (1999), "Appendix II."
110. Lori Montgomery (1999), "Some Female Kosovo Refugees Are Falling Prey to Criminal Gangs in Albania," *South Coast*, May 22, available at http://www.s-t.com/daily/05-99/05-22-99/c07/wn125.htm (4 pp.).
111. Claire Doole (2001), "Albania Blamed for Human Trafficking: Gangs Use Albania to Lure Women into Prostitution," BBC News, April 17, available at http://www.uri.edu/artsci/wms/hughes/ukraine/allblame.htm (3 pp.); Montgomery (1999), op. cit.
112. Kennedy et al. (2002), op. cit., p. 3.
113. Richard (1999), "Appendix II."
114. Montgomery (1999), op. cit., p. 3.
115. Xhudo (1996), op. cit.; Montgomery (1999), op. cit.; "UNICEF Sees Prostitution Among Kosovo Albanians" (1999), Reuters, May 20.
116. "MSNBC: Albanian Nationalists Profit from Sex Slavery and Drugs in Macedonia" (2002), *Reality Macedonia*, May 13, available at http://www.realitymacedonia.org.mk/web/news_page.asp?nid=1877 (3 pp.); Xhudo (1996), op. cit.
117. "MSNBC: Albanian Nationalists" (2002), op. cit.
118. Human Rights Watch (2002), "Bosnia and Herzegovina: Hopes Betrayed: Trafficking of Women and Girls to Post-Conflict Bosnia and Herzegovina for Forced Prostitution," 14 (November); Hank Hyena (2000), "Albanian Gangsters Kidnapping Women and Girls to Service Troops," *Urge* [salon.com], February 9, available at http://archive.salon.com/health/sex/urge/world/2000/02/09/kosovo (3 pp.).
119. Michael Voss (2001), " 'Slave Trade' Thrives in Bosnia: High Unemployment Makes Women Easy Prey," BBC News, March 8, available at http://www.uri.edu/artsci/wms/hughes/ukraine/slavebosnia.htm (2 pp.).
120. Daniel Simpson (2002), "Bosnia: Policemen Fired for Aiding Sex Traffic," *The New York Times*, October 18, A-5, p. 6; Doole (2001), op. cit.
121. Junger (2002), op. cit.
122. Kennedy et al. (2002), op. cit., p. 1. Also, more generally, see Orhant (2001), "Republic of Ireland."

123. Richard (1999), "Appendix II"; Molo Songololo (2000), *The Traffic of Women into the South African Sex Industry*. [Cited in "South Africa's Child Sex Trafficking Nightmare" (2000), BBC News, November 23, available at http://news/bbc/co/uk/2/hi/world/africa/1027215.stm.]
124. International Organization for Migration (1997/1998), op. cit.
125. Ibid.
126. Graham Rayman (2001), "Stripped of Their Dignity: Czech Women Lured to Work at NYC Sex Clubs," Newsday.com, March 13, available at http://www.newsday.com/news/local/newyork/ny-smuggled-easteeurope,0,4558166.story (6 pp.).
127. Adriatik Kelmendi (2001), "Kosovo Prostitution Racket Flourishes," Institute for War and Peace, March 28.
128. Brian Freemantle (1995), *Europe in the Grip of Organized Crime* (London: Orion).
129. Richard (1999), "Appendix II."
130. Ibid.
131. Ibid., p. 5.
132. Rayman (2001), op. cit.
133. International Organization for Migration, Skopje (2003), "Dilaver Bojku-Leku Escapes," *Counter-Trafficking*, June 21, available at http://www.iomskopje.org.mk/CT/news/news_062103.html; "US: $10,000 Reward for Dilaver Bojku Alias Leku," *Reality Macedonia* (Vest), January 7 (3 pp.), available at http://www.realitymacedonia.org.mk/web/news_page.asp?nid=2652; Preston Mendenhall (retrieved September 29, 2003), "Top Fugitive in Sex Trade Arrested," *MSNBC News*, February 10, available at http://stacks.msnbc.com/news/870996.asp (5 pp.); Preston Mendenhall (n.d., retrieved February 22, 2002), "Sex Slaves in Europe," *MSNBC News*, available at http://www.msnbc.com/news/725802.asp?Osp=v3z2 (9 pp.).
134. Meena Menon (1998), "Women in India's Trafficking Belt," *Third World Network Features*, March 22, available at http://www.hartford-hwp.com/archives/52a/062.html (4 pp.); Robert I. Friedman (1996), "India's Shame: Sexual Slavery and Political Corruption Are Leading to an AIDS Catastrophe," *The Nation,* 262, April 8.
135. "Current Situation of Organized Crimes in Trafficking Stolen Vehicles, Card Fraud, Money Laundering and Major Transnational Organized Criminal Groups" (retrieved October 16, 2003), Resource Material Series no. 58, available at http://66.218.71.225/search/cache?p=Dawood+Ibrahim+organized+crime&url=UR9goFj8. This mafia is named after its leader, Dawood Ibrahim, currently believed to be living in exile in Pakistan, from where he is still thought to be running his mafia. Ibrahim has been accused as the ringleader responsible for

the 1993 bombings in Bombay, in which 257 people were killed. For more about Ibrahim's alleged activities in Pakistan, see Suketu Mehta (2002), "Gangsters in Exile," *TIME Asia*, May 6, available at http://www.time.com/time/asia/magazine/article/0,13673,50102056-233995,00.html (3 pp.); B. Muralidhar Reddy (2003), "Is Dawood Running Underworld Empire in Karachi?" *The Hindu*, September 22, available at http://www.hindu.com/3002/22/stories/2003092204190100.htm (2 pp.).

136. Celia W. Dugger (1998), "As Bombay Piles on Wealth, Gangsters Get Their Cut, Too," *The New York Times*, November 12; Friedman (1996), op. cit.
137. Ibid.
138. Ibid.
139. Melanie Orhant (2001), "News/US: His Own Private Berkeley," *Stop-traffic*, November 29, available at http://fpmail.friends-partners.org/pipermail/stop-traffic/2001-November/001756.html (8 pp.).
140. The Protection Project (2002), op. cit., "Bangladesh," "Nepal"; Hughes et al. (1999), op. cit., "Bangladesh"; S. M. Tumbahamphe and B. Bhattarai (retrieved November 1, 2002), "Trafficking of Women in South Asia" (ANNFSU-Asian Students Association), available at http://www.ecouncil.ac.cr/about/contrib/women/youth/english/traffic1.htm; Human Rights Watch (1995), "Rape for Profit: Trafficking of Nepali Girls and Women to India's Brothels" (New York).
141. "Child Trafficking Creates Panic" (2002), *The Independent*, September 6. (Associated Press), available at http://www.walnet.org/csic/news/world_2002/independent-020906.html (3 pp.).
142. "Combating International Crime in Africa," (1998), U.S. House of Representatives, Subcommittee on Africa, Committee on International Relations (Washington, D.C.) [Testimony of subcommittee], available at http://commdocs.house.gov/committees/intlrel/hfa50884.000/hfa50884_0.HTM. Various forms of financial fraud, known overall as "419 fraud," solicit funds, usually to be deposited in Nigerian banks, guaranteed to make money for the contributor; even if the solicited person doesn't actually transfer funds to the Nigerian bank, any identity information he or she might provide may be used for identity theft or other fraud.
143. Richard (1999), "Appendix II."
144. Hughes et al. (1999), op. cit., "Nigeria."
145. "Combating International Crime in Africa" (1998), op. cit., statement of Phil Williams, Director, Center for International Security Studies, University of Pittsburgh.
146. Ibid.

147. Allison Loconto (2001), "The Trafficking of Nigerian Women into Italy," *TED Case Studies* 656 (January), available at http://www.american.edu/TED/italian-trafficking.htm; Mark Taylor (2001), U.S. Embassy in Nigeria, Protection Project fact-finding mission, Lagos, Nigeria (July) [Cited in The Protection Project (2002), op. cit.]; Hughes et al. (1999), op. cit., "Italy."
148. "French Police Bust Nigerian Prostitution Ring" (2002), *Asia Intelligence Wire* (*Financial Times*), September 15, available at http://www.walnet.org/csis/news/world_2002/aiw-020915.html (2 pp.).
149. International Organization for Migration (1997/1998), op. cit.
150. "Often Prostitutes Are Merchandise" (2002), *Het Parool*, September 10, available at http://www.walnet.org/csis/news/world_2002/parool-020910.html (2 pp.).
151. Stephan Faris (2002), "Italy's Sex Trade Pulls Teens Pushed by Poverty," *Women's News*, August 15, available at http://www.womensnews.org/article/cfm/dyn/aid/1005/context/archive (4 pp.); Richard (1999), "Appendix II"; Shannon (1999), op. cit.
152. Richard (1999), "Appendix II."
153. Ibid.
154. "Combating International Crime in Africa" (1998), op. cit., statement of Phil Williams.
155. The Protection Project (2002), op. cit., "South Africa"; Molo Songololo (2000), op. cit.
156. Melanie Orhant (2003), "Report/Southern Africa: IOM Study on Human Trafficking in Southern Africa Released," *Stop-traffic*, May 12, available at http://fpmail.friends-partners.org/pipermail/stop-traffic/2003/002999.html (4 pp.).
157. Molo Songololo (2000), The Trafficking of Children for Purposes of Sexual Exploitation—South Africa (Cape Town, South Africa).
158. Orhant (2003), op. cit.
159. Richard (1999), "VI. The Traffickers."
160. Phil Williams (1998), "The Nature of Drug-Trafficking Networks," *Current History* 97, pp. 154–159.
161. Shannon (1999), op. cit.
162. Human Rights Watch (2000), op. cit.
163. Bagley (2001), op. cit.
164. Peter Landesman (2004), "The Girls Next Door," *The New York Times Magazine*, January 25, pp. 30–39, 66–67, 72, 74.
165. The Cadena family lied to or kidnapped young women from or near their own hometown in Mexico and trafficked them into prostitution in Florida and neighboring U.S. states. See Chapter 3 for a fuller discussion of the family crime group's sex trafficking activity.

166. Landesman (2004), op. cit., p. 36.
167. The Protection Project (2002), op. cit., "Dominican Republic"; International Organization for Migration (1996), "Trafficking in Women from the Dominican Republic for Sexual Exploitation" (June), (Budapest: Migration Information Programme).
168. Alison Phinney (2002), "Trafficking of Women and Children for Sexual Exploitation in the Americas" (Washington D.C.: Pan American Health Organization/World Health Organization).

5

From Here to There: Sex Trafficking Flows and the Economic Conditions That Drive Them

It would seem that one way of making sense out of sex trafficking flows would be simply to map them. But a look at such efforts reveals the difficulty of such a task. The mapping of routes to and from different countries and regions in The Protection Project's report on sex trafficking is illustrative. Its maps show, for example, that routes to and from Russia alone involve 47 countries. Even less prominent former Soviet republics use a variety of routes; in Ukraine, for instance, trafficking routes involve 29 countries. Western countries are also globally implicated—49 countries are included in U.S. trafficking routes, 30 in Germany's routes. Regional routing is, of course, even more dense—for Africa, 66 countries are included in the map; for Southeast Asia, there are 54 countries and for the Middle East, 52 countries.[1]

Another difficulty is capturing the trajectories of sex trafficking flows. While some countries, such as Russia and Ukraine, are primarily *source sites*—that is, they send women out to other destinations—other countries are *bidirectional,* in that they both send out and receive trafficked women. Across regions, still other countries have evolved into centers, or *hubs,* for sex trafficking. Hubs provide venues through which women can be purchased and exchanged by multinational traffickers, then either taken elsewhere or incorporated into the hub country's own sex industry. The sex market in a hub country is typically most active in one or more of its major cities—Bangkok in Thailand, or Guatemala City in Guatemala, for example. Although they do not constitute hubs, most source and bidirectional countries also serve as transit stops for women as they are moved around the globe.[2] Furthermore, most countries that traffic women to other destinations also traffic women internally for prostitution in their own country.

Finally, some—mostly affluent—countries are almost exclusively *destinations* for trafficked women. In the map just described, for example, all U.S. trafficking routes bring women to, rather than away from, the United States. Although such countries are typically not *global* traffickers of their own women, they may engage in the internal trafficking of both imported and local women.

While these multifaceted arrangements create a complex sex trafficking maze, it is in many ways a patterned one. The roles of particular countries and regions in the sex trafficking industry are related to local economic conditions, which are increasingly affected by global conditions—economic markets and development and globalization policies. Although the match is not perfect, a country's level of human development, rates of poverty and joblessness, and size of per capita income or gross domestic product (GDP) tend to be related to its primary sex trafficking role. As might be expected, source countries that mainly traffic women elsewhere are likely to be less affluent or less economically stable than the destination countries that receive the women.

Based on the literature, and most heavily on the by-country findings published by The Protection Project in its *Human Rights Report on Trafficking in Persons, Especially Women and Children: A Country-by-Country Report on a Contemporary Form of Slavery,* I have identified 99 countries that have been documented as actively involved in sex trafficking—and that I have classified as source, hub, bidirectional, or destination sites.[3] Table 1

Table 1

Selected Sex Trafficking Countries ($n = 99$) by Region and Primary Sex Trafficking Role

Region	Source	Hub	Bidirectional	Destination	Total
CEE/NIS	17	2	8	1	28
Western Europe/ North America*	0	0	0	21	21
East/South/ Southeast Asia	6	4	5	3	18
Latin America	6	2	1	3	12
Africa	7	1	1	2	11
Middle East	1	0	1	7	9
Total	37	9	16	37	99

*This category also includes Australia and New Zealand.

shows the number of countries in each of these four trafficking roles by region. The largest number of involved countries are from Central and Eastern Europe (CEE), including the newly independent states (NIS). The great majority of countries in the CEE/NIS region (about 86%) are either source or bidirectional countries. In Africa too, source countries are in the majority.[4]

Taken together as a Westernized bloc, Western Europe and North America (along with Australia and New Zealand) have the second highest number of sex trafficking countries, and *all* of them are destination sites.[5] While fewer in number, trafficking countries in the Middle East are also largely destination sites. More trafficking role variation is found in East and Southeast Asia and Latin America, where all roles are represented by at least one country.

The lack of sufficient revenues, including money to pay their workforce, pushes many source (and some bidirectional) countries to send women out of the country for work, with the hope, and sometimes the requirement, that they will send money back home. The greater their country's need for revenues, the less likely a government is to check thoroughly on the conditions of work for their temporary emigrants. Should they be vigilant and find poor working conditions, they often lack the resources to do much about it.

High rates of joblessness and poverty in developing and transitional countries ensure a large pool of women who are desperate for work. In many instances, women take the risk of foreign job offers because they are responsible for the care of family members—parents, grandparents, or young children. They often expect to work out of the country for a short period of time, send money home, and then return home with savings. Says Pot, a Thai woman recruited to go to Japan in 1990 for what she thought was a legitimate job:

> A friend I knew from the market . . . told me about the opportunity to work in factories in Japan. I had divorced my Thai husband when I was four months pregnant and now my son was three years old and I had to raise him by myself and was finding it difficult to make enough money. My parents asked me not to go, but I thought if I went for just one year I could make money for my family and my son.[6]

Kaew, another woman trafficked into prostitution in Japan, explained that she too had to make money in order to support her children. Although Kaew was married, her husband was an abusive alcoholic who did not have a job. In 1992, Kaew traveled to Japan on a 90-day tourist visa, hoping to find work and then return to her village in Thailand. "I had three kids, my husband drank, and we had no money," she said, "so I had to do something." Kaew found work as a prostitute, but after 2 years, she was arrested and sent back to Thailand. Back home, she expressed her fear that her sons would be ashamed of her and the work she did when they were younger: "Whenever I think too much, I get sad. But then I remember when I could only feed my children rice and soup. My husband didn't help, so my kids had to stay with my mother while I went to earn money." While the work helped her support her family, Kaew remains saddened by her experience abroad.[7]

Women's Poverty, Joblessness, and Poor Working Conditions in Source Countries

Around the world, women's poverty and unemployment rates are almost always higher than those of men. Moreover, if women are employed, they typically have lower pay and poorer working conditions than men. When economies are unstable and joblessness spreads, women, whose jobs are more tenuous than men's to begin with, are likely to lose even more.[8] This clearly happened in Eastern European countries in the 1990s as they struggled to cope with the fall of the Soviet Union. In Ukraine, for example, by the mid-1990s, 80% of those without jobs were women.[9] Traditional beliefs aggravate the problem of women's joblessness in difficult economic times. In spite of the high numbers of women who are the sole or main breadwinner for their families around the world, it is often assumed that it is more important to provide men with jobs than women. As Russia's Labor Minister Gennady Melikyan put it when joblessness in Russia soared in the mid-1990s, "Why should we employ women when men are out of work?"[10]

In developing countries, women are commonly found in the informal sector of the labor market, in which work tends to be underpaid, or not paid at all, and without regulation of any sort.[11] The informal labor market largely consists of small-scale family or individual enterprises, in which work is done with "traditional technology and labor-intensive methods,"[12] characteristics that aptly describe much of women's work in developing countries. And, whether in agriculture, street vending, or home-based piecework (e.g., sewing garments at home for a company that pays the worker for each garment or garment part), workers in the informal market incur costs (e.g., equipment, space, utilities, inventory) that in the formal market are sustained by the employer.

Furthermore, workers in the informal sector are frequently isolated, which limits their ability to organize for workers' rights. Sometimes they are not even recognized as part of the labor force. An example of such invisibility is the woman farmer, often referred to and treated not as a farmer, but rather as the farmer's wife. This representation remains in spite of the fact that these "invisible" female farmers produce an estimated 50% of the world's food "for direct consumption."[13] Formal farming business activities—applying for loans, purchasing farm equipment, and even purchasing the farm itself—are usually done in the name of the (male) head of household, making him the "real" agricultural worker in the family. This lack of recognition is exacerbated by the fact that much of women's agricultural work is unpaid. Lack of pay for women is common in, but not unique to, agricultural work. In fact, according to several reports, whether agricultural, domestic, industrial, or vending, *most* of the work that women do around the world is unpaid.[14]

At the end of the 1990s, the majority of women working in developing countries, with perhaps the exception of Latin America, were in the informal sector of the labor market.[15] Throughout much of Africa, over a third of women working in something other than agriculture were working in the informal sector, often doing home-based work.[16] And in Latin America, the informal work sector is increasing. In fact, over 80% of new jobs created in Latin America and the Caribbean between 1990 and 1993 were in the informal sector.[17]

Although women continue to be heavily represented in the informal market sector in both developing and transitional countries, they also have increasingly become industrial workers in the formal market. But here, women tend to be located in the manufacturing industries or companies that are the least well represented by labor unions,[18] where their working conditions are often similar to those in the informal market. In developing countries, much of the manufacturing work overall is unorganized. Take India and Pakistan, for example—both developing countries and active sex trafficking hubs. In these two countries 70% and 75%, respectively, of all manufacturing jobs are unorganized.[19]

With such poor working conditions, even women who are working are vulnerable to recruitment for seemingly better jobs in a larger city or a foreign country. For young, rural women working in the informal sector, opportunities described by recruiters often seem too good to pass up. Some parents, thinking they are helping their daughters find a better life, agree to their daughters' travel and only afterward learn of their mistake. The story of Jinlian and her parents is illustrative.

Jinlian and her parents were eager to take advantage of an opportunity for the 15-year-old girl to leave their small village in China and go to a nearby town to learn to be a seamstress. The family "scraped together" enough money and sent her off. When interviewed by a journalist, Jinlian's parents sat clinging to a picture, "their only keepsake" of her. It had then been 3 years since she left, and in all that time, they had heard nothing from her. Most likely, according to sources familiar with this kind of situation, Jinlian was the victim of a bride abduction, sold into a new life from which she could not escape.[20]

Although labor and financial woes stem from somewhat different circumstances in former socialist countries making the transition to private market economies than in developing countries, such woes also affect women more harshly than men.[21] As one author notes, in the 1990s, as Eastern European and NIS countries "privatized industries and established new market economies, labor demands . . . shifted and competition for jobs, and economic survival" became "fiercely aggressive."[22] Under socialism, women had jobs mainly in "manufacturing and agriculture or in government-funded offices and scientific-research institutes. Now those jobs, once guaranteed by the state, either no longer exist or have gone to enduring downsizing and gender-based layoffs."[23] Like women in developing countries, women in the NIS and other Eastern European countries have increasingly turned to the informal sector—in many cases to street vending, selling crafts they have made or food and flowers they have grown.[24]

The personal economic problems of women worldwide, and particularly of women from sex trafficking source countries (both developing and transitional), stand in stark contrast to their contributions to the economic well-being of global and local economies, as well as that of their own families. Says Mahbub ul Haq, the primary author of the United Nations 1995 *Human Development Report*:

> There is an unwitting conspiracy on a global scale to undervalue women's work and contributions to society. . . . In virtually every country of the world, women work longer hours than men, yet share less in the economic rewards. If women's work were accurately reflected in national statistics, it would shatter the myth that men are the main breadwinners of the world.[25]

Nevertheless, it is useful to keep in mind that poverty is a driving force behind much of men's, as well as women's, involvement in sex trafficking. Women, of course, are more likely to be the trafficked commodity, but traffickers at the low end of the industry (often recruiters) are commonly women and men who are poor and without other work. As the U.S. Agency for International Development (USAID) points out: "Trafficking is inextricably linked to poverty. Wherever privation and economic hardship prevail, there will be those destitute and desperate enough to enter into the fraudulent employment schemes that are the most common intake systems in the world of trafficking."[26]

Conditions in Developing and Transitional Source Countries

As indicated above, economic problems in source countries have fueled the expanding recruitment of women and girls for global sex trafficking in the 1990s and early 2000s. Many source countries have fledgling, unstable market systems that have increasingly become linked to the powerful global market dominated by Western powers.

The newer, transitional trafficking countries, including many of the former Soviet republics and other Eastern European countries, were relatively isolated from Western destination countries prior to the breakup of the Soviet Union in 1991. As has been discussed,[27] the infrastructure collapse that accompanied the Soviet breakup was followed by struggles of various ethnic enclaves in the region to establish identity and build quasi-independent economic and social structures. New governments lacked the resources to subsidize industries or to support the establishment of new markets, and economic decline was the norm throughout the 1990s.[28]

Many of the developing source countries, on the other hand, suffered under lengthy oppressive colonial rule, followed by hard-fought struggles for independence and then for economic and social stability.[29] In order to maximize their own economic interests, colonizers have typically favored the production of export or cash crops in their colonies over subsistence economies that feed the local people and thus provide them with a measure of independence.[30] Moreover, colonial powers have introduced their own gender inequalities into the territories they have seized. Suzanne LaFont points out that colonial practices aimed at moving colonies toward market economies favored men, who were "given the tools, technology, training, credit, and opportunities to succeed in the market economy," while the "status of women was devalued as they were left behind in the transition from 'traditional' to 'modern' society."[31]

Developing source countries found a new high-demand export or cash crop in their young women and girls, who could be trafficked for prostitution to specific destination countries, often former colonial powers. Women's lack of status and economic opportunity under colonial rule continued following independence and helped legitimate their trafficking victimization.

Conditions in Affluent Destination Countries

Cliché though it may be, it still bears repeating that the "rewards and costs of economic change are not distributed evenly between as well as within nations."[32] And there are real concerns that globalization is contributing to the growing inequality between nations and regions, as well as to that between the sexes.[33] Economic conditions in affluent Western destination countries are not always optimal, and they are definitely not optimal for everyone, but they are far better overall than conditions in developing and transitional source countries. Affluence in Western countries provides many with ample discretionary income to spend on luxury goods, recreational activities, and an expanding set of services.[34] As more middle-class women have moved into the labor market, and as the population ages, there is an increasing demand in affluent Western countries for domestic and caretaking labor, filled in part by local minority women, but also by foreign women migrating specifically for wage-paying jobs.

Demand for foreign labor generally, and for female domestic labor specifically, is also strong in (oil-) wealthy Middle Eastern destination countries, such as the United Arab Emirates (U.A.E.) and Kuwait. Many women have been trafficked to Middle Eastern destination countries for domestic work, where they labor under unacceptable working conditions, including sexual abuse and exploitation. A plethora of reports about the abuse of their female emigrant domestic workers in several Persian Gulf countries has prompted governments in South and Southeast Asia to call those workers back home.[35] The supply of foreign female labor, however, has been easily replenished in the era of globalization.

Globalization and Its Macrolevel Ends

While trafficking in women is not a new business, it has expanded and taken on new dimensions with the emergence of a global market system with specific goals and specific strategies for achieving them. Globalization features at least three economic ends, all of which are highly valued by the global power elite:[36]

- Privatization and integration of global and local markets

- Liberalization of trade and other market exchanges
- Spread of production through foreign investment by multinational corporations

Market Privatization

Central among the goals of globalization is the buildup of a global, privatized market economy to which local market economies are linked. Developing and transitional countries are encouraged to privatize their economies—that is, to adopt capitalistic economies based theoretically on the law of supply and demand.[37] In such market systems, the state plays a lesser role in the economy, including a lesser involvement in the provision of economic security (e.g., jobs, unemployment compensation, minimum wage, social services) for workers.[38] In countries that are industrializing or moving from a socialist or government-secured economic system to a capitalist one, poverty and joblessness can and often do increase. Furthermore, many of the jobs that have emerged in the privatized global economy have involved "irregular, often precarious forms of work"—part-time, self-employed, or home-based, again without protection or regulation from any governing body.[39]

With the integration of local and global markets, developing and transitional countries are also more dependent on the state of global economic affairs, over which they have very little, if any, control.[40] Economic crises in the global system (or in affluent countries) reverberate in individual nations, and when local crises result, women tend to be hit harder. Development specialists point out that during the Asian financial crisis in the late 1990s, for example, it became clear that "greater integration to the world economy increases vulnerability to outside shocks," and that the "cost of economic crisis" in Asia was "disproportionately borne by women."[41]

Market Liberalization

Liberalization refers to the opening up of markets—the breaking down of barriers to allow more and freer trade around the globe. One strategy for achieving this goal, of course, is literally to open up borders, making it easier for people, goods, and services to move from country to country and from region to region. Now, for example, residents of Central European countries (newly) affiliated with the European Union do not need a visa to enter other European Union countries, a change that has greatly facilitated the trafficking of women from transitional source and bidirectional countries to destination countries in Western Europe.[42] Movement goes back and forth between poor and affluent countries, with the poor likely to migrate for work (including sex work) and the affluent likely to travel for recreation (including sex tourism).

But it is not just people, or even other commodities, that move with greater ease and speed across the globe today. Money is transferred across international borders and financial markets on a daily basis, and the amount vastly exceeds the value of internationally traded goods and services.[43] Advanced communication technologies have increased not only the volume, but also the complexity of global financial transactions. Both their volume and their complexity make illegal transactions, including the transfer and laundering of illegal money, more difficult to detect or track.[44]

Finally, the barely regulated Internet has further opened the door to sex trafficking and sex tourism. Marketed to the masses or to targeted groups are a multitude of sex goods and services, including individual prostitutes and mail-order brides, video sex shows, and all-inclusive sex tours. Moreover, the ease of purchase by credit, most commonly by Visa or MasterCard, allows the consumer to shop and buy without cash.[45]

Spread of Production Through Foreign Investment

The third globalization end—the expansion of foreign investment and the spread of production—also affects sex trafficking. First, production is often spread around the world by exploiting vulnerable and cheap labor supplies. As Min Choi puts it, "Global capital roams around the world looking for cheaper and more obedient labour, exploiting local women or those who have migrated to rich countries to escape poverty." Among such women, according to Choi, "the exploitation of sex workers has reached disproportionate levels."[46]

A second problem for women is that foreign investments to help stimulate production in developing and transitional countries have often been based on gender-biased beliefs and values. Here again, agriculture is a good example. Loans and other resources for agricultural development have typically been given to male farmers, perhaps reflecting a Western lack of understanding of the very important role of women in agriculture, particularly in developing countries.[47] All too often women have been denied access to technological resources that might allow them to do well in commercial farming, and thus have been relegated to the more tedious, labor-intensive, subsistence farming that does nothing to move them out of poverty.[48] This scenario repeats itself in the industrial sector, in which foreign capital in the form of overseas factories has provided local male populations with better jobs, ironically within a numerically female-dominated industrial labor force. An estimated 80% of workers in world-market factories are women.[49]

In a careful analysis of the evidence on globalization, liberalization, and foreign capital, Nobel laureate and economist Joseph Stiglitz concludes that "opening markets to short-term, speculative capital flows increases economic instability and that economic instability contributes to insecurity and poverty."[50] He offers the example of China and its relative success in recent years in achieving economic growth and reducing poverty. But China, he points out, has *not* "fully liberalized." Moreover, China's development strategies have explicitly included policies that promoted equity. Liberalization, according to Stiglitz, increases globalization, but does not necessarily lead to economic growth. What slight growth may occur often goes hand in hand with an increase in poverty. In fact, globalization often leaves "disadvantaged groups" behind; and as it has operated thus far, the benefits of globalization, in Stiglitz's view, have "disproportionately gone to rich people."[51]

Development Policies: Loans, Debts, and Austerity and Structural Adjustment Programs

As developing nations struggled to stabilize their economies following declarations of independence in the 1960s and 1970s, transnational lending institutions, such as the World Bank and the International Monetary Fund (IMF), stepped in to offer them sizable loans, along with economic "advice." Many developing countries took the money, soon acquiring debts that they were unable to repay.[52] The same scenario repeated itself in the 1990s in the transitional countries, particularly the NIS.[53] Theoretically in order to help them pay down their debts and strengthen their economies, global organizations outlined economic policy plans for indebted countries. Most notably, these plans called for the affected countries to

- build up their tourism industry where possible

- accommodate wealthy foreign corporations (and foreign or global capital generally) interested in setting up operations in their countries
- cut back services to their people

Each of these policy dictates feeds into the trafficking and sexual exploitation of women and girls. The buildup of tourism typically includes the buildup of a local sex industry, along with a supply of women for that industry. In fact, the market for sex tourism has expanded numerically and geographically.

Also moving forward is the encouragement of foreign corporations' relocation in developing and transitional countries. One such strategy, introduced by the IMF, is the establishment of "structural adjustment" policies, especially in heavily indebted countries. Structural adjustments include the setting up of export processing zones (EPZs), where multinational companies can locate profitable businesses, using the cheap local labor supply, virtually unimpeded by regulations that would protect workers and ensure decent working conditions. The industrial and high-tech labor supply has been drawn heavily from local populations of women, based in part on the belief that women can be paid less and will be less likely than men to complain about poor working conditions.[54] Moreover, EPZs are sex industry–friendly, providing both unregulated spaces for female and child labor and a potential customer pool of foreign or local working men.

Another globalization project is the implementation in indebted countries of "austerity" programs (i.e., government cutbacks and revenue-saving programs), which often reduce or terminate services to already economically strained local populations. Austerity programs have resulted in a loss of social services that women have relied on to help them care for their families, making their "double shift" of paid labor and family caretaking doubly difficult. With their resources thus reduced even further, women in indebted countries have become highly motivated to look for better-paying jobs, often requiring travel away from their homes.

Global and Local Conditions and Sex Trafficking Flows: Concluding Comment

Globalization ends and policies have affected the economies of developing and transitional countries, already struggling to stabilize as they move out from under colonial rule and begin to industrialize or make the transition from socialism to a market system. The mix of global policies and local economic conditions in particular countries or regions can help explain sex trafficking flows—why countries and regions with particular economic characteristics get involved in sex trafficking in particular ways.

The final sections of this chapter provide a more in-depth look at the economic status of source, hub, bidirectional, and destination countries in various regions. Statistical data are examined for their support of claims regarding relationships between local economic conditions (both within and across trafficking roles) and trafficking flows.

Relationships Between Trafficking Roles and Countries' Economic and Gender Status

Measures of Economic and Gender Status

As used in the analysis to follow, the term "economic status" incorporates measures of countries' human development, per capita GDP, internal economic inequality, and poverty. The measures and the data presented here are drawn largely from the United Nations *Human Development Report*. Published annually by the United Nations Development Programme, the *Report* provides statistical information on the human development status of countries (n = 175 in the 2003 edition) around the world. Its base measure is the Human Development Index (HDI), calculated using four variables: life expectancy at birth, adult literacy, school enrollment of children, and GDP per capita. (Per capita GDP is based on U.S. dollars and converted for purchasing power parity (PPP)—that is, matched with what those dollars will buy in a given country.)[55] Each country is assigned an HDI value, as well as an HD rank and level (high = ranks 1–55; medium = ranks 56–141; low = ranks 142–175).

Internal inequality is measured by the amount of income of—or, in some countries, consumption by—the richest 20% of the population. Poverty is represented by the Human Poverty Index (HPI-1), a measure of the percentage of people in a country who are poor, calculated from the percentages of people surviving to age 40, literate adults, people using improved water sources, and children who are underweight. The HPI-1 is calculated for developing countries only; for industrialized countries, "probability at birth of not surviving to age 60" is used as a proxy for poverty.

The *Report* also contains data on the economic activity rate, which represents the percentage of a country's population (age 15 and over) that is active in the labor market at a given time. The female economic activity rate as a percentage of the male rate, used in the following analysis, provides a measure of how many women are in the labor market (female employment) compared to the number of men. If this statistic were, for example, 80%, that would mean that for every 100 men in the labor market, there are 80 women. The second gender status indicator is women's political representation in a particular country, which is measured by the percentage of parliament seats that are held by women.

Human Development Level and Primary Trafficking Roles

Of the 99 countries involved in sex trafficking, 21 are Western destination sites. These countries are among the most highly developed, with a median HD rank of 12. The median HD rank of non-Western destination countries is 45 (see Table 2), considerably lower than that of the Western destination sites, yet higher than that of source, hub, or bidirectional countries.

In Table 2, the 78 non-Western trafficking countries are shown by their primary trafficking role (along with the median HD rank of each trafficking role type) and their HD level. As indicated, source countries fare most poorly in terms of human development (their median HD rank is 107). Only 3 (8%) of the 37 source countries (all from the CEE/NIS region) have a high HD level. At the other extreme are the (non-Western) destination countries, 10 (63%) of which have a high HD level, with the remainder at the medium level. Bidirectional countries are more evenly divided between the high and medium HD levels, with only one country—Côte d'Ivoire—at the low level. Hubs constitute the smallest sex trafficking category. Hubs' HD status is similar to that of source countries, and their median HD rank is only slightly better than that of source countries.

While these HD ranks are clearly consistent with the arguments presented earlier about the relationship between levels of development and trafficking roles, there are also regional variations in human development and other economic and equality indicators that cut across trafficking roles.

Table 2

International Sex Trafficking Countries (n = 78) by Primary Trafficking Role, Median Human Development Rank of the Role Type, and Human Development Level (Excluding Developed Western Countries)

HD Level	Source (n = 37)	Hub (n = 9)	Bidirectional (n = 16)	Destination(n = 16)
Median HD rank*	107	96	54	45
High	**CEE/NIS** Belarus Croatia Slovakia	**Latin America** Mexico	**Asia** Korea **CEE/NIS** Czech Republic Estonia Hungary Latvia Lithuania Poland Slovenia	**Asia** Hong Kong Japan Singapore **CEE/NIS** Cyprus **Latin America** Costa Rica **Middle East** Bahrain Israel Kuwait United Arab Emirates Qatar
Medium	**Africa** Algeria Ghana Togo **Asia** Bangladesh Indonesia Laos Myanmar Vietnam	**Asia** India Philippines Thailand **CEE/NIS** Albania Turkey **Latin America** Guatemala	**Asia** Cambodia China Malaysia Sri Lanka **CEE/NIS** Bosnia–Herzegovina **Latin America** El Salvador	**Africa** Morocco South Africa **Latin America** Belize Jamaica **Middle East** Saudi Arabia Syria

	CEE/NIS Armenia Azerbaijan Bulgaria Georgia Kazakhstan Kyrgyzstan Moldova Romania Russia Serbia-Montenegro Tajikistan Turkmenistan Ukraine Uzbekistan **Latin America** Brazil Colombia Dominican Republic Honduras Nicaragua		**Middle East** Jordan
Low	**Africa** Benin Ethiopia Kenya Senegal **Asia** Nepal **Latin America** Haiti **Middle East** Afghanistan	**Africa** Nigeria **Asia** Pakistan	**Africa** Côte d'Ivoire

*From highest = 1 to lowest = 175, as ranked in United Nations (2003), *Human Development Report.*

Regional Variations in Economic and Gender Status and Trafficking Roles

Regional and Modified Regional Categories

Table 3 presents trafficking role and economic data on nine regional or modified regional sex trafficking areas, along with two exclusions. The first modification treats as a single category the economically similar, Westernized, Organization for Economic Cooperation and Development (OECD) countries. Seventeen of these countries are in the same region (i.e., Western Europe), but the category also includes the United States, Canada, Australia, and New Zealand. Two other modifications involve categorical separations within a region. In East and Southeast Asia, there are notable differences between sex trafficking countries with a high HD level and those with a medium HD level, so separate statistics are presented for these two blocs. Similarly, differences between the NIS and the other CEE trafficking countries led to the decision to treat these two parts of the region separately. Finally, because they differ considerably from other trafficking countries in their regions, Israel and South Africa are independently considered. In the discussion below, individual countries in these regional groupings, along with their HD ranks, are listed.

Westernized OECD Countries ($n = 21$):

Norway (1), Iceland (2), Sweden (3), Australia (4), the Netherlands (5), Belgium (6), United States (7), Canada (8), Switzerland (10), Denmark (11), Ireland (12), United Kingdom (13), Finland (14), Austria (16), France (17), Germany (18), Spain (19), New Zealand (20), Italy (21), Portugal (23), Greece (24)

As shown in Table 3, the Westernized OECD countries have much in common: not only are they all sex trafficking destination countries, but they have the highest mean HD rank, the highest per capita GDP, the lowest poverty rate, and the highest rate of female political representation of all sex trafficking regions. However, they are not much better off than other regions in regard to internal income inequality, and their female work rate is about in the middle of the overall across-regions range. Interestingly, the United States, which has the highest per capita GDP ($34,320) of the grouping, also has the highest poverty rate (12.6%) and the highest level of internal income inequality, with the richest 20% getting 46.4% of the income.[56] The highest HD ranks, the least income inequality, and the

Table 3

Regional Trafficking Roles and Economic and Gender Status Means, Listed in Order of Mean Regional Human Development Rank

Region (number of countries)	Trafficking role of countries in region	HD rank	Per capita GDP, PPP$ 2001	Female economic activity rate (% of male rate)	% parliament seats held by women	Income inequality (richest 20%)	Poverty (% poor)*
OECD [Westernized bloc] (*n* = 21)	All ***destination***	12.1	25,574	73.0	25.5	40.5	9.4
East/Southeast Asia [high HD bloc] (*n* = 4)	All but 1 ***destination***	23.3	21,937	66.5	9.2	43.2	. . .
Central/Eastern Europe (*n* = 13)	Mainly ***bidirectional*** & ***source***	52.6	10,291	75.5	13.7	38.8	15.3
Middle East [excludes Israel] (*n* = 8)	All but 1 ***destination***, no source	64.0	11,321	38.4	3.3	. . .	. . .
Russia and NIS (*n* = 15)	Mainly ***source***, some bidirectional	79.4	4,872	81.7	11.6	42.3	21.9
Latin America (*n* = 12)	***Mixed***, with all role types	87.1	5,480	53.7	13.9	57.5	**15.9**
East/Southeast Asia [medium HD bloc] (*n* = 9)	***Mixed***, but no destination	104.2	3,667	78.8	16.3	48.0	**23.6**
South Asia (*n* = 5)	***Mixed***, but no destination	130.4	2,166	58.0	8.8	43.5	**35.2**
Africa [excludes South Africa] (*n* = 10)	Mainly ***source***, with all role types	144.6	2,020	67.3	8.0	49.5	**38.6**
OVERALL MEANS		77.2	10,083	65.6	13.2	45.5	. . .
Israel	***Destination***	22.0	19,790	67.0	15.0	44.3	. . .
South Africa	***Destination***	111.0	11,290	59.0	30.0	66.5	**31.7**

Source: United Nations (2003), *Human Development Report*.

*HPI-1, a measure of the percentage of the population that is poor (calculated from percentages surviving to age 40, literate adults, people using improved water sources, & children underweight), is calculated for developing countries only. An alternative measure, percentage with probability at birth of not surviving to age 60, is used as a proxy for poverty for developed countries. Numbers in **bold** designate regions where the most common poverty measure (by country) is HPI-1.

lowest poverty rates are found in the Scandinavian destination countries of Norway, Iceland, and Sweden.

East/Southeast Asia [high HD bloc] (*n* = 4):

Japan (9), Hong Kong (26), Singapore (28), Korea (30)

Second highest in HD rank and per capita GDP is the high HD level bloc of East/Southeast Asia, which includes Japan, Hong Kong, Singapore, and Korea. All but Korea (a bidirectional) are destination countries. As shown in Table 3, women's economic activity and political representation, as well as internal economic inequality, are about average (close to the overall means). Among the four countries, Japan stands at the top, with the highest HD rank (9) and per capita GDP, and the least inequality. The lowest HD rank and per capita GDP are found in Korea, the only country in this grouping that is not primarily a destination site.

Central/Eastern Europe (*n* = 13):

Cyprus (25), Slovenia (29), Czech Republic (32), Poland (35), Hungary (38), Slovakia (39), Croatia (47), Bulgaria (57), Bosnia–Herzegovina (66), Romania (72), Albania (95), Turkey (96), Serbia-Montenegro (n.a.)

Five of the CEE trafficking countries are bidirectionals, five are sources, two are hubs, and only one is a destination country. This region has the third highest mean HD rank, at 23.3 (excluding unranked Serbia-Montenegro), and the fourth highest per capita GDP (slightly behind the Middle East). But, as Table 3 shows, per capita GDP is less than half that in the high HD East/Southeast Asia regional bloc. While their political representation is at the norm (close to the overall mean), women's economic activity rate in the CEE region is higher than that in either the OECD or the high HD East/Southeast Asia groupings. Moreover, internal inequality is much less than in either of the latter two regional groupings. Of the countries within the region, Cyprus has the highest HD rank (25); and the two hubs—Albania and Turkey—have the lowest, at 95 and 96, respectively.

Middle East (*n* = 8) [excludes Israel]:

Bahrain (37), Qatar (44), Kuwait (46), U.A.E. (48), Saudi Arabia (73), Jordan (90), Syria (110), Afghanistan (n.a.).

Here we have the third primarily destination region: all but two of the eight Middle Eastern sex trafficking countries are destination sites (Jordan is a bidirectional country, and Afghanistan is a source country). Four of the eight Middle Eastern countries (typically referred to as Persian Gulf countries) are in the high HD category and are notably set off from the other four (following the U.A.E, with a rank of 48, is Saudi Arabia, with a rank of 73). As indicated in Table 3, while overall the Middle East region lags behind the CEE region in human development, its average per capita GDP is slightly higher.

The most notable feature of the Middle Eastern sex trafficking countries, however, is women's exceptionally low economic activity rate and parliamentary representation. Only 3.3% of parliament seats are held by women, and, at 38.4%, the female economic activity rate is far below the next lowest—Latin America's 53.7% rate. Data on poverty are unavailable for all but three of the previously listed Middle Eastern countries. Saudi Arabia and Syria have poverty rates of 16.3% and 18.8%, respectively, whereas Jordan has a relatively low poverty rate of 7.5%. In Jordan, the only one of these countries for which there are inequality data, the richest get 44.4% of the income, on a par with the overall mean.

Israel, a destination country, is much better off than other sex trafficking countries in the Middle East, and thus is described separately in Table 3. It has a very high HD rank (22), the highest per capita GDP in the region, and far better female workforce and political representation than elsewhere in the Middle Eastern region.

Russia and the Other NIS (n = 15):

Estonia (41), Lithuania (45), Latvia (50), Belarus (53), Russia (63), Ukraine (75), Kazakhstan (76), Turkmenistan (87), Georgia (88), Azerbaijan (89), Armenia (100), Uzbekistan (101), Kyrgyzstan (102), Moldova (108), Tajikistan (113)

The great majority (n = 12) of NIS countries are source sites. The other three—all Baltic states—are bidirectionals. There are no destination or hub countries in this region. The Baltic bidirectionals have the highest per capita GDP in the region and represent three of the four countries in this region with a high level of human development (Belarus is the fourth). Overall, the NIS region is closest to the overall across-regions mean in its own mean HD rank (see Table 3). However, its per capita GDP is relatively low and its poverty rate relatively high. On the other hand, the NIS region has the highest female economic activity rate (81.7%) of all regions.

Latin America (n = 12):

Costa Rica (42), Mexico (55), Colombia (64), Brazil (65), Belize (67), Jamaica (78), Dominican Republic (94), El Salvador (105), Honduras (115), Guatemala (119), Nicaragua (121), Haiti (150)

The Latin American region is quite mixed in regard to trafficking roles. There are six source countries, three destinations, two hubs, and one bidirectional. The three destination countries—Costa Rica, Belize, and Jamaica—are all popular tourist sites and are experiencing growth in sex tourism. Unlike most other destination countries, those in Latin America are not particularly affluent. In fact, Jamaica's per capita GDP is $3,720; and Belize's, at $5,690, is not much above that.

The Latin American region has an average HD level in the medium category and slightly below the overall, across-regions mean. The range of HD ranks among the trafficking countries in the region is considerable, from a high of 42 in Costa Rica to a low of 150 in Haiti. But, as illustrated in Table 3, the Latin American region stands out most notably in two ways—it has the highest level of internal inequality of any region (over 57% of the income goes to the richest 20%) and the second lowest female economic activity rate.

East/Southeast Asia [medium HD bloc] (*n* = 9):

Malaysia (58), Thailand (74), Philippines (85), China (104), Vietnam (109), Indonesia (112), Cambodia (130), Myanmar (131), Laos (135)

Other than destination sites (of which there are none), the medium HD bloc of East/Southeast Asia is mixed in regard to trafficking roles. Four of the countries are sources, three are bidirectionals, and two—Thailand and the Philippines—are hubs. All of the countries have a medium HD level; but, as shown in Table 3, mean per capita GDP is very low at $3,667. Three countries—Cambodia, Myanmar, and Laos—have per capita GDPs below $2,000. However, gender status measures indicate relatively heavy participation by women: the female economic activity rate is the third highest across regions, and female political representation is second only to that of the Westernized OECD countries.

South Asia (*n* = 5):

Sri Lanka (99), India (127), Bangladesh (139), Nepal (143), Pakistan (144)

Among the five South Asian sex trafficking countries, there are two sources, two hubs, and one bidirectional (Sri Lanka, which also has the highest HD rank in the region). The average HD rank and the per capita GDP are even lower in South Asia than in the East/Southeast Asia medium HD bloc (see Table 3). Three South Asian countries are in the medium HD category, and two are in the low category. Per capita GDP is only slightly over $2,000; and at 35.2%, the poverty rate is the second highest of all regions. In the countries with the three lowest HD ranks—Pakistan, Nepal, and

Bangladesh—poverty rates are over 40%. Women's economic participation and political representation in the region are relatively low.

Africa (n = 10) [excludes South Africa]:

> Algeria (107), Morocco (126), Ghana (129), Togo (141), Kenya (146), Nigeria (152), Senegal (156), Benin (159), Côte d'Ivoire (161), Ethiopia (169).

Six of the ten sex trafficking countries in Africa are source sites, two more are bidirectionals, one (Morocco) is a destination, and one (Nigeria) is a hub. Africa is the worst off of all the regions. As indicated in Table 3, the African region is the only one whose mean HD rank places it in the low HD category. Moreover, the per capita GDP is barely over $2,000, and the mean poverty rate, again the highest of all regions, is close to 40%. In fact, in the African countries with the five lowest HD ranks, the poverty rate is over 40%. Four countries have per capita GDPs below $1,000. In the poorest country, Ethiopia, per capita GDP is $810, and an appalling 56% of the population is poor.

South Africa, a destination country, shows a somewhat different profile from the other African sex trafficking countries, and so is described separately in Table 3. South Africa's per capita GDP is relatively high at $11,290 (the next highest in the region is that of Algeria, at $6,090). However, inequality is considerably greater in South Africa than elsewhere in the region; in fact, it is higher than in any other region, with over 66% of the income going to the richest 20%. Moreover, women's economic activity rate is a good deal lower in South Africa than in other trafficking countries in Africa.

Conclusions from Trafficking Role and Regional Analyses

It seems quite clear from the data presented above that sex trafficking flows are driven in large part by countries' human development, economic, and gender status, which in turn have been driven in part by global conditions and globalization policies, and in part by local histories. Although local conditions and the global spurs behind them vary by region, they make sense in regard to the particular sex trafficking roles that regions, and countries within those regions, play.

Most of the destination countries are one of three types:

1. very affluent Westernized nations, with relatively high rates of female employment and female political representation, but with levels of internal inequality similar to those in other regions;
2. very affluent East and Southeast Asian countries, where women's employment and political representation are on the moderate to low side; and
3. affluent Middle Eastern countries with very poor female employment and political representation.

Source countries typically are one of two types:

1. poor, developing countries with notable gender inequality, or
2. economically depressed, transitional countries, but with a history of high female employment.

While women trafficked from transitional countries are more likely than those trafficked from developing countries to have higher-level work skills and employment backgrounds, their status has been weakened by the economic depression being experienced in their countries, making negotiation for their own welfare not much easier than it is for women in developing countries.

Bidirectional countries are less easily classified. Many are in CEE, and most are countries that are relatively well off, where gender conditions are relatively good and internal economic inequality is less than in other regions. Much of the CEE region (including the Baltic states) has been negatively affected economically by the demise of the Soviet Union, but not nearly as severely as most of the actual former (largely source) Soviet republics. Bidirectional countries and their female populace may not, on average, be as desperate for income and employment as source countries and the women in them. However, they are often geographically (and sometimes politically) well positioned to send their own women, as well as women from neighboring source countries, on to nearby destination sites. At the same time, the bidirectional countries (with a collective level of human development higher than that of either source or hub countries) are also likely to have a pool of local, relatively affluent customers for their own local sex industry.

Outside of the CEE region, other, less affluent countries are well positioned for, or have special circumstances that lend themselves to, the bidirectional role. Côte d'Ivoire, for example, has one of the higher poverty rates of the African sex trafficking countries and does traffic women out of the country, mainly to Western Europe or the Middle East. But with a big urban center (Abidjan), Côte d'Ivoire is also a West African destination for trafficked women and children. In Sri Lanka, a relatively poor developing country that traffics some women out, there are thriving sex tourism and child pornography industries, drawing pimps and "their women" into the country.[57] And Cambodia, whose sex industry burgeoned with the stationing of peacekeeping troops there in the early 1990s, still receives women, but poor Cambodian women are also vulnerable to recruiters promising them good jobs out of the country.[58]

Like the bidirectionals, the hub countries also emerge at least in part due to positioning or special circumstances, but on average, the hubs are poorer and have less gender equality than the bidirectionals. Some hubs, such as Albania, Turkey, and Pakistan, are poor and well positioned geographically (close to both source and destination countries) for sex trafficking and have well-organized criminal networks. Albania has capitalized on the criminal trafficking of a variety of products, and its criminal trafficking networks have expanded greatly in recent years. Turkey has become an important country for the smuggling of humans in general, providing migrants from a variety of countries (e.g., Afghanistan, Iran, China), as well as its own citizens, with illegal entry into Western European countries.[59] Turkey's location close to Western European countries and its membership in the European Union are both facilitative of trafficking. Pakistan and India are well located for trafficking women and girls from poor South Asian countries into Persian Gulf destination countries as well as into its own sex industry. And Nigeria, the most populous country in Africa, is located in the generally poor West African area of the continent, where internal labor smuggling and trafficking is rampant. Criminal networks in Nigeria have evolved into highly sophisticated units that participate in the global trafficking not only of women and children, but also of other products, as well as in a variety of international theft scams.[60]

Other hubs (such as Thailand and the Philippines) have highly developed sex industries and related services that have grown out of historic demand for prostitution by military personnel and that can be used by foreigners for their trafficking transactions. In recent years, these countries, along with India, have expanded their sex industries by increasing their value as sex tourism destinations.

Mexico is a hub country that is, of course, heavily involved in human as well as drug smuggling, and its established routes and criminal networks are increasingly used for sex trafficking. Finally, the sex industry in Guatemala—and in particular, Guatemala City—has shown enormous growth in recent years, so that some now refer to Guatemala as "the new Thailand."[61]

Across regions and trafficking role types, women are disadvantaged. This absolute reality is central to any full examination of the "whys" of the sex trafficking supply. As noted above, gender inequalities vary in level and type across and within regions and by trafficking role type, but they are substantial everywhere. The 20% of parliament seats held, on average, by women in destination countries seems quite robust in comparison with the 12%, on average, in source, bidirectional, and hub countries. But women account for over half the population worldwide, so why should their political representation be so meager? Moreover, although again there is some variation, women's rate of participation in the workforce is, on average, two-thirds that of men. Much of women's labor, of course, goes uncounted and is unpaid. Even with missing data from countries known to have some of the worst conditions for women, women around the world are earning, on average, not much more than half of what men earn. In fact, according to available *Human Development Report* data, the mean ratio of female to male income is not much above 50 in bidirectional (57.9), destination (56.4), and source (52.5) countries. In hub countries, the mean female to male income ratio is only 45.6. Why is it that, across regions and role types, women are earning so much less than men?

Chapter 6 moves to this and related questions with an examination of patriarchal customs and beliefs across cultures that feed into and justify the sexual exploitation of women. The chapter begins with a look at the cross-cultural normalization of militarized rape and sexual enslavement in war, and the way in which such wartime violence against women fosters sex trafficking and the sex trade. This is followed by an examination of patriarchal belief systems' characterizations of women and their "place" in men's lives, both of which seem to prescribe and legitimate male entitlement to control and sexually use women.

Notes

1. The Protection Project (2002), *Human Rights Report on Trafficking in Persons, Especially Women and Children: A Country-by-Country Report on a Contemporary Form of Slavery*, 2nd ed., "Maps" (The Paul H. Nitze School of Advanced International Studies, Johns Hopkins University).
2. My decision to classify sex trafficking countries as source, destination, bidirectional, and hub countries is adapted from Kathleen Barry (1995), *The Prostitution of Sexuality* (New York: New York University Press). Barry classified sex trafficking countries as source, destination, and sex-industrialized (similar to my category of hubs). Barry also examined the level of human development (high, medium, low) of countries with various trafficking roles.

3. My primary source for identifying and classifying sex trafficking countries was, as stated, The Protection Project (2002), *Human Rights Report on Trafficking in Persons, Especially Women and Children: A Country-by-country Report on a Contemporary Form of Slavery*, 2nd ed. (The Paul H. Nitze School of Advanced International Studies, Johns Hopkins University). This report describes each country by its sex trafficking role(s) and summarizes the research on sex trafficking in each country. Other sources referred to for corroboration or additional information were U.S. State Department (2002), "Country Narratives," Trafficking in Persons Report (Washington D.C.: Office to Monitor and Combat Trafficking in Persons), available at http://www.state.gov/g/tip/rls/tiprpt/2002/10679.htm, as well as numerous articles (referenced throughout the book) on sex trafficking in particular countries or regions. Again, however, inclusion and classifications remain problematic. Particularly difficult was the distinction between bidirectionals and hubs. Often hubs began as bidirectionals, not qualifying for my hub category unless/until (1) there was evidence supporting the assertion that they were centers for the sexual exchange of women, and (2) they had become firmly sex-industrialized and were discussed as such in the literature.
4. The decision to include (or not) countries in Africa as sex trafficking countries (and of what type) was particularly difficult. Many, if not most, African countries engage in a good deal of back-and-forth, internal human trafficking, much of it for labor, especially child labor. [See, for example, Matthias Muindi (2001), "The Bitter Taste of Chocolate: Child Labour in Côte d'Ivoire and Ghana," *AFRICANEWS*, (July), available at http://www.globalmarch.org/child-trafficking/news-articles/thebittertasteofchocolate.htm; U.S. Department of State (2001), *Country Reports on Human Rights Practices* (Africa) (Bureau of Democracy, Human Rights, and Labor), available at http://www.state.gov/g/drl/rls/hrrpt/2000/af/773.htm.] Sexual exploitation can and does occur in the course of human trafficking, but the former may not be acknowledged. Moreover, trafficking in a variety of goods and services in Africa is increasingly common, with the choice of particular goods and services changing in accordance with opportunity or other circumstances at a given time. In the end, I chose to include those countries that were most frequently covered in the literature on sex trafficking, and for which there seemed to be reliable evidence of such trafficking.
5. Taken together, this bloc of Western countries, along with Australia and New Zealand, allows for a comparison of countries that are similar in their sex trafficking roles, in their (very or relatively affluent) economic status and high level of human development, in their

market economies, and in many ways, in their Westernized cultural beliefs and values, with other, varied regions (or "regional blocs").

6. Human Rights Watch (2000), "Owed Justice: Thai Women Trafficked into Debt Bondage in Japan" (September), available at http://www.hrw.org/reports/200/japan4-profiles.htm (p. 1 of 11).
7. Ibid., pp. 3–5.
8. See, for example, United Nations (1999), *1999 World Survey on the Role of Women in Development: Globalization, Gender and Work*, Report of the Secretary-General A/54/227 (110 pp.), available at www.un.org/womenwatch/daw/followup/a54227.pdf; Rosalind Marsh (1996), "Introduction: Women's Studies and Women's Issues in Russia, Ukraine and the Post-Soviet States," pp. 1–28 in *Women in Russia and Ukraine*, ed. by R. Marsh (Cambridge/New York: Cambridge University Press); Human Rights Watch (1995), "Russia: Neither Jobs nor Justice: State Discrimination Against Women in Russia," 7 (March) (30 pp.) (Washington D.C.: Women's Rights Project).
9. Kristin von Kreisler (1997), "E. European Women Battle for a Better Workplace," *The Christian Science Monitor*, August 8, available at http://search.csmonitor.com/durable/1997/08/08/feat/feat.1.html (4 pp.).
10. Ibid., p. 2.
11. United Nations (2000), *The World's Women 2000: Trends and Statistics* (New York: U.N. Department of Economic and Social Affairs); Maciej Grabowski (retrieved November 26, 2003), "Informal Labor Market and Informal Economy During Transition—The Polish Perspective," Gdansk Institute for Market Economics (20 pp.); Amanullah Khan and Asthma Fozi Qureshi (n.d.), "Women in the Informal Labor Market in a Developing Metropolis: Agents for Change," Department of Community Health Sciences, The Aga Khan University, Karachi, Pakistan.
12. Khan and Qureshi (n.d.), op. cit.
13. Arturo Escobar (1995), *Encountering Development: The Making and Unmaking of the Third World* (Princeton, N.J.: Princeton University Press).
14. United Nations (2002), "Women and Gender Inequality," *State of World Population 2002: People, Poverty and Possibilities*, United Nations Population Fund (UNFPA), available at http://www.unfpa.org/swp/2002/english/ch4/page2.htm (5 pp.); United Nations (1995), *Human Development Report* (New York: Oxford University Press).
15. United Nations (1999), op. cit.
16. Ibid.
17. Ibid.
18. Victoria S. Lockwood (2001), "The Impact of Development on Women: The Interplay of Material Conditions and Gender Ideology," pp. 529–543 in *Gender in Cross-Cultural Perspective*, 3rd ed., ed. by Caroline

B. Brettell and Carolyn E. Sargent (Upper Saddle River, N.J.: Prentice Hall); United Nations (1999), op. cit.

19. Ibid.
20. Elisabeth Rosenthal (2001), "Harsh Chinese Reality Feeds a Black Market in Women," *The New York Times*, June 15.
21. United Nations (1999), op. cit.
22. Kreisler (1997), op. cit, p. 1.
23. Ibid., p. 2.
24. Ibid.
25. United Nations (1995), op. cit.
26. Allison Loconto (2001), "The Trafficking of Nigerian Women into Italy," *TED Case Studies* 656 (January), available at http://www.american.edu/TED/italian-trafficking.htm (p. 3 of 16). See also Isabella Gyau Orhin (2002), "Sex Trafficking Rife—Police," *AllAfrica Global Media*, November 5, available at http://allafrica.com/storiesprintable/200111060034.html (3 pp.).
27. Refer especially to Chapter 1.
28. United Nations (2003), *Human Development Report* (New York: Oxford University Press).
29. Veronica Dujon (2000), "Women and Global Capitalism," *Against the Current* XV (March–April), p. 1.
30. Lockwood (2001), op. cit.; Aida F. Santos (1999), "Globalization, Human Rights and Sexual Exploitation," in *Making the Harm Visible: Global Sexual Exploitation of Women and Girls*, ed. by Donna M. Hughes and Claire Roche (North Amherst, MA: Coalition Against Trafficking in Women), available at http://www.uri/edu/artsci/wms/hughes/mhvglo.htm (8 pp.).
31. Suzanne LaFont (1999), "Male Economies and the Status of Women in the Post-Communist Countries," available at http://geocities.com/suzannelafont/eewomen.htm (p. 1).
32. United Nations (1999), op. cit., p. xv.
33. See, for example, Joseph E. Stiglitz (2002), *Globalization and Its Discontents* (New York: W.W. Norton); Pax Christi USA (2001), "Toward a Globalization of Solidarity," PCUSA National Council, November 10, available at http://www.paxchristiusa.org/globalization.html.
34. In addition to an expansion of personal child care and housework and (for men) landscape and yard maintenance, newer services (often provided by minorities) in the United States, for example, include staffing of assisted living and other senior care facilities and special occasion labor (e.g., putting up outdoor Christmas lights and similar displays).
35. Melanie Orhant (2000), "Saudi Arabia: Asian Migrant Workers Face Rights Abuses in Saudi Arabia: Amnesty," *Stop-traffic*, July 3, available

at http://www.friends-partners.org/partners/stop-traffic/1999/0871.html; Melanie Orhant (2000), "India-Kuwait: India Bans Domestic Workers Going to Kuwait Due to Abuses," *Stop-traffic,* March 7, available at http://www.friends-partners/org/partners/stop-traffic/1999/0707.html; United Nations (1999), op. cit.

36. To begin with, persons concerned about global elitist power typically are referring to economic rather than cultural globalization, and point out that globalization "understood as increasing internationalization of ideas, science, communication and technology, must be distinguished from economic globalization, which *transforms trade and finance in favour of powerful global actors* [italics mine]" [World Council of Churches (2003), "Economic Globalization," available at http://www.wcc-coe.org/wcc/what/jpc/globalization.html]. As used, the term "global power elite" typically refers to elites heading or influencing global institutions such as the World Bank, the World Trade Organization, and the International Monetary Fund, along with the argument that ideology and practice in these institutions favors wealthy (and Western) nations over developing nations. Referring to the "inequities in the global trading system" promoted by such global institutions, economist Joseph Stiglitz suggests that "few—apart from those with vested interests . . . defend the hypocrisy of pretending to help developing countries by forcing them to open up their markets to the goods of the advanced industrial countries while keeping their own markets protected, policies that make the rich richer and the poor more impoverished—and increasingly angry" [Stiglitz (2002), op. cit., excerpt available at http://www.wwnorton.com/catalog/spring03/032439 excerpt.htm (p. 6 of 7)]. Others go beyond the leading global financial institutions to examine "elitist" global policies imposed by affluent nations that reflect their vested interests. Nobel Peace Prize winner Adolfo Perez Esquivel, for example, criticizes the Free Trade Area of the Americas (FTAA), scheduled to be implemented in 2005, as an "example of the globalised totalitarianism that the US is attempting to impose on the entire world through commercial agreements, militarisation and the so-called 'single thought'" [Adolfo Perez Esquivel, quoted in World Council of Churches (2003), "Nobel Peace Laureate Warns Churches Against Free Trade Area of the Americas," available at http://www2.wcc-coe.org/pressreleasesen.nsf/index/pu-03-19.html (p. 1 of 2)]. The point is often made that because they control economic resources worldwide, global elite institutions often go unchallenged, certainly by developing nations who depend on them for economic survival. It is also argued that global institutions are not structured as, and were never intended to be, democratic bodies. [See,

for example, Dan Plesch (2002), "How to Democratize Global Institutions," *Observer*, November 10, available at http://www.globalpolicy.org/globaliz/politics/1110democracy.htm (3 pp.); Stiglitz (2002), op. cit.; Pax Christi USA (2001), op. cit.]

37. While free market *theory* argues that the market fluctuates/controls itself in accordance with the "law of supply and demand," and thus requires a "hands-off" approach, market policies imposed by global institutions involve numerous interventions—that is, hands are not kept off of the workings of the global market.
38. Santos (1999), op. cit.
39. United Nations (1999), op. cit.
40. Ibid.
41. Ibid. This survey report points out that costs were also disproportionately borne by women under the structural adjustment programs of the 1980s in a number of developing countries.
42. Gerben J. N. Bruinsma and Guus Meershoek (1999), "Organized Crime and Trafficking in Women from Eastern Europe in the Netherlands," pp. 105–117 in *Illegal Immigration and Commercial Sex: The New Slave Trade*, ed. by Phil Williams (London/Portland, OR: Frank Cass).
43. United Nations (1999), op. cit.
44. Donna M. Hughes (2000), "The 'Natasha' Trade: The Transnational Shadow Market of Trafficking in Women," *Journal of International Affairs*, Special Issue: "In the Shadows: Promoting Prosperity or Undermining Stability?" 53 (Spring), pp. 625–651, available at http://www.owl.ru/eng/research/thenatasha.htm.
45. Vanessa von Struensee (2000), "Globalized, Wired, Sex Trafficking in Women and Children," *Murdoch University Electronic Journal of Law* 7, available at http://www.murdoch.edu.au/elaw/issues/v7n2/struensee72_text.html (14 pp.); Aurora Javate de Dios (1999), "Confronting Trafficking, Prostitution and Sexual Exploitation in Asia—The Struggle for Survival and Dignity," in *Making the Harm Visible: Global Sexual Exploitation of Women and Girls*, ed. by Donna M. Hughes and Claire Roche (North Amherst, MA: Coalition Against Trafficking in Women, available at http://www.uri.edu.artsci/wms/hughes/mhvasia.htm; Santos (1999), op. cit.
46. Min Choi (2001), "Globalization and Sex Trade in South-East Asia," available at http://picis.jinbo.net/english/women/sextrade.htm. [Translation of the Korean original in *People's Solidarity Social Progress (PSSP)* monthly magazine, March 2001, and "Feminine Thoughts, Global Resistance," *PICIS*, June 2001.]
47. Marilyn Porter and Ellen Judd (1999), *Feminists Doing Development: A Practical Critique* (London/New York: Zed Books).
48. Lockwood (2001), op. cit.; United Nations (1995), op. cit.

49. Lockwood (2001), op. cit.; Santos (1999), op. cit.
50. Joseph E. Stiglitz (2003), "Poverty, Globalization and Growth: Perspectives on Some of the Statistical Links," p. 80 in United Nations (2003), *Human Development Report* (New York: Oxford University Press).
51. Ibid.
52. Dujon (2000), op. cit.
53. Gillian Caldwell, Steve Galster, Jyothi Kanics, and Nadia Steinzor (1999), "Capitalizing on Transition Economies: The Role of the Russian Mafiya in Trafficking Women for Forced Prostitution," pp. 42–73 in *Illegal Immigration and Commercial Sex: The New Slave Trade*, ed. by Phil Williams (London/Portland, OR: Frank Cass).
54. Dujon (2000), op. cit.; United Nations (1999), op. cit.
55. No data on per capita GDP were available in the *Human Development Report* for five trafficking countries—Afghanistan, Myanmar, Qatar, and Serbia-Montenegro. For these countries, per capita GDP data were taken from The Protection Project's *Human Rights Report*. Some of these data were from years other than 2001. Also, per capita GDP of the United Arab Emirates (given in the *Human Development Report*) was from 1998 rather than 2001.
56. Other than HD rank, economic data on individual countries are not shown in the text, but can be found in the United Nations (2003) *Human Development Report*.
57. Susannah Price (1999), "South Asia: '100 Kids Abused Daily' in Sri Lanka," BBC News, February 9, available at http://news.bbc.co.uk/2hi/world/south_asia/276054.stm.
58. Liz Kelly (2000), "Wars Against Women: Sexual Violence, Sexual Politics and the Militarised State," pp. 45–65 in *States of Conflict: Gender, Violence and Resistance*, ed. by Susie Jacobs, Ruth Jacobson, and Jennifer Marchbank (New York: Zed Books).
59. Molly Moore (2001), "Smuggling of Humans into Europe is Surging," *Washington Post*, May 28. [Cited in The Protection Project (2002), op. cit., p. 556.]
60. "Combatting International Crime in Africa" (1998), U.S. House of Representatives, Subcommittee on Africa, Committee on International Relations (Washington D.C.) [Testimony of subcommittee], available at http://commdocs.house.gov/committees/intlrel/hfa50884_0.htm.
61. Yifat Susskind (2002), "Violence Against Women in Latin America," *Madre*, available at http://www.madre.org/art_violence.html; End Child Prostitution and Trafficking of Children in Central America (2001), "Sexual Exploitation and Trafficking of Children in Central America," 36 (September), available at http://www.ecpat.net/eng/Ecpat_interIRC/articles.asp?articleID=195&NewsID=24.

6

Militarized Rape and Other Patriarchal Hostilities: Fueling and Legitimating Male Demand for a Sex Trade

During the volatile civil conflict that resulted in the partition of India and Pakistan in 1947, women were regularly raped and used as sexual slaves by men of opposing ethnicities or religions. Often, according to one source,

> abduction followed or accompanied rape, untold numbers of women were sold into slavery and prostitution, and in many places their bodies were marked with deliberate, carefully chosen humiliations: tattoos of the symbols of the other religion, slogans of a similar nature, the cutting off of their breasts, parading them naked in the streets.[1]

Two years after the end of this war, an estimated 75% of the abducted girls and young women were still being bought and sold—"from one man to another."[2]

Almost 30 years later, in 1971, violence erupted again in the region during East Pakistan's fight for independence and eventual emergence as the nation of Bangladesh. Over the 11-month course of the war for independence, hundreds of thousands of Bengali women were raped by Pakistani soldiers.[3] Afterward, the women's suffering was recognized by Bengali leader Sheikh Mujibur Rahman, who designated them as *biranganas* (war heroines) and asked their families and neighbors to welcome them back into their homes and communities. But, to many, the raped and prostituted women were tainted and shameful, no longer acceptable as family members, or even as neighbors. As one victim describes it, the women often felt they had no choice but to stay with, and remain as sexual slaves to, their captors:

> We went with them *voluntarily* because when we were being pulled out from the bunkers by the Indian soldiers, some of us half-clad, others half-dead, the hatred and deceit I saw in the eyes of our countrymen standing by, I would not raise my eyes a second time. They were throwing various dirty words at us . . . . [italics mine][4]

And thus we see the familiar, age-old woman problem—the loss of chastity (outside of marriage) degrades a woman (but not a man), making her permanently "damaged goods," unfit for marriage or even acceptance back into her family of origin. The circumstances of her "loss" are irrelevant—whether through rape or consensual sex, she has moved to the "whore" side of the infamous madonna/whore split. To some, this scenario may seem a thing of the past—no longer applicable in today's more gender-liberated world. However, in some time period in virtually *all* cultures, and in some cultures *today*, this scenario is the reality. In many parts of the contemporary world, women who have been victims of rape and other sexual assaults are cast out, and prostitution may be their most viable, or their only, option; so, like the woman above, they "voluntarily" give in. Even in cultures today in which sexually active women are not permanent outcasts, a "bad reputation" can still ruin much in a young woman's life; and overall, prostitutes are still at the bottom of the female social status scale.

But, there's another rub. For many men—in virtually all cultures and time periods—rape and the sexual enslavement of women have been normalized under *some* circumstances, and men have been given (or assume they are entitled to) sexual access to *some* women all of the time. War, for example, is a "circumstance" in which rape and sexual enslavement have been, and continue to be, normalized, and soldiers on rest and recreation (R & R) time are given access to prostitutes whenever they so choose.

This chapter examines the normalization of rape and sexual enslavement in war, along with societal belief systems that legitimate male entitlement to control and sexually use women. It argues that the forces that lead to the organization of the sex trade, and to male demand for it, are rooted in patriarchal constructs about women and men and the relations between them. War rape and wartime prostitution occur within the patriarchal structure of the military, in which women, and the "feminine" more generally, are devalued while the "masculine" is elevated. Moreover, assaults on the enemy's property, including women, are normalized and, in victory, seen as legitimate spoils of war. Wartime normalization of rape and prostitution, along with the militarized view of women as both male property and inferior to men, sets the stage for the commodification of women and the legitimation of the commercial trafficking of women for prostitution.

War Rape, Wartime Prostitution, and Sex Trafficking: Connections

Rape, enslaved prostitution, and other sexual violence against women have been a part of war for all of recorded history—across *all* cultures, and in all kinds of wars, be they religious, colonizing, or revolutionary. And, as one author points out, rape during warfare "is not bound by definitions of which wars are 'just' or 'unjust'."[5] Although rape and other sexual assaults on women still occur with impunity in virtually every armed conflict, they have begun to garner public attention through the reporting of several especially egregious cases, most notably during the brutal "ethnic cleansings" in the civil wars in Bosnia and Rwanda.[6]

At first glance, the rape of women by warring soldiers may seem unconnected to soldiers' use of prostitutes for R & R *away from* combat, and perhaps even further from the problem of global sex trafficking. But they have much more in common than one might think. First, war rape and recreational military prostitution both occur within the context and under the "auspices" of militaristic structures, in which (largely) male combatants fight against designated enemies in an effort to kill and conquer them.[7] Moreover, both rape and use of prostitutes are thought to be inevitable, if not normal, behaviors of warring soldiers. Military leaders recognize that soldiers will rape women during warfare—an expectation succinctly captured by General George Patton during World War II, when he told an aide that in spite of efforts to thwart it, "there would unquestionably be some raping" by American GIs.[8] R & R prostitution is often organized by the military under the assumption that providing soldiers access to prostitutes will reduce wartime raping—when, in reality, the two are complementary.

Women as Objects and Property

Rape and prostitution both hinge—especially during war—on the view of women as objects or commodities belonging to or used by men. The often-stated belief that men fight wars to protect "their" women and children (and other property) assumes that warring factions are attempting to take or defile the others' property, including their women. In fact, civilian rape laws were written, according to one well-accepted feminist perspective, to protect the female property rights of men. Rape, then, violates a man's honor by taking from him his exclusive right to sexual possession of a woman (e.g., wife, daughter, niece) or women.[9]

The raping and looting of the enemy's property during or following a battle affirms not only the construction of women as male property, but also the belief that "access to a woman's body" is "an actual reward of war."[10] Like rape in war, militarized prostitution for R & R rewards soldiers away from the battlefield by giving them sexual access to and use of others' (not their own) women. In her classic analysis of rape and war, Susan Brownmiller highlights the connection between militarized rape and prostitution as the spoils of war:

> Because access to women after a battle has been a traditional reward of war, it is impossible to discuss rape in warfare without touching also on prostitution, since the two have been linked in history. Not that if prostitutes are not readily available men will turn to rape "to satisfy their needs," but that the two acts—raping an unwilling woman and buying the body and services of a more or less cooperating woman—go hand in hand with a soldier's concept of his rights and pleasure.[11]

Another argument is that battlefield rape and militarized prostitution—particularly when done by groups of men on the bodies of objectified others—provide a misogynous (i.e., reflecting hatred of or hostility toward women) form of masculine bonding among soldiers that builds group solidarity in preparation for battle.[12] In civilian life as well, men and boys sometimes "do masculinity" in this perhaps unapproved, but nevertheless understood, manner. As noted, gang rapes are common experiences for women trafficked into prostitution servicing civilian as well as military customers. Also, according to a growing body of research, some number of "normal" young college men appear to engage in masculine bonding through fraternity gang rapes.[13] Perhaps nowhere, however, is masculine socialization more extreme than in the military. Acting out the hyper-hetero-masculinity to which soldiers are socialized can include both raping women while in combat and using the services of a prostitute on breaks from combat.

Making Men out of Boys: Military Socialization

When the U.S.-led invasion of Iraq moved forward in 2003, many young American men were exposed to graphic war violence for the first time. They, like other combat soldiers before them, were expected to respond to war violence in accordance with enduring norms of militarized masculinity. One lesson to this end was reported by U.S. media in November 2003, when "[the] Army dismissed a cowardice charge and filed a lesser count against an Army interrogator who sought counseling after he saw the body of an Iraqi man cut in half by U.S. fire." After he saw the "mangled corpse," the soldier reported, he "began shaking and vomiting and feared for his life." Subsequently, he "had trouble sleeping and started suffering what he thought were panic attacks." The company commander stated that he thought the new charge, dereliction of duty, was more appropriate for the soldier's (alleged) "misconduct."[14] What's this? A visceral reaction to the blowing apart of another human being is characterized as cowardice (or even dereliction of duty, for that matter) *and* is a punishable military crime? Is it a military crime if the mutilated victim is a comrade–soldier, or only if the victim is the enemy? Regardless of the answers to these questions, the story alone is a reminder of the military's expectations of soldiers. Fear, timidity, panic, inability to handle the sight of violence—these are traits stereotypically thought of as feminine, not masculine,[15] and as such they are unacceptable in soldiers.

Some have argued that this military disdain for all that is feminine—and particularly where and when it appears in men—helps create or preserve masculine detachment and aggressiveness and thus the will to kill. The degradation of the feminine prepares soldiers for the dehumanization of the other—the enemy (and his women).[16] While this military socialization may be functional for combat, it is dysfunctional in myriad other ways.

Military socialization to "make a man out of the boy" not only attempts to obliterate all that is feminine, but may also breed misogynous heterosexuality in the soldier. Liz Kelly argues, for example, that the use of pornography is, at least in modern Western-style militaries, "virtually compulsory" for soldiers.[17] Numerous military stories, songs, and other symbols also link male prowess to violence against—and especially to the sexual misuse and abuse of—women.[18] Moreover, male soldiers not exhibiting hyper-hetero-masculinity are hit with derisive female or homosexual labels—pussy, cunt, fag. The interchangeability of gender and sexual orientation descriptors reflects the misogynous/heterosexist belief that to be a gay man is to be like a woman. And gay or "feminine" men often themselves become victims of soldier violence.

Finally, serving in the military is often linked to being a masculine man or to "manhood" in itself. In describing the Serbian–Bosnian conflict, Cynthia Enloe reports that there is evidence that "the warrior is a central element in the twentieth-century cultural construction of the Serbian ideal of masculinity."[19] Convincing men that manhood is best reflected in, or is achieved only through, soldiering helps build armies. According to Enloe, "militarization of ethnic nationalism often depends on persuading individual men that their own manhood will be fully validated only if they perform as soldiers, either in the state's military or in insurgent autonomous or quasi-autonomous forces."[20]

Battlefield Rape and Prostitution: One and the Same

The most straightforward connection between battlefield rape and prostitution, however, is that they are often one and the same. As shown in the example at the beginning of the chapter, the Bengali women caught in the middle of men's armed conflict were sexually assaulted—sometimes once (which we think of as rape), and sometimes again and again as captives (which certainly describes enslaved prostitution). Moreover, many women captured by the enemy during war are used sexually for the R & R of their captors, temporarily away from but close to the actual battlefield.

Militarized Rape, Sexual Enslavement, and Patriarchy

Whether the victim of a single rape, a single incident of gang rape, or prolonged enslaved prostitution, women war victims, as indicated earlier, are often ostracized and cut off from networks where they might be afforded some protection and care. Prior victimization, then, provides a potential pool of women to service soldiers as well as civilians for recreational prostitution. As one author says, "massive rape in war produces sex-industry commodities. These populations of women, who are raped and therefore disgraced to their families and in their communities, are particularly vulnerable to the procurers of the [sex] industry."[21] In some instances, women who have been sexually enslaved in war camps are simply sold to procurers, who then traffic them into the general commercial market. This exchange of women effects a direct connection between war rape and commercial prostitution. Moreover, through this connection, information about trafficking patterns and routes—in fact, the "ins and outs" of the sex trade business—can be communicated to soldiers and their leaders by civilian sex traffickers.

Sexual enslavement in war camps is not unlike the debt-bonded enslavement that women trafficked into commercial prostitution experience. For women who have been sexually victimized in war, similar victimization in a commercial market may feel familiar. Therefore, previously brutalized women may be more easily trafficked into enslaved prostitution. The normalization of sexual enslavement during wartime also legitimates the sex trafficking and enslavement of women in a commercial and civilian market. Research on sexual violence suggests that the normalization of men's sexual abuse of women in war desensitizes them to the sexual abuse of women generally. In the words of one author, "War rape diminishes sensitivity to human suffering and intensifies men's sense of entitlement, superiority, avidity, and social license to rape."[22]

Finally, wartime rape and sexual enslavement, militarized recreational prostitution, and the trafficking of women into debt-bonded prostitution in the commercial market are all rooted in and backed by patriarchal systems that operate across societies. To fully understand the connections among the three, and why they thrive, some understanding of patriarchy is useful.

Patriarchy and Masculine Dominance

Patriarchy can be understood as an organizational form or system, with supporting norms, that (1) is hierarchical and has a small group of high-status men at the top of the power structure; (2) rules over and/or discriminates against all women, but especially low-, minority-, and deviant-status women *and* low- or minority-status men; (3) devalues the feminine and elevates the masculine; and (4) maintains power by violence or the threat of harm.[23] This definition is of patriarchy as an *ideal type*. In the real world, particular societies or institutions within them (e.g., the economic or political system, the family, the military, education, religion) commonly fall somewhere on a continuum between patriarchal and egalitarian. Across cultures, however, the military typically matches the ideal type of patriarchy, as do particular cultural or temporal systems—such as historic feudal societies with their landed estates and lords (patriarchs), and the nineteenth-century slavery systems in the United States and other parts of the Americas.

Another institution that typically fits closely with the patriarchal ideal type *across cultures* is religion, or more specifically, the major world religions—but with a twist. The major world religions almost always espouse some egalitarian norms and beliefs and often speak out against violence (except perhaps as a last resort).[24] But religious words and deeds are not always the same, and a good deal of violence and injustice has been committed in the name of religion. Moreover, the writings in religious texts are often inconsistent, and they are often subject to more than one interpretation. Nevertheless, religious hierarchies are overtly sexist, with all high positions held by men and, most often, forbidden to women. The subjugation of the "lesser" female is often said to be religiously ordained, and religion is used to legitimate men's rule over, and even their violence against, women.

The remainder of this section provides examples of war rape and sexual enslavement. The section following describes some of the patriarchal beliefs found in major world religions that help set up and legitimate men's control of and sexual access to women. Without such patriarchal underpinnings, the normalization of sex trafficking and the success of the sex industry would have been much more difficult to achieve, and the male demand for and sense of entitlement to sexual services from women would be less forthcoming.

Examples of Wartime Rape and Sexual Enslavement

The rape or sexual enslavement of their women in wartime can destabilize an enemy in several ways. It may lead to feelings of humiliation, emasculation, and demoralization among the enemy soldiers, thus weakening their resolve; indeed, rape of the opponent's women is as much a symbol of defeat for one side as of victory for the other. At another level, war rape can be taken as a serious affront to, or even a defilement of, the other's culture or religion. If war rape results in pregnancy, it can be seen as literally impurifying the enemy's race, ethnicity, or religious identity—sometimes serving as one of several strategies in what has come to be known as ethnic cleansing or ethnic genocide.[25]

The importance to men of maintaining ethnic or religious purity is illustrated by the actions of some combatants during the armed conflict over the India–Pakistan partition. Reportedly, the fear that their women would be raped and impregnated by the enemy, resulting in the "pollution and impurity" of their religion, led some men (particularly Sikh village men) to murder their own women. Afterward, these women were described as having been martyred rather than murdered.[26]

Whether myth or reality, the ancient story of the rape of the Sabine women by Roman warriors highlights the theme of women as a commodity for the taking by men through battle. Without women of their own, the Romans are said to have asked the neighboring Sabines for their wives and daughters. When the Sabines refused to hand their women over, the Romans took them by force, raped them, and made them their wives. A series of battles followed, and the more powerful Romans prevailed. The rape of the Sabines is said to have led to the founding of Rome.[27]

While the Sabine women were raped prior to major warfare, they were nevertheless part of the booty or bounty of a dominant warrior class. Throughout history, certain groups of men have been forced—sometimes through warfare and other times because they lacked status or power—to give their women to the dominant class of men. A Roman tradition that survived in Europe even after the Empire's fall was to force the bride of a commoner to have sex with the lord of the estate on her wedding night. In the United States, of course, the institution of slavery included the sexual enslavement of African slave women, who were regularly raped and abused by their white owners. The pattern was the same in Latin America and the Caribbean, where indigenous women were expected to sexually service plantation owners, foremen, and supervisors.[28] Thus conquerors may deal with threats or perceived threats to their dominance (and their putative superior masculinity) by raping or sexually enslaving the subordinates' women. This same masculinized struggle is played out again and again on the battlefield of war.

According to Joshua Goldstein, wartime strategy in ancient Greece and the Middle East was often intended to "literally feminize a conquered population by executing male captives, raping the women, then taking women and children as slaves."[29] In another example, the British army abruptly put an end to an insurrection in the Scottish Highlands in the 1746 Battle of Culloden, during which the Highlands women were assaulted and sexually mutilated. As he led his soldiers forward following the main battle, Lord George Sackville permitted his men to rape the women in the town. Afterward, the women were forced to stand by and watch as the victors killed their husbands, sons, and brothers.[30] And in one of many examples in World War II, as the German army invaded small villages in Poland and Russia, soldiers dragged out Jewish girls and assaulted and raped them, often in front of their parents.[31] Even more recently, the Indonesian military has used rape as a weapon of war in its attempt to put down the resistance of East Timorese revolutionaries. Reports indicate that Indonesian soldiers have raped East Timorese women in front of their families, and in some cases have even forced East Timorese men to rape their own women in front of the troops.[32] In the armed conflict in Mozambique during the 1990s, young women were also raped in front of others to humiliate not only the women, but perhaps more importantly, their men. The testimony of one woman raped in Mozambique attests to this systematic and public violence:

> The soldiers like to punish us. They would select girls aged 12 to 14 and ask them to take off their clothes and then rape them while all of us stood watching. . . . Sometimes we were raped by 10 men. I felt I wanted to die because I felt I wasn't worth anything anymore.[33]

Colonial conquests of indigenous peoples are rife with examples of the raping of the subordinated women. The European conquest of Latin America in the 1500s is one of many takeovers in which "indigenous women have been disproportionately targeted for rape as a weapon of war." At times, young women were "given" by the indigenous peoples to the conquering Spanish and Portuguese armies as "sexual peace offerings," another route through which women were commodified.[34]

Patterned sexual assaults on indigenous women have continued to the present, as in the armed conflict in Chiapas, Mexico. To quell the actions of largely indigenous rebels (known collectively as the Zapatista National Liberation Front, or simply as "Zapatistas"), government-backed forces have often escalated the level of violence in the area. Since 1994, close to 700 assaults on native women in Chiapas have been formally documented; 300 of those were specifically identified as rapes, perpetrated primarily by government forces.[35] In 1997, government-backed paramilitaries massacred 45 people (mostly women and children) at Acteal in Chiapas. Locals have told reporters that prior to the massacre, the word was put out that "first the wives" and then the "daughters of Zapatistas will be raped."[36]

In another example of advance notice, during World War I, an eyewitness to the German siege of Louvain, Belgium (in 1914), told British historian Arnold Toynbee that some "German soldiers came up to me sniggering and said that all the women were going to be raped" and that the soldiers had "explained themselves by gestures."[37]

Whether announced in advance or not, the rape of women by soldiers, paramilitaries, or bandits is so commonplace that, at the least, it seems to reflect a sense of masculine entitlement. This sense of entitlement is reinforced because, in spite of the large number of victims, such rapes rarely get much public attention or result in punishment for the perpetrators. How well known is it that during the civil conflicts in Central America in the 1980s, "tens of thousands of indigenous and other poor, mostly rural women were raped and murdered,"[38] or that during the ongoing conflict in Algeria, women of "entire villages" have been raped and killed?[39] Is it known that at least 5,000 Kuwaiti women were raped by Iraqi soldiers during the invasion of Kuwait by Iraq in 1990,[40] or that, in addition to Kuwaiti women, numerous foreign women working in Kuwait were also raped during that invasion?[41]

At times, soldiers rape not just enemy women, but even the women they are supposedly saving *from* the enemy. When the victorious European allies marched into Germany in May and June of 1945, they raped not only German women, but also Jewish women who had survived the Nazis and were being "liberated."[42] And, during continuing battles following the takeover of Afghanistan by the Taliban, ethnic minority women who were in the midst of the fighting were subject to rape and sexual enslavement by "all parties to the conflict."[43]

In some cases, "rogue soldier groups"[44] abduct women at random for sexual enslavement and even temporary or permanent "marriage." The Algerian government believes, for example, that in recent years some 1,600 young women and girls have been abducted and sexually enslaved by "roving bands from armed Islamic groups."[45] And, in both Sierra Leone and Myanmar, there is evidence that "rebel, paramilitary, and military contingents force women and girls into sexual slavery and, in some cases, marriage."[46] Interviewed in a refugee camp in South Africa, one woman from Sierra Leone told how she had been chosen to be the "wife" of a commander, adding that others, including her own children, were "given as 'wives' to other soldiers."[47]

Victims of war rape or sexual enslavement are often understandably unsure of whom to trust with their stories, and they are fearful that reporting the assaults will bring even greater harm to themselves or their families. In the early 1990s, an estimated 4,000 Somali women in Kenyan refugee camps were raped by roaming bands of Somali men. Because of both fear of reprisals and fear of being ostracized for being rape victims, fewer than 200 women came forward to tell of the assaults. In 1993, the U.N. put out an appeal for $1 million to help protect Somali women from being raped in refugee camps. Regarding the response to this appeal, Christiane Berthiaume, spokesperson for the U.N. Commission for Refugees, reported that "it interests no one."[48]

There are no exact lines between wartime rape that is committed to express or maintain masculine dominance, to humiliate or defile an enemy, to play out a misogynous hostility toward women, or in celebration of or as a reward for victory. In many cases, all the above motives are involved. But as the following well-documented and better-publicized cases of *systematic* rape and massacre demonstrate, war "tends to intensify the brutality, repetitiveness, public spectacle, and likelihood of rape."[49]

The Rape of Nanking Women

In December 1937, the Japanese army invaded the city of Nanking in China, and within the first month of their occupation, they raped and sexually tortured at least 20,000 women, most of whom they killed afterward.[50] Reports indicate that Japanese soldiers systematically singled out women for rape and "sexual torture games."[51] The subsequent testimonies of eyewitnesses were frighteningly similar, describing "abducted women forced to perform sex shows for troops at play; fathers forced at gunpoint to rape their own daughters." When "a group of soldiers was finished with a captured woman, a stick was sometimes pushed up into her vagina; in some cases the woman's head was severed."[52] Such brutality is far from a single, isolated wartime incident.

The Rape of Women at My Lai during the Vietnam War

That American soldiers regularly raped Vietnamese women during the Vietnam War is now fairly commonplace knowledge.[53] In fact, one American squad leader in Vietnam told journalist Seymour Hersh that such rape was "an everyday affair," and that "you can nail just about everybody on that—at least once. The guys are human, man."[54] The rape and massacre at My Lai in Vietnam, however, was over the top. On March 16, 1968, American soldiers entered My Lai and systematically began shooting the town's residents—mainly women, children, and elderly men. During the slaughter, in which up to 567 people were killed,[55] soldiers raped and brutalized the women. Hersh reported on one case in which several soldiers pulled a girl of about 15 from a group and began to tear her clothes off. An older woman in the group rushed to the young girl's defense and fought with the soldiers until one hit her with the butt of his rifle. In spite of the fact that army photographers were there, one soldier took care of the situation by stepping up and fatally shooting both women. A photograph, snapped just before the murders, appeared in *Life* magazine.[56]

Rape, Ethnic Cleansing, and Terror in Rwanda and Bosnia

The civil war in Rwanda that began in 1990 became increasingly brutal in the years to follow. Between April and June of 1994 alone, soldiers and civilians murdered from 500,000 to 1,000,000 people.[57] Sexual violence took place on a "massive scale," with at least 500,000 women suffering "brutal forms of sexual violence."[58] By most accounts, rape and murder were intended by the dominant Hutu extremists not only to invoke terror in the Tutsi enemy, but to conduct ethnic genocide against them.

During the Bosnian war of 1992–1995, amid numerous assaults and murders, an estimated 20,000 women were raped, tortured, and sexually enslaved.[59] The rape of Muslim women by Bosnian Serb soldiers was also purposeful, intended to impregnate them—thus, in a classic case of ethnic/religious cleansing, forcing them to bear "Serbian babies."[60] Although, according to the U.N. Commission to Investigate the Human Rights Situation in the Former Yugoslavia, Croatian and Muslim soldiers also raped their enemies' women during the war, the majority of the rapists were Serbs, and the majority of the victims were Muslim women.[61]

For the first time, however, international tribunals have convicted a small number of Rwandan and Bosnian men of rape as a crime against humanity. In September 1998, the International Criminal Tribunal for Rwanda found Jean-Paul Akayesu, the mayor of a Hutu village in Rwanda, guilty of genocide and other crimes, including rape, specified as a crime against humanity *and* as an "instrument of genocide."[62] Tribunal Judge Navanethem Pilllay ruled that Akayesu should be punished for the rapes he had ordered, and he was eventually sentenced to life in prison.[63]

In February 2001, the International Criminal Tribunal for the Former Yugoslavia convicted three Serbian army commanders of raping Bosnian Muslim women and girls from 1992 to 1993. The three defendants, Dragoljub Kunarac, Radomir Kovac, and Zoran Vukovic, were sentenced to 28, 20, and 12 years, respectively, for their roles in multiple rapes and in the enslavement of women and girls in "rape camps."[64] Presiding Judge Florence Mumba of Zambia told the three defendants that "lawless opportunists should expect no mercy," and that whether in peace or war, "men of substance do not abuse women."[65]

While these rulings are groundbreaking and offer some hope for other past as well as future victims, they are still drops in the bucket. Moreover, there is always the chance that the convictions will be overturned. In fact, another Rwandan, Alfred Musema, convicted by the Rwanda tribunal in January 2000 of genocide and rape, had his three rape convictions overturned on appeal, although his genocide conviction (for taking part in the murders of 500,000 Tutsis and moderate Hutus) was upheld.[66]

Military rape and sexual enslavement are backed, at least indirectly, by patriarchal systems across cultures that legitimate male control over and sexual access to women. Among them are the major world religions, which have had an enormous impact on social thought throughout history and are often referred to for norms on gender relations. The cultural reach of the major religions is substantial and certainly goes beyond even the approximately 1.9 billion adherents of Christianity, 1.1 billion of Islam, 781 million of Hinduism, 324 million of Buddhism, and 14 million of Judaism worldwide.[67]

Organized Religion, Misogyny, and the Sexual Use of Women

Religious texts, and interpretations of them, have had a good deal to say about women and their relationship to men. Many who have probed religious writings for their take on gender have found considerable evidence of misogyny.[68] Some argue, however, that it is not the original or seminal religious texts (e.g., the Qur'an [Koran], the Bible), but rather patriarchal interpretations of them, that are misogynistic.[69] Such interpretations may appear in religious writings authored not by a prophet said to be bearing the words of an almighty deity, but rather by socially influenced interpreters one or more steps removed from the prophet's message (sometimes referred to as exegetes). A related argument is that interpretation is necessary because religious writings, even the "original" ones, are often contradictory, and their meaning is not always self-evident. If this is so, then the likelihood of selective interpretation—to fit with the interpreter's own beliefs—increases. Still other arguments are that religious writings are gender-egalitarian (although perhaps prescribing different roles for women and men), but that discriminatory, antiwoman actions that do not reflect those writings are taken in the name of religion.[70]

While this debate about religious "truths" regarding gender is an important one, it is not particularly relevant to the purpose at hand. Whether in seminal or post-seminal writings or in the policies and other actions of religious or politico-religious leaders, religion-based misogyny can facilitate or legitimate the sexual misuse and subjugation of women by men, thus establishing the climate for sexual enslavement and the trafficking of women into the sex industry. The examples from religious writings that follow constitute neither a representative nor a random sample. Nevertheless, they do *appear* in religious writings and, as such, are definitive; moreover, they are strikingly *similar* across the major world religions.

While almost no one claims that all references to women in religious writings are misogynistic, across religious texts women are repeatedly characterized as the "flawed other"—inferior (to man), deceitful, sexually provocative, and imbued with evil. Men are warned to beware of women's sexuality and their attempts to seduce or trick them. Religious prescriptions also mirror one another in their calls to men to keep women silenced and subjugated. Woman's earthly role is to serve and obey her husband. The specific examples that follow (chosen largely from critical or feminist studies of religion and the treatment of women) illustrate the similarity of such messages across religions.

Human life begins, in the biblical version, with a man, from whose rib woman is then born. Woman's secondary birth, however, is trumped by Eve's role in leading Adam—and thus all men—into (original) sin. It is this betrayal or "seduction" that perhaps most notably tarnishes womanhood and rationalizes subsequent female subjugation.[71] Interpreting this story, the Christian priest Tertullian (ca. 150–230) projected it onto all women: "Do you know that you are each an Eve? On account of your desert even the Son of God had to die." Augustine (ca. 54–430) later echoed his words: "It is still Eve the temptress that we must beware of in any women."[72] In the *Ramayana*, a religious text of ancient India, women are also said to be "impure by their very birth."[73] And, influenced by the cultural beliefs of Aryan nomadic tribes, the sage Manu, believed by some to be a voice of God, wrote into early Hindu law: "When God created woman, he allotted to them . . . impure desire, wrath, dishonesty, malice and bad conduct."[74]

During the Christian Inquisition in the Middle Ages, women's "gross sexuality" was highlighted by Dominican priests Kramer and Sprenger in their 1486 treatise, *Malleus Maleficarum* [the Hammer of Witches]. Witches, these two inquisitors claimed, were likely to be women because "all witchcraft comes from carnal lust which is in women insatiable."[75] The righteous priests also accused women witches of various sexual perversions, including orgies with the devil. The violence incited by these and related claims was massive, resulting in the murder of up to 10 million "witches" during the Inquisition.[76]

Descriptions of women as deceitful, sexually wanton, and witchlike are also found in the writings of other religions. In one Hindu text—the *Devi Bhagaveta*—woman is described as the "embodiment of . . . [or] a mine of vices . . . she is practically a sorceress and represents vile desire."[77] And a Jewish religious work states, "Even the most righteous of women has witchcraft."[78]

Across religions, then, women are characterized as impure, untrustworthy, and generally defective. What messages to men flow from such characterizations? A Jewish morning prayer provides one: "Blessed art thou, O Lord our God, King of the universe, who hast not made me a woman."[79] But misogyny calls for more than just gratitude for not *being* a woman. One suggestion for dealing with "the feminine" can be found in a Buddhist belief in the need for the "sacrifice of the feminine principle," deemed essential in order to attain the highest level of spiritual being. Solutions for women to their flawed femininity include reincarnation as a man, or striving to have a "man's state of mind." One part of the religious texts known as the *Sutras* suggests that women who are able to "awaken to the thought of enlightenment" can attain "the great and good person's state of mind, a man's state of mind, a sage's state of mind."[80]

Sometimes, women are told to subjugate themselves, as in the New Testament command: "Wives, submit yourselves unto your own husbands, as unto the Lord. For the husband is the head of the wife. . . ."[81] Or, "I permit no woman to teach or to have authority over men; she is to keep silent."[82] Many religious prescriptions, however, seem to be directed more to men in their call for and legitimation of male domination over all women, and in their likening of women to slaves. As stated in the Qur'an: "Men are in charge of women, because Allah hath made the one of them to excel the other."[83] And in one strain of Hindu-related laws, "In childhood a female must be subject to her father, in youth to her husband, when her lord [husband] is dead to her sons; a woman must never be independent."[84] Researcher Daniela Kramer points out that the Hebrew "*Babylonian Talmud* often places together women and slaves" (in one verse, women, slaves, and children, and in another verse, women, slaves, and cattle).[85]

Obedience to a husband (or other male relative) is a hallmark of the ideal woman, and major religions typically allow some level of violence against a disobedient wife. While pointing out that the level of Islamic violence against women witnessed today is not approved of in Islam, researcher Maria Holt notes that "according to the Qur'an, Islam permits moderate physical punishment by men of their wives in certain circumstances."[86] And, in one Hebrew writing, men are told that "anything a man wants to do with his wife, he shall."[87] The messages here are overtly patriarchal, calling for female subjugation and the rule of the husband/father, by violence or the threat of violence if necessary.

Oppressive control of and violence against women today is often committed in the name of religion-based and other patriarchal traditions or writings—as in dowry killings, in which husbands (and their families) murder their wives for their failure to provide adequate property; and in honor killings, in which women are murdered by (mainly) male relatives for having shamed their family—in some cases, for having been the victim of a rape! In the second half of the 1990s, in the region around Pakistan's capital, Islamabad, one women's nongovernmental organization reported having dealt with some 5,000 cases of honor-related crimes against women. Moreover, an estimated 40% of the total number of cases go unreported.[88] In 2001 alone, there were 221 honor-related murders of women in the Pakistan province of Sindh and 227 in Punjab; in most cases, the woman's killer was her husband or brother.[89] Honor killings are pervasive in other countries as well; in both Egypt and Jordan, they have accounted for close to one-fourth of all homicides in recent years.[90]

For Hindus and Muslims in several countries, religious "personal laws" that control and restrict women's behavior take precedence over state laws. In India in the late 1980s, state legislation allowing greater maintenance payments to wives and divorcées was heavily protested by fundamentalist Muslims, and eventually was countered by the Muslim Women's Act, which effectively "denies [Muslim] women the option of exercising their rights under the provisions of secular legislation."[91] Punitive in the extreme is the Islamic law of Shari'ah, invoked in recent death-by-stoning sentences for women in northern Nigeria and elsewhere. These death sentences have been meted out for the commission of adultery—even, again, in cases in which women have reported that they were raped.[92] The revival of extreme religious fundamentalism in northern Nigeria that calls for the severe punishment of (sexually) immoral women has, ironically, occurred at the same time that the trafficking of women into prostitution by Nigerian traffickers has increased.

Patriarchal religious images pair female carnality and sexual wantonness with the need for female obedience and subjugation. So perhaps it is not so surprising that restrictions on and punishment for women's sexual behavior coexist with the sexual exploitation and abuse of women by men—including that by clerics themselves.

Clerics and Sexual Enslavement

In his book entitled *Unzipped: The Popes Bare All: A Frank Study of Sex and Corruption in the Vatican*, Arthur Frederick Ide reveals a history of clerical concubinage in the Euro-Christian Roman Catholic Church. He reports, for example, that Pope Innocent VII "turned his court into a colourful and barbarically loose brothel,"[93] and that Pope Benedict III kept a special log on clerical sexual exploits.[94] He describes the preoccupation with sex of the French clergy, and says that by the eighth century, it was common knowledge that French "priests, monks, and bishops kept in their beds four or five concubines or more."[95] Ide concludes that the "Vatican itself became a pornocracy, with licentiousness more common than chastity for more than half of its existence."[96] Whether or not his accounts are this generalizable, Ide does seem to have uncovered a religiously deviant pattern normalized by some Roman Catholic clergy at particular times in history.

In another example, Rachel Bundang reports that when the Spanish colonized the Philippines and converted its population to Christianity in the mid-1500s, they set up a virtual "friarocracy" to rule over the land. The clerical leaders, brought to the Philippines from foreign lands, ruled the local population with brutality, and systematically sexually abused and enslaved the women.[97]

Of course, behaviors by male clergy in specific papacies or other clerical dominions are not necessarily institutionalized in the religion itself. In the examples to follow, sexual enslavement is a formal part of religious practice.

Religious Sexual Enslavement

In the *Devadasi* religious system practiced in parts of India, Nepal, and Sri Lanka, young, prepubertal girls are dedicated or "married" to the gods. Living in the temple, the dedicated girls (known as *jogini*) serve as enslaved

prostitutes for priests and sometimes for upper-status community members as well. Real marriage is forbidden to these girls. When they reach puberty, jogini are typically cast out of the temple and are often auctioned off to sex traffickers.[98] Some believe that the first devadasis (the name means "servant of god") were Buddhist nuns, and that their sexual enslavement occurred when Buddhist temples were taken over by the Brahmins and their priests.[99] Regardless, the system is still practiced today, and devadasis are thought to account for about 10% of the total number of women and girls trafficked into the sex trade in India.[100]

When she was 12 years old, Ghanian Abia Kotor was given to the village priest in atonement for her uncle's rape of her mother—an assault that resulted in her mother's pregnancy and Abia's birth. The offering of Abia was part of a traditional religious practice known as *Trokosi,* in which young virgin girls are given to priests as a "way of appeasing the gods for crimes committed by family members."[101] Once again, the sacrificed girls are sometimes considered to be "married" to a god and his human counterpart, the priest. (The word *trokosi* means "slaves of the gods.")[102] Trokosi girls may live in the shrine for several years or all of their lives, but even if they are allowed to leave, they are forever the sexual property of the priest. If the girl dies, or the priest is not happy with her, her family must replace her with a new virgin girl. Today, the Trokosi practice is outlawed in Ghana, and human rights groups have worked to end the tradition and bring perpetrators to justice. Partly as a result of these efforts, as of 2002, some 2,900 women and girls (thought to be about half of all trokosi in Ghana) had been freed from Trokosi enslavement.[103] The practice, however, continues unabated in many areas of Ghana.

Finally, religion sometimes offers prostitutes redemption in exchange for their acceptance of their "lot in life." An interpretation of the Buddhist law of karma, said to be popular among prostitutes, holds that an inferior or looked-down-upon status (including being a woman per se) is the result of a failure to behave appropriately in a past life; accepting one's condition or place in this life and serving others in accordance with that place will produce a better status in one's next incarnation.[104]

Because patriarchal systems share common features, they typically coexist comfortably, with each system providing support or legitimacy for the other. No wonder, then, that the military's take on women and gender relations parallels that of major world religions. Whether by their "original" prophetic edicts or by written or behavioral interpretations of them, major religions provide gender and gender-relations constructs that mimic and legitimize men's military experiences. As one author puts it, "militarism makes use of the dominant patriarchal structures which perpetuate the enduring exploitation and degradation of women."[105]

The next chapter looks at the organization of militarized prostitution for soldiers' recreation in modern wars and its role in the sex industrialization of developing countries, primarily in East and Southeast Asia. The chapter also provides examples of "congregational prostitution"—that is, organized recreational prostitution in places where sizable groups of men congregate for instrumental purposes (e.g., jobs, peacekeeping) away from home and family.

Notes

1. Urvashi Butalia (1997), "A Question of Silence: Partition, Women and the State," p. 99 in *Gender and Catastrophe*, ed. by Ronit Lentin (London/New York: Zed Books). See also Anuradha M. Chenoy (1998), "Militarization, Conflict, and Women in South Asia," pp. 101–110 in *The Women and War Reader*, ed. by Lois Ann Lorentzen and Jennifer Turpin (New York: New York University Press), for more on this topic.
2. Butalia (1997), op. cit., p. 99, quoting records kept by Anis Kiwai, a social worker in Muslim camps in Delhi during the Partition conflict.
3. Santi Rozario (1997), " 'Disasters' and Bangladeshi Women," pp. 254–268 in *Gender and Catastrophe*, ed. by Ronit Lentin (London/New York: Zed Books).
4. Nilima Ibrahim (1994), *Ami Birangana Balchi*, Part I (Dhaka, Bangladesh: Jagriti Prashani), p. 59. [Quoted in Rozario (1997), op. cit.]
5. Susan Brownmiller (1975), *Against Our Will: Men, Women and Rape* (New York: Fawcett Columbine), pp. 32–33.
6. The United Nations Security Council established the International Criminal Tribunal for the Former Yugoslavia in May 1993 and, less than 2 years later, in November 1994, the International Criminal Tribunal for Rwanda. The two tribunals have played an active role in prosecuting persons for their role in the brutal killings (often referred to collectively as ethnic genocide) and assaults during the civil armed conflicts in these countries during the early 1990s. Both the killings and the tribunals have been widely covered by the media. For more, see Daisy Sindelar (2001), "World: International Justice—Rwandan and Yugoslav Tribunals," Radio Free Europe/Radio Liberty, available at http://www.rferl.org/features/2001/09/04092001125355.asp.
7. Cynthia Enloe (2000), *Bananas, Beaches and Bases: Making Feminist Sense of International Politics* (Berkeley: The University of California Press); Meredeth Turshen (2001), "The Political Economy of Rape: An Analysis of Systematic Rape and Sexual Abuse of Women During

Armed Conflict in Africa," pp. 55–68 in *Victims, Perpetrators or Actors: Gender, Armed Conflict and Political Violence*, ed. by Caroline O. N. Moser and Fiona C. Clark (London/New York: Zed Books).

8. George S. Patton, Jr. (1947), *War as I Knew It* (Boston: Houghton Mifflin). [Quoted in Brownmiller (1975), op. cit., p. 31.]
9. Rhonda Copelon (1998), "Surfacing Gender: Reconceptualizing Crimes Against Women in Time of War," pp. 63–79 in *The Women and War Reader*, ed. by Lois Ann Lorentzen and Jennifer Turpin (New York: New York University Press); Susan Griffin (1971), "Rape: The All-American Crime," *Ramparts* 10, pp. 26–35.
10. Brownmiller (1975), op. cit., p. 35.
11. Ibid., p. 35.
12. Nelia Sancho, ed. (1998), "The Case of the Filipino Comfort Women, Part II," *War Crimes on Asian Women: Military Sexual Slavery by Japan during World War II* (Manila: Asian Women's Human Rights Council).
13. See, for example, Peggy Sanday (1990), *Fraternity Gang Rape: Sex, Brotherhood, and Privilege on Campus* (New York: New York University Press); Patricia Yancey Martin and Robert A. Hummer (1989), "Fraternities and Rape on Campus," *Gender & Society* 3, pp. 457–473; Julie K. Ehrhart and Bernice R. Sandler (1985), *Campus Gang Rape: Party Games?* (Washington, DC: Association of American Colleges).
14. "Army Lessens Charge Against Interrogator" (2003), *The Oregonian*, November 7, A14.
15. Janet Spence, R. L. Helmreich, and J. Stapp (1974), "The Personal Attributes Questionnaire: A Measure of Sex Role Stereotypes and Masculinity-Femininity," *JSAS Catalog of Selected Documents in Psychology*, 4 MS 167; Inge K. Broverman, S. R. Vogel, D. M. Broverman, F. E. Clarkson, and P. S. Rosenkrantz (1972), "Sex-role Stereotypes: A Current Appraisal," *Journal of Social Issues* 28, pp. 59–78.
16. Gwyn Kirk, Rachel Cornwell, and Margo Okazawa-Rey (retrieved September 9, 2002), "Women and U.S. Military Presence" [KAISA-KA study], East Asia-US Women's Network Against US Militarism, available at www.yonip.com/main/articles/womenmilitary.html; Gwyn Kirk, Rachel Cornwell, and Margo Okazawa-Rey (1999–2000), "In Focus: Women and the U.S. Military in East Asia," *Foreign Policy in Focus* 4 (July), a joint project of the Interhemispheric Resource Center and Institute for Policy Studies, ed. by Tom Barry (IRC) and Martha Honey (IPS), available at http://www.globalspin.org/women_asia_usmilitary.html; Sister Mary Soledad Perpinan (1990), "Militarism and the Sex Industry in the Philippines," reproduced (slightly edited) from pp.149–153 in *ISIS Women's World* 1990–1991, 24 (Winter).

17. Liz Kelly (2000), "Wars Against Women: Sexual Violence, Sexual Politics and the Militarised State," pp. 45–65 in *States of Conflict: Gender, Violence and Resistance,* ed. by Susie Jacobs, Ruth Jacobson, and Jennifer Marchbank (New York: Zed Books).
18. Ibid.; Cynthia Enloe (1993), *The Morning After: Sexual Politics at the End of the Cold War* (Berkeley: University of California Press); Marilyn French (1992), *The War Against Women* (London: Hamish Hamilton).
19. Cynthia Enloe (1998), "All the Men Are in the Militias; All the Women Are Victims: The Politics of Masculinity and Femininity in Nationalist Wars," pp. 54 in *The Women and War Reader,* ed. by Lois Ann Lorentzen and Jennifer Turpin (New York: New York University Press).
20. Ibid., p. 55.
21. Margit J. Horvath (retrieved January 4, 2004), "Sex, War, and Tourism: An International Affair," available at http://www.runet.edu/~peace/ippno/papers/pl.html (p. 4 of 12).
22. Rhonda Copelon (1998), op. cit., p. 75. See also Peggy R. Sanday (1981), "The Socio-Cultural Context of Rape: A Cross-Cultural Study," *Journal of Social Issues* 37, pp. 5–27, for a discussion of societal and group characteristics that encourage rape.
23. The term "patriarchy" commonly appears in feminist discourse on causes of the exploitation and subjugation of women, but its precise meaning varies. The definition of patriarchy used in this text seems to me to accurately reflect the role of race and class in structures of male privilege. That is, it recognizes that not all men are in positions of power in a patriarchy, and that the level of subjugation and devaluation of women varies by their class and race (and deviance) status.
24. Keep in mind that patriarchy as an ideal type is at one end of a continuum. Major religions may vary in their place on that continuum, and most certainly, the views of those making the placements are going to vary. Overall, however, the major world religions have a number of characteristics (as described in the definition above) that qualify them as more on the patriarchal than on the egalitarian side of the continuum.
25. Jeanne Ward (2002), "If Not Now, When? Addressing Gender-Based Violence in Refugee, Internally Displaced, and Post-Conflict Settings," The Reproductive Health for Refugees Consortium, available at http://www.reliefweb.int/w/rws.nsf (15 pp.); Butalia (1997), op. cit.; Ruth Seifert (1994), "War and Rape: A Preliminary Analysis," pp. 54–72 in *Mass Rape: The War Against Women in Bosnia-Herzegovina,* ed. by Alexandra Stiglmayer (Lincoln: University of Nebraska Press); Brownmiller (1975), op. cit.
26. Butalia (1997), op. cit.

27. "Myth of the Rape of the Sabines, The" (retrieved January 16, 2004), available at http://www2.students.sbc.edu/dwarzski00/sabines1.html; "Sabines" (2002), *The Columbia Encyclopedia*, 6th ed., available at http://www.bartleby.com/65/sa/Sabines.html; Brownmiller (1975), op. cit.
28. Yifat Susskind (2002), "Violence Against Women in Latin America," *Madre*, available at http://www.madre.org/art_violence.html.
29. Joshua S. Goldstein (2001), *War and Gender: How Gender Shapes the War System and Vice Versa* (Cambridge: Cambridge University Press).
30. Brownmiller (1975), op. cit., p. 38.
31. Ibid., p. 50.
32. Ward (2002), op. cit.; Project Ploughshares (2001), "Indonesia-East Timor," *Armed Conflicts Report 2003*, available at http://www.ploughshares.ca/CONTENT/ACR/ACR00/ACR-IndonesiaETimor.html.
33. [Quoted in A. J. Franco (1999), "Mozambique and the Civil War," paper presented at the Aftermath Conference, University of the Witwatersrand, Johannesburg, South Africa, July 20–22.]
34. Susskind (2002), op. cit., p. 1.
35. Wells Staley-Mays (retrieved January 15, 2004), "Massacre Victims and Survivors in Acteal, State of Chiapas, Mexico," available at http://www.peaceactionmme.org/Acteal.html; "Women's Work, Women's Struggle in Chiapas, Mexico" (1998), compiled by the International Wages for Housework Campaign, available at http://flag.blackened.net/revolt/mexico/comment/women_jul98.html (2 pp.).
36. "Women's Work" (1998), p. 2.
37. [Quoted in Brownmiller (1975), op. cit., p. 41.]
38. Charles M. Goolsby (2003), "Dynamics of Prostitution and Sex Trafficking from Latin America into the United States," p. 10 in *2003 Report on Latin America to U.S. Sex Trafficking*, Libertad Latina, available at http://www.libertadlatina.org/LL_LatAm_US_Slavery_Report_01_2003.htm. See also Susskind (2002), op. cit.; Goldstein (2001), op. cit.
39. Valerie Oosterveld (2000), "Recognizing Rape and Sexual Violence as War Crimes," pp. 32–34 in *War Crimes*, ed. by Henny H. Kim (San Diego, CA: Greenhaven). [Reprinted from "When Women Are the Spoils of War" (1998), *UNESCO Courier* (August).]
40. Ibid.
41. Ibid.
42. Seifert (1994), op. cit.
43. Ward (2002), op. cit.
44. Includes groups variously referred to as insurgents, revolutionaries, paramilitaries, mercenaries, or bandits.

45. Oosterveld (2000), op. cit., p. 33.
46. Ward (2002), op. cit., p. 2.
47. [Quoted in T. Sideris (1999), "Rape in War and Peace—Same Category Different Experiences?" paper presented at the Aftermath Conference, University of the Witwatersrand, Johannesburg, South Africa, July 20–22.]
48. "Somali Refugees Arrive in Portland" (1993), *The Oregonian*, October 29.
49. Copelon (1998), op. cit.
50. Brownmiller (1975), op. cit.
51. Goldstein (2001), op. cit.
52. Brownmiller (1975), op. cit., p. 59.
53. Philip Johnston (2002), "A Brutal Weapon of Ancient and Modern Warfare," *News.telegraph.co.uk*, January 6, available at http://www.telegraph.co.uk.news/main.jhtml/xml=/news/200201/24/wbeev124.xml; Brownmiller (1975), op. cit.
54. Brownmiller (1975), op. cit., pp. 104–105.
55. Accounts vary by source.
56. Brownmiller (1975), op. cit.
57. Turshen (2001), op. cit.
58. Oosterveld (2000), op. cit.
59. David J. Craig (2001), "Wartime Rape Convictions Overdue, Says Women's Studies Scholar," *Boston University Bridge* IV (March 16), available at http://www.bu.edu/bridge/archive/2001/03-16/rapte.html (3 pp.); Pamela Goldberg (1995), "Where in the World Is There Safety for Me? Women Fleeing Gender-based Persecution," pp. 345–355 in *Women's Rights Human Rights: International Feminist Perspectives*, ed. by Julie Peters and Andrea Wolper (New York: Routledge); Alexandra Stiglmayer (1994), "The Rapes in Bosnia–Herzegovina," pp. 82–169 in *Mass Rape: The War Against Women in Bosnia–Herzegovina*, ed. by Alexandra Stiglmayer (Lincoln: University of Nebraska Press).
60. Human Rights Watch (2000), "Kosovo: Rape as a Weapon of Ethnic Cleansing" (March); Catherine A. MacKinnon (1994), "Turning Rape into Pornography: Postmodern Genocide," pp. 73–81 in *Mass Rape: The War Against Women in Bosnia–Herzegovina*, ed. by Alexandra Stiglmayer (Lincoln: University of Nebraska Press); Sally Hargreaves (2001), "Rape as a War Crime: Putting Policy into Practice," *Lancet* 357, no. 9258 (March 10); Anna Quindlen (1993), " 'Gynocide': Rape of Bosnian Muslim Women," *The Oregonian*, March 14, C9.
61. Stiglmayer (1994), op. cit.
62. Kelly Askin (2001), "Legal Precedents in Rwanda Court," *The Tribunals* (May), Crimes of War Project, available at http://www.crimesofwar.org/tribun-mag/rwanda.html.

63. Sindelar (2001), op. cit.
64. Craig (2001), op. cit.; Marlise Simons (2001), "3 Bosnian Serbs Are Convicted in Wartime Rapes," *The New York Times*, February 23, available at http://www.freeserbia.netArticles/2001RapeInFoca2.html.
65. Barbara Crossette (2001), "A New Legal Weapon to Deter Rape," *The New York Times*, February 4, available at http://www.globalpolicy.org/wldcourt/tribunal/2001/0204rape.htm.
66. "Rwandan Escapes Sentence, Gets Life for Genocide" [Africa: Central Africa] (2001), News24, November 16, available at www.news24.com/News24v2/ContentDisplay/genericFrame/0,6178,2-11-39_1109505,00html.
67. Daniela Kramer, with Michael Moore (2002), " 'Women Are the Root of All Evil': The Misogyny of Religions," The Secular Web, available at http://www.secwe.org/asset.asp?AssetID=203 (25 pp.); "Major Religions of the World Ranked by Number of Adherents" (2002) (September 6), available at http://www.adherents.com/Religions_By_Adherents.
68. Kramer (2002), op. cit.; Rosemary Reuther (1983), *Sexism and God-Talk: Toward a Feminist Theology* (Boston: Beacon Press); Gerda Lerner (1986), *The Creation of Patriarchy* (Oxford: Oxford University Press); Pamela J. Milne (1989), "The Patriarchal Stamp of Scripture: The Implications of Structuralist Analyses for Feminist Hermeneutics," *Journal of Feminist Studies in Religion* 5, pp. 17–34; Mary Daly (1985 [1968]), *The Church and the Second Sex* (Boston: Beacon Press).
69. Karen Armstrong (1993), *A History of God* (New York: Ballantine); Raqiya Abdallah (1982), *Sisters in Affliction: Circumcision and Infibulation of Women in Africa* (London: Zed Press).
70. Armstrong (1993), op. cit.
71. Kramer (2002), op. cit.; Uta Ranke-Heinemann (1990), *Eunuchs for the Kingdom of Heaven: Women, Sexuality and the Catholic Church* (Harmondsworth, U.K.: Penguin); Daly (1985 [1968]), op. cit.
72. [Quoted in Kramer (2002), op. cit., p. 5.]
73. [Quoted in Kramer (2002), op. cit., p. 9.]
74. Manu (n.d.), *Manava Dharma-shastra* IX.17. [Quoted in Roderick W. Marling (retrieved January 1, 2004), "History: A Spiritual Analysis," KamaKala Publications, available at http://www.kamakala.com/history.htm (27 pp.).]
75. See Mary Daly (1978), *Gyn/Ecology: The Metaethics of Radical Feminism* (Boston: Beacon Press), for a good discussion of *Malleus Maleficarum.*
76. Daly (1978), op. cit.
77. Terry Flower (1986), "Holy Prejudice," in "Women Are the Devil's Gateway," *New Internationalist* 155 (January), available at http://www.newint.org/issue155/gateway.htm.

78. Haim Nahman Bialik and Y. H. Ravnicki, eds. (1948), no. 118, pp. 489, in *Sefer Ha-Aggada* (The Book of Legends), 3rd ed. (Tel Aviv: Dvir) (in Hebrew). This book is a compilation of legends and sayings from the *Talmud* and the *Midrashim* (both are Jewish religious works) collected by the authors. [Cited in Kramer (2002), op. cit.]
79. J. H. Hertz, ed. (1959), *The Authorised Daily Prayer Book of the United Hebrew Congregations of the British Empire*, revised ed. (London: Shapiro Vallentine). [Cited in Kramer (2002), op. cit.]
80. Diana Y. Paul (1985), *Women in Buddhism: Images of the Feminine in the Mahayana Tradition*, 2nd ed. (Berkeley: University of California Press), pp. 175–176. [Quoted in Victor Trimondi and Victoria Trimondi (2003), "Buddhism and Misogyny—An Historical Overview," Part I, "Ritual as Politics," in *The Shadow of the Dalai Lama*, available at http://www.trimondi/de/SDLE/Part-1-01.htm (13 pp.).] Keep in mind, however, that there are opposing voices that argue that a particular religious writing is not the "true word," or is misinterpreted. Regarding sutras, for example, Reverend Myoshu Agnes Jedrzejewska says that "Sutras . . . are neither written by any Buddha, nor [do] they carry only the words of the Buddha." [Quoted in Myoshu Agnes Jedrzejewska (2003), "The Female Disciples of Buddha—An Understanding of Shinran's Teachings for Our Present Times," available at http://jodoshinshu.republika.pl/jodoe/dharma/sanfrancisco2003.htm (11 pp.).]
81. From Ephesians 5:22–23. [Quoted in Kramer (2002), op. cit., p. 6.]
82. From 1 Timothy 2:11–14. [Quoted in Kramer (2002), op. cit., p. 6.]
83. From the Qur'an IV:34. [Quoted in Maria Holt (2002), "A Habit of Violence Grown Ordinary: Constraints on Muslim Women's Participation in War," *Minerva: Quarterly Report on Women and the Military* (Spring), available at http://www.findarticles.com/cf_ds/mOEXI/1_20/98079155/print.jhtml (23 pp.).]
84. From Manu (n.d.), *Manava Dharma-shastra*, v. 28. [Quoted in Marling (2004), op. cit., p. 6.]
85. Kramer (2002), op. cit., p. 4.
86. Holt (2002), op. cit., p. 1.
87. Bialik and Ravnicki (1948), op. cit., no. 165, p. 491.
88. Goldstein (2001), op. cit.
89. Ibid.
90. Ibid.
91. T. K. Rajalakshmi (2001), "Women's Rights: An Inequitous Proposal," *India's National Magazine* [from the publishers of *The Hindu*] 8, July 7, available at http://www.flonnet.com/fl1814/18140890.htm (3 pp.).

92. "Shari'ah Law, Adultery and Rape" (retrieved January 25, 2004), International Society for Human Rights. Frankfurt, Germany, available at http://www.ishr.org/activities/campaigns/stoning/adultery.htm.
93. Arthur Frederick Ide (1987), *Unzipped: The Popes Bare All: A Frank Study of Sex and Corruption in the Vatican* (Austin, TX: American Atheist Press). [Quoted in Kwame Nantambu (2002), "Sexual Abuse in Roman Catholic Church," *News and Views*, August 13, The Trini Center, available at http://www.trinicenter.com/kwame/2002/Aug/142002.htm, p. 4 of 5.]
94. Ibid., p. 4.
95. Ibid., p. 3.
96. Ibid., p. 3–4.
97. Rachel Bundang (1999), "Scars ARE History: Colonialism, Written on the Body," pp. 53–69 in *Remembering Conquest; Feminist/Womanist Perspectives on Religion, Colonization, and Sexual Violence*, ed. by Nantawan Boonprasat Lewis and Marie M. Fortune (New York: Haworth).
98. Samantha Chattoraj (2002), "The Devadasi System," available at http://iml.jou.ufl.edu/projects/Spring02/Chattaraj/index2.html (6 pp.); Corie Hammers (2001), "International Trafficking in Women in the Asian Region in the Era of Globalization," unpublished master's thesis, Portland State University, Portland, OR; M. Luhan and P. Thapa (1993), "World of the Girl Child," pp. 20–25 in *Tulasa and the Horrors of Child Prostitution: Sold and Resold Body and Soul* (Bombay: Indian Health Organization).
99. Chattoraj (2002), op. cit.
100. Hammers (2001), op. cit.
101. "Slavery in Ghana: The *Trokosi* Tradition" (2002), *Equality Now* (May), available at www.frauen.spoe.at/download/international/sclavery_in-ghana.pdf (2 pp.). See also Benjamin Rinaudo (2003), "Trokosi Slavery: Injustice in the Name of Religion," African Studies Association of Australia and the Pacific 2003 Conference Proceedings—Africans on a Global Stage, available at http://cp.yahoo.net/search/cache?p=Trokosi+religious+tradition&url=xrWD3CS33p8J; Byron Woods (2002), "Unwilling Sacrifices," *Independent*, available at http://indyweek.com/durham/2002-04-17ae3.html (3 pp.).
102. "Slavery in Ghana" (2002), op. cit.
103. Woods (2002), op. cit.
104. Nantawan Boonprasat Lewis (1999), "Remember Conquest: Religion, Colonization and Sexual Violence: A Thai Experience," pp. 5–17 in *Remembering Conquest: Feminist/Womanist Perspectives on Religion, Colonization, and Sexual Violence*, ed. by Nantawan Boonprasat Lewis and Marie M. Fortune (New York: Haworth).
105. Sancho (1998), op. cit., p. 4.

7

The Organization of Military Prostitution in Modern Times: Building a Sex Trade from Militarized Demand

As noted in the last chapter, militaries have been instrumental in ensuring soldier access to prostitution across time and cultures. The extent to which military leadership has been proactive in or supportive of the organization of prostitution during modern wars has varied. By the time of World War II, however, some military leaders had determined that prostitution was too important to their soldiers to be left to develop on its own. In fact, the U.S. military thought back on World War I, when prostitution for its troops was available, but not regulated, and STD infection rates among GIs were high.[1] In World War II and thereafter, the U.S. military took a more proactive role in organizing and regulating prostitution for its troops.

The organization of prostitution close to military bases and installations has resulted, in many instances, in the evolution of prostitution or entertainment economies in towns or areas nearby. During "boom times"—of war or war threat—the demand for prostitutes is frequently met by trafficking women to those towns from within or outside the region. When troops leave, the prostitution towns lose their customer base, and many women in the business are left without jobs or incomes. Now the flow reverses, with women trafficked from those towns or countries for work elsewhere. Perhaps nowhere is there a better modern example of this phenomenon than in the Philippines during and after World War II.

Organized Military Prostitution and Prostitution Economies: An Example

Following the closure of Clark Air Force Base and the Subic Bay Naval Station in the Philippines in 1992, the entertainment towns that had built up to serve them—Angeles City and Olongapo—languished. Many of the thousands of women who had made their living as bar girls there found themselves without work and as the sole support of their children, some of whom had been fathered by American GIs. In their heyday during World War II, and later during the Korean and Vietnam wars, Angeles City and Olongapo served a steady stream of largely American troops stationed in the Philippines or sent there for R & R. Sex businesses proliferated and added new services, including special events such as "foxy boxing," in which women "were forced to fight each other until they drew blood or showed bruises." If no "demonstrable injuries" were forthcoming, the women were not paid.[2]

Prior to the base closures, over 25,000 U.S. military personnel were stationed at Clark Air Force Base. Five thousand were stationed at Subic Bay, and an additional 70,000 troops were intermittently on the islands as their aircraft and ships stopped for "repairs and renovations" there.[3] Business was booming in the towns around the bases. In Angeles City, a town of almost 280,000, there were over 1,500 registered bars, brothels, and massage parlors in 1990.[4] And, in Angeles City and Olongapo together, at least 55,000 Filipina women and girls were working as "entertainers."[5]

Olongapo and Angeles City were, in one author's words, "whoredoms" that grew out of the organization of militarized recreational prostitution services for American troops during World War II.[6] The Philippines remained a crucial strategic military location for the United States after World War II and throughout the cold war. Following the U.S. occupation of the Philippines at the end of World War II, the two governments signed the RP-US Military Base Agreement (MBA), which provided the United States with "unhampered" use of the Philippines for military bases and other facilities for 44 years. With troops regularly on board, the entertainment businesses of Olongapo and Angeles City thrived. However, when the MBA expired, in 1991, the Philippines declined to renew the agreement, thus forcing the closure of the Clark and Subic Bay bases.[7]

When the bases closed, brothels and bars suffered from the loss of customers, and a number of Filipina women and girls who had worked near the bases migrated to other countries for work. Some went to U.S. military base sites in Guam, Okinawa, and Germany, where they continued to serve American troops. And, as the United States made new R & R agreements and renewed old ones with countries such as Australia, Singapore, Malaysia, Korea, and Japan, Filipinas were among the women from around the world who went or were trafficked to those countries to provide R & R services for soldiers.[8] Of the estimated 7 million to 8 million overseas Filipino workers at the end of the 1990s, six to eight of every ten were female, and among the females, the two most common jobs were domestic worker and sex worker.[9]

Since the mid-1990s, over 5,000 women and girls, most of whom are Filipinas, have been trafficked to South Korea for prostitution.[10] The Korea Special Tourism Association, an organization made up of 189 club and bar owners near U.S. military camps in South Korea, has helped bring "entertainers" into the country, considering them to be essential to the survival of prostitution businesses there. According to an International Organization for Migration report, cooperation with the association in providing troops with prostitution services near bases was the "de facto" policy of the U.S. military.[11] The redeployment of some Clark and Subic Bay troops to Japan, adding to the more than 40,000 U.S. troops already located there, also encouraged sex trafficking. In the late 1990s, there were over 150,000 foreign women working as prostitutes in Japan; over half of them were Filipinas.

In 1999, 8 years after Clark and Subic Bay were closed, the United States negotiated another agreement with the Philippines, this one known as the Visiting Forces Agreement (VFA)/Status of Forces Agreement (SoFA). The SoFA, ratified by the Philippine Senate in May 1999, allowed the U.S. military to use 22 Philippine ports (with access to airports on the main islands) for purposes such as repairs, refueling, military exercises, and R & R services for troops.[12] Olongapo and Angeles City, both of which had negative growth rates between 1990 and 1995, began to grow again in the late 1990s. Even before the ratification of the SoFA, however, the Philippines, with its long history as a site for U.S. military installations, was on a pathway toward sex industrialization.

Today there are at least 400,000 women working in the Philippines as registered prostitutes; added to that are an unknown number of unregistered prostitutes.[13] As of 2000, there were 4,356 registered prostitutes in Olongapo and 3,430 in Angeles City. According to one source, if unregistered prostitutes were also counted, the total number of working prostitutes would be somewhere around 9,000 in Olongapo and 7,000 in Angeles City.[14] Moreover, sex industry growth has not been limited to these two towns. In Davao (the second largest city in the Philippines, with a population of almost 875,000), the number of prostitution establishments went from 80 in 1993 to 135 in 1997. And the number of registered prostitutes in Davao went from 868 in 1993 to 1,525 in 1996.[15] In Cebu (the third largest city in the Philippines, with a population of almost 750,000), the number of registered prostitutes jumped from 1,500 in 1993 to 4,500 in 1997.[16]

At least one-fourth of the prostitutes in the Philippines are children, and in Olongapo and Angeles City, the risk of becoming a prostitute is particularly high among the Amerasian children fathered by American GIs. Left with only their mothers to support them, and stigmatized and isolated in their communities, Amerasian children (thought to number around 30,000 in the country) have few opportunities for the future.[17] In her talks with bar women in Olongapo and Angeles City 2 years after the base closures, Kathleen Barry reported hearing one theme "reiterated over and over again,"—the women's "belief, hope, wish, that the GIs who had fathered their children would return to take them to the United States as their wives." Barry pointed out that for these women, work in the Philippines other than prostitution seemed an impossibility, so that "marrying an American becomes one of the only dreams of getting out of prostitution and poverty."[18]

Sex industry customers in the Philippines today consist of more than just American soldiers. The availability of services brings in local customers, and there is a newer crop of foreign men traveling to the Philippines through an expanding arm of the sex industry—prearranged sex tours. Ads promoting sex tours to the Philippines are showing up around the world. In 1998, for example, *Philippine Adventure Tour* offered a sex tour for $1,645, which included round-trip airfare from Los Angeles, hotel accommodations, and guided tours to bars where men could buy prostitutes starting at $24. The owner–operator of the tour told potential customers that they "never sleep alone on this tour," and he even suggested that customers hire a different prostitute every day, or "two if you can handle it."[19] Whether for a group or for individuals, sex tourism promotions often draw on racism for their appeal. In an article in *Playboy* entitled "Why They Love Us in the Philippines," the author describes Olongapo as a place "with beaches and bars and girls and everything cheap," and as the "last frontier where you can have what you want—get a blow job, see a female boxing bout and oil wrestling, and have fun with LBFMs" (i.e., Little Brown Fucking Machines), a racist euphemism that has been used elsewhere to describe women of color in the sex industry, usually in Third World countries.[20] In addition, the Philippines has become a popular site for pedophile sex tours from the United States and Europe. Child prostitution is not a new phenomenon in the Philippines, but by all accounts, it grew and expanded dramatically during the 1990s. Estimates put the number of child prostitutes in the Philippines somewhere between 60,000 and 100,000.[21] In the mid-1980s, child sex rings were operating in 7 Philippine provinces; by the end of the 1990s, the number of involved provinces had increased to 37.[22]

The Philippines may be seeing more male sex tourists, but they've not seen the last of American troops. After the September 11 terrorist attacks that obliterated the World Trade Center in New York and devastated parts of the Pentagon in Washington D.C., President George W. Bush identified the Philippines as America's "second front" in the war against terrorism, and several thousand troops were immediately deployed to the islands. Most of these troops are stationed in the southern port town of Zamboanga, where there are now about 2,000 women and girls working as prostitutes, compared to only a handful prior to this newest deployment.[23]

Of particular concern, given this latest military buildup, is a section of the SoFA that grants U.S. troops virtual immunity from criminal prosecution by the Philippine government. This section reads in part that in recognition of the "responsibility of the United States military authorities to maintain good order and discipline among their forces, Philippine authorities will, upon request by the United States, waive their primary right to exercise jurisdiction except in cases of particular importance to the Philippines." It goes on to say that if the Philippine government finds a case involving American military personnel of particular importance to them, they can so notify the U.S. military commander, who will then make a determination regarding the Philippine notification.[24] Although U.S. military authorities are to "take full account of the Philippine position," the transfer of the case to Philippine authorities is by no means automatic. In fact, under the earlier MBA (which had a similar "immunity clause"), more than 50 cases of rape, murder, assault, and other serious crimes of violence allegedly committed in the Philippines by U.S. servicemen were never placed under Philippine jurisdiction; moreover, the alleged offenders were typically shipped out of the country under what was described as "normal troop rotation."[25]

Violence against prostitutes committed by servicemen, although often unreported, is widespread.[26] In their research, Aida Santos and Cecilia Hofmann found that prostitutes working in bars around military bases or installations "were often hurt, hit or raped if they resisted anal sex or giving blow jobs, clients putting objects in their vaginas or other acts."[27] In one especially brutal murder of a prostitute by a serviceman, the victim "was found with part of her uterus scraped out by a broken bottle and with three barbecue sticks stabbed into her vagina." The killer was convicted of the murder and served 1 year in prison before being released.[28]

The situation in the Philippines is perilous in many ways. Prostitutes are clearly put at risk for violence and disease, and their already unstable livelihoods are constantly affected by changing relations between foreign militaries and their own government. The country is now economically dependent on its sex industry, as well as on revenues from the out-migration work of its citizens. The Philippines provide a particularly potent example of the ways in which massive military recreational prostitution contributes to the growth and expansion of a sex industry that eventually can permeate an entire country.

Military prostitution does not typically arise and flourish on its own—that is, by the law of unfettered supply and demand. In fact, in major modern wars, military leadership has virtually always been engaged at some level in the organization of prostitution services for its troops. In the next section, the role of militaries in organizing prostitution during World War II and the Korean and Vietnam wars is examined more closely.

The Military's Role in Organizing Prostitution in Modern Wars

Soldiers' desire and need for sexual services has been regarded as a given in virtually all military undertakings that take men away from their families. As Liz Kelly puts it: "Sexual access to women has been explicitly organised by the military for centuries, demonstrating a fundamental connection between militarism and coercive heterosexuality."[29] In the late 1500s, for example, the Spanish army set out to invade the Netherlands, and on their march forward took with them "40 mounted whores and 80 on foot" who were under the command of officers as providers of R & R services for soldiers—a support unit of sorts.[30] Even earlier, during the formation of the mighty Roman Empire, one of the new government's first tasks was to set up and manage brothels as a regular service for its army.[31]

This section examines military organization of recreational prostitution in three modern wars—World War II, the Korean War, and the Vietnam War—as well as ways in which military prostitution in these wars led to the buildup of sex industries and sex trafficking in Southeast Asia. The following section looks at the organization of recreational prostitution in places where men congregate for quasi-military or even civilian work.

World War II

Sex industrialization in Southeast Asia got a big boost with the massive deployment of U.S. and Japanese troops in the region during World War II. Joint planning by foreign militaries and local governments resulted in the buildup of prostitution economies in Okinawa and, as discussed previously, the Philippines. Military prostitution was also organized, regulated, and routinized around U.S. bases in Hawaii during World War II.

Okinawa

On the southern Japanese islands constituting Okinawa, local women and women from neighboring countries served as prostitutes for Japanese troops during World War II and then for U.S. troops following the war. In the final days of World War II, according to Ryan Masaaki Yokota, Japan was using Okinawa as "the last military staging ground of the Pacific war,"[32] which made it a site of particularly devastating sieges. In fact, in a single battle (the Battle of Okinawa) in 1945, 200,000 Okinawans were killed, and the island itself was heavily damaged.[33] When Japan surrendered a short time later, it gave Okinawa to the United States for its continuing military operations, thus beginning the U.S. occupation of Okinawa that was to continue for the next 27 years. According to research professor Yasutaka Oshiro of Okinawa International University, prostitution zones "were created by U.S. officials following World War II," with the hope that they would "counter the problem of U.S. troops raping local women with abandon."[34] In these zones, the sex industry could operate "with impunity." The brothels in the designated zones were initially filled with local women, many of whom either had been raped and sexually enslaved by Japanese troops during the war, or had lost their husbands or other male relatives during the war and were desperate for money to support themselves and their children.[35]

The prostitution economy in Okinawa also benefited from the Korean and Vietnam wars, when U.S. soldiers were either stationed in or sent for R & R to the islands. By 1969, some 8,000 prostitutes in Okinawa were servicing U.S. troops there.[36]

Although Okinawa was officially returned to Japan in 1972, the American military presence there remains strong, and the islands are considered to be an important strategic site for U.S. troops. In the late 1990s, there were still 30,000 U.S. troops stationed at some 39 U.S. bases and installations in Okinawa (occupying about 20% of the land area).[37] Okinawa currently serves as an R & R site for the 47,000 U.S. troops stationed throughout Japan. As the sex industry has grown, demand has overtaken local supply, and in the 1990s, women from other countries were being trafficked to Okinawa for prostitution in increasing numbers. Today, for example, there are at least 7,000 Filipina women working in Okinawa on entertainment visas; most are working as prostitutes and are mainly employed around U.S. bases.[38]

The Philippines

The Philippines served as a colonial pawn from the beginning to at least the middle of the twentieth century. As a Spanish colony in the late 1800s, the Philippines were ceded to the United States at the end of the Spanish–American War in 1898. In 1935, the Philippines became a self-governing commonwealth of the United States, enjoying some independence but required to accommodate the United States in a number of ways—one of which was the allowance of a substantial number of U.S. bases and installations there. Then, on the same day that they attacked Pearl Harbor, the Japanese attacked the Philippines; the fighting ended in 1942 with the latter's surrender to and occupation by Japan. Although Japan had designated the Philippines as an independent republic in late 1943, with the U.S. victory over Japan, the Philippines once again found themselves in a dependency relationship with the United States. In 1946, the United States acknowledged the Republic of the Philippines as an independent nation, but retained military rights in the islands through the Military Base Agreement discussed earlier.

As noted, the rise of a prostitution economy in the Philippines was due almost entirely to the organization of military prostitution around Clark Air Force Base and the Subic Bay Naval Station, with the full knowledge and support of the U.S. military leadership. In fact, the U.S. military worked out an agreement with local authorities mandating medical exams for all prostitutes working around the bases. As Cynthia Enloe reports, local authorities were to provide the U.S. military with IDs of women found to have an STD.[39] At the bases, pictures of "infected" Filipina prostitutes were hung up on a wall so that soldiers would recognize and avoid them. As a demeaning gesture, the pictures of the women were hung upside down—that is, with their genital area as the focal point.[40] Here, as at other military sites, the concern was always and only that prostitutes would or could infect the GIs. No thought was given to the possibility of transmission in the other direction—from the men to the women—certainly a far greater likelihood in the case of young prostitutes. As a further sign of their exclusive concern for their men, the U.S. military was unwilling to provide or even contribute to health care for prostitutes who tested positive for an STD.[41]

Another U.S. strategy aimed at preventing soldiers from acquiring STDs was the decision to allow prostitutes to spend the night on the base with a soldier "boyfriend." The theory here was that if soldiers had a regular girlfriend, they would be less frequently exposed to STD transmission. If a soldier did get an STD, the name of the prostitute from whom he *thought* he had contracted the disease was commonly given back to the employer at her brothel. As a result, she often lost her job.[42]

The prostitution economy established in the Philippines during World War II also thrived during the Korean and Vietnam wars, when soldiers were sent to the islands for R & R. By the late 1960s, the Philippines were providing R & R services, including at least 55,000 prostitutes, for about 10,000 servicemen each day.[43]

Hawaii

The U.S. military and the Hawaiian government also worked together to set up a system regulating prostitution for troops stationed in Hawaii and soldiers brought in for R & R during World War II. As elsewhere, the protection of American troops from STDs was a top priority.[44] Again, the health risk for the prostitutes was a nonissue, even though there was evidence that Hawaiian prostitutes were at particularly high risk of STDs transmitted to them by their customers.[45]

Although Hawaii had passed a national law in 1941 criminalizing prostitution, planning for military prostitution went forward as U.S. military and local authorities (including the governor's office and the police department) worked out a regulatory system.[46] Initially, 250 prostitutes were registered as entertainers with the Honolulu Police Department. In addition to paying an annual fee of $1.00, these licensed "entertainers" were required to have regular medical exams and to refrain from buying any property in Hawaii, owning a car, going out after 10:30 p.m., or marrying a member of the U.S. armed forces.[47] At the same time, the U.S. Army and Navy opened condom distribution centers in areas with a high level of prostitution activity.[48]

Organized military prostitution in Hawaii built on a history of racism in the prewar sex industry on the islands. Before World War II, brothels appeared to be segregated, in that there was one entrance for white male customers and another for customers of color. This strategy was predicated on the belief that white men did not want prostitutes who they thought were also having sex with men of color. Although the same women often serviced both white men and men of color, the separate doors gave the illusion of prostitute, as well as customer, separation. During the war, when a greater share of the customers were white (military) men, brothel owners became increasingly concerned about offending prejudiced white soldiers; many brothels simply stopped serving men of color altogether.[49]

Monrovia, Liberia

Much less well publicized is the organization of prostitution for troops stationed in the African country of Liberia during World War II. A U.S. battalion, consisting of mainly white officers and mainly black enlisted men, was secretly stationed at the Firestone Plantation in Monrovia, where it guarded the production of rubber used by the United States for military equipment. According to one of the officers stationed there, the U.S. military expressed concern about the unregulated and unprotected sex that its enlisted men were purportedly engaging in with local women. The military leadership responded to this concern by building and operating two brothels—"Paradise" and "Shangra La"—open *only* to African-American troops—another example of the acting out of racism in militarized prostitution. The brothels were open daily from 6 to 10 p.m., and the prostitutes working in them were regularly checked by U.S. Medical Corps staff for STDs and other infectious diseases.[50] The objective, as usual, was to protect the health and well-being of the soldiers.

Japan's "Comfort Women"

Perhaps the most notorious militarized prostitution of the World War II era was the Japanese military's sexual enslavement of Asian women for the recreational use of its troops. Between 1942 and 1945, as many as 200,000 Asian women were forced to serve as prostitutes, or "comfort women," for Japanese troops. The great majority (an estimated 80%) of "conscripted" women were Korean, but Filipina, Chinese, Burmese, and Thai women were also among those enslaved during the war.[51] The women were usually abducted—taken from their homes or communities—and often beaten and raped before being enslaved in makeshift housing around military bases, where they were forced to provide sex to as many as 100 soldiers a day.[52] "Comfort stations" were located in virtually all places occupied by Japanese troops. In fact, the World War II enslavement of women followed at least a decade of militarized captive prostitution by the Japanese Imperial Army. In the mid-1930s, following its invasion of China, the Japanese military organized and opened army brothels for Japanese troops in China.[53] It also operated brothels for its troops in the Philippines, Korea, and Malaysia.[54]

During World War II, the comfort women were forcibly trafficked around East and Southeast Asia. As the U.N. Special Rapporteur on Violence Against Women describes it, the government of Japan "shipped girls and women like military supplies throughout the vast area of Asia and the Pacific that Japanese troops controlled from the Siberian border to the equator."[55] Japanese records show comfort women placed on supply lists, under the headings of "ammunition" or "amenities."[56] In Korea, some women were said to be "recruited" under an "official labor draft," called into service to "strengthen the Japanese war effort." The Japanese name for this draft translates in English to "Voluntarily Committing Body Corps for Labor."[57]

Once placed in a comfort station, the women–amenities were subjected to a rigid set of behavioral rules and the requisite regular medical exams. Their lives were filled with extreme and routinized acts of violence, including rapes, physical assaults, and murders. In fact, an estimated 70%–80% of the comfort women did not survive the violence they endured at the hands of the Japanese army![58] Some of them were executed by Japanese soldiers as World War II came to an end. In one mass murder, in Micronesia, the Japanese army executed 70 comfort women in one night, just prior to the arrival of U.S. troops.[59]

After Japan was defeated and occupied by Allied—largely U.S.—soldiers, the Japanese government opened up its existing comfort stations to U.S. troops.[60] The U.S. military subsequently asked for additional comfort stations to be built for their use. In a 1945 meeting between the surgeon general of the U.S. Army and the chief of Tokyo's public health system, a decision was made to divide responsibility for old and new comfort stations between the Tokyo public health system and U.S. Colonel C. F. Sams, chief of the U.S. Army's Public Health and Welfare Department.[61] At the end of the war, about 400,000 U.S. troops occupied Japan; 2 years later, about half of them were still there.[62]

Comfort women enslaved during the war have courageously come forth in recent years to tell their stories and to demand recognition and reparations from the Japanese government.[63] Their stories are horrific. One woman, for example, testified that she was repeatedly and brutally raped and eventually became pregnant. Soldiers used a bayonet to cut out her fetus and then her uterus.[64] Tomasa Salinog, a Filipina former comfort woman, told how soldiers broke into her home in the middle of the night, decapitated her father, and dragged her to a military installation, where she was raped by two soldiers and beaten until she was unconscious. Tomasa was 13 years old at the time.[65] And, in an article that appeared in *Ms.*, reporters gave voice to Julia Porras, also kidnapped at age 13 from her home in the Philippines by Japanese troops.[66] Julia described being enslaved in a tunnel, where she was raped by four to five soldiers every day for 8 months during the latter part of the war. Julia told no one about her torture for the following 48 years, until, emboldened by the testimony of another victim, she spoke out: "I knew nothing about sex. . . . I wept and wept because of the pain. My body shook, I passed out. Every day, different soldiers came to rape me. That whole time, my vagina was bloody and swollen and all I had was a towel to cover myself."[67]

After many victim testimonies and unheeded calls for recognition, eighteen Filipina former comfort women filed a class action suit against the Japanese government calling for an apology and monetary compensation.[68] Finally, in 1993, the Japanese government admitted to and apologized for wrongfully sexually enslaving comfort women during World War II, and stated that these actions were a "grave affront to the honor and dignity of large number(s) of women."[69] In 1995, a private fund (initiated by the Japanese government) was set up to pay compensation to 300 former comfort women. The fund, however, has failed to raise much money, and payment, at any rate, is limited to a very small percentage of the former comfort women.[70] The Japanese government itself has refused to pay reparations, claiming that it is not their responsibility to do so.[71] While advocacy for reparations continues, nothing can repair the damage done to these women by the Japanese army, which organized and operated the comfort stations with a "vast infrastructure and [set of] resources" at their disposal.[72]

Today, Japan's sex industry is one of the most sizable and profitable in the world. Earnings from the sex sector account for from 1% to 3% of Japan's gross domestic product; and child prostitution, pornography, and sex tourism are all on the rise.[73] Japan is a major destination site for women trafficked for prostitution from all over the world, including the Asian countries from which many of the comfort women were taken in the 1930s and 1940s. At the beginning of the 2000s, there were well over 150,000 foreign women working as prostitutes in Japan. Over half of them are Filipinas, and sizable numbers are from Thailand, the NIS, and other Eastern European countries; but women are trafficked to Japan for prostitution from all over the world, including Indonesia, Malaysia, Myanmar, Cambodia, Laos, Vietnam, Korea, and Sri Lanka in Asia, as well as countries in Africa and Latin America.[74]

The Korean War

Like the Philippines, Korea was under Japanese rule until the end of World War II, when Allied troops—mainly U.S. troops in the south and Soviet troops in the north—occupied the country. Although there was some expectation that the north and south would eventually be reunited, disagreements between the occupying Americans and Soviets could not be resolved, and the land remained divided. The split between the north and the south erupted into the Korean War in 1950, and active combat continued until 1953. During and after the Korean War (up until the early 1970s, when the United States finally withdrew the bulk of its troops), some 6 million American soldiers served in Korea.[75] The north and south remained divided and are known today as the communist state of North Korea (officially the Democratic People's Republic of Korea) and the more capitalist, Westernized state of South Korea (officially the Republic of Korea).

The occupation of South Korea by American forces after World War II was accompanied by an increase in "camptown" (in Korean, *kijich'on*) prostitution, in which Korean women moved to and congregated around military bases, selling sex and sometimes other services (e.g., laundry, shopping) to soldiers.[76] These emergent camptowns were initially dependent on a military customer base. Camptown prostitution prior to the occupation had operated informally and without regulation; but with the arrival of U.S. troops, militarized prostitution became more organized, evolving eventually into a well-developed sex industry.

During and after the Korean War, camptowns were organized by American and Korean authorities working together. Military prostitutes were required to register with the Korean government, and bar and brothel owners were enlisted to specialize in R & R services around military bases.[77] The war left many women without food or shelter and with a need to escape the bombs and gunfire; the camptowns provided them a means of survival.[78] Although the active combat eventually ended, the camptowns survived, changing over the years to accommodate alterations in military presence and civilian consumer demand

In the late 1950s, the United States and the Republic of Korea signed the Mutual Defense Treaty, identifying each other as "alliance partners" and formally giving the United States the right to keep troops in Korea, along with a guarantee of the provision of R & R sites for American soldiers stationed in or visiting the country.[79] At the end of the 1960s, as Katharine Moon notes, there were in South Korea more than "20,000 registered prostitutes available to 'service' approximately 62,000 U.S. soldiers."[80]

Today, the United States and the Republic of Korea have a Status of Forces Agreement similar to that between the United States and the Philippines. The SoFA provides for a continuing U.S. military presence in Korea, as well as a "supportive environment for the US military forces." Again, U.S. soldiers are for the most part protected from criminal prosecution by Korean authorities.[81] As of 2003, there were 37,000 U.S. troops stationed at 96 sites throughout Korea.[82] In addition to these soldier–customers, there are a growing number of male sex tourists who come to Korea through organized group tours.[83]

According to official sources, there are currently an estimated 18,000 registered and at least 9,000 unregistered prostitutes working around U.S. military bases in Korea; some believe the numbers are much higher.[84] An estimated 5,000 of these women have been trafficked to Korea from other countries. Among them are approximately 1,000 Filipinas and a substantial number of women from the NIS and other Eastern European countries, as well as from China. Although their numbers are not yet as large, more and more women are being trafficked into the South Korean sex industry from Sri Lanka, Nepal, and Bangladesh, as well as from countries in South America.[85]

The 12 largest U.S. military stations in South Korea all have neighboring camptowns with bars licensed by the Korean government, but which are off-limits to Koreans. In 2000, an estimated 2 million customers spent time in these camptowns.[86] *Time* magazine reporter Donald Macintyre describes the camptown in Tongduchon, which is "barely 100 meters from [U.S.] Camp Casey's main gate," as a "seedy mile of sleazy bars, greasy-spoon restaurants and shops," but says that it is "the bars that rule the strip: dimly lit dives with names like U.S.A., Las Vegas and Sexy Club," and fronted by (largely Filipina and Russian) prostitutes urging the soldiers to come inside.[87] One of the soldier–customers told Macintyre that the "women here have been tricked" in that they are "told they're going to be bartending or waitressing, but once they get here, things are different." According to Macintyre, "the fact that the women may have been forced into prostitution doesn't seem to bother most of their soldier–patrons."[88]

The Vietnam War

The Vietnam War, like the Korean War, was a civil conflict between the north (a communist stronghold) and the south (a more capitalist and Western-influenced region). Concerned about "communist insurgencies" into the south, U.S. President Dwight Eisenhower approved the deployment of 760 U.S. troops to South Vietnam in 1959. By the early 1960s, the U.S. troop buildup in Vietnam was well under way (the number rose to 11,300 by 1961, and to 16,300 in 1962). At its peak in 1968, some 536,000 U.S. soldiers were fighting alongside South Vietnamese against North Vietnamese.[89]

The bar and club scene in Vietnam expanded with the growth in the number of military bases, installations, and soldiers in the country.

Throughout the 1960s, brothels opened around the military bases, and prostitution increased in designated prostitution zones in towns close to the bases as well as in Saigon.[90] In addition, the U.S. military leadership allowed military "brothels" to operate at some bases. That is, soldiers could bring prostitutes onto the base, where the women were officially treated as "local national guests." Such was the case at the U.S. base at Longbinh, near Saigon, where, reportedly, "soldiers could take onto the base as a local national guest any of the 50 to 60 girls who waited outside."[91]

By the late 1960s, the demand for prostitution services began to outstrip the supply of local women, and recruitment efforts expanded. In addition to the procurement of prewar "bar girls," war refugees, and war rape victims in Vietnam, recruitment spread to neighboring countries, such as Laos and Thailand.[92] According to Susan Brownmiller, when it came to trafficking, the U.S. military "kept its hand partially clean by leaving the procurement and price arrangements to Vietnamese civilians." Once the women had been successfully recruited, however, the "health and security features of the trade" were "controlled and regulated" by the United States.[93]

In 1967, militarized prostitution for Vietnam War soldiers took a new turn when the U.S. military signed a treaty with Thailand for the latter's provision of R & R services for U.S. troops visiting or stationed there.[94] Together with Thai officials, the United States successfully obtained funds from international lending institutions such as Chase Manhattan and Bank of America for the Thai government to build up the R & R industry. These funds (altogether approximately $4 million) were formally referred to as "investments," but in fact they were used to build many new R & R sites—which some soldiers came to refer to as "intoxication and intercourse" sites.[95] During the Vietnam War there were at least five U.S. military bases in Thailand, where 40,000 to 50,000 soldiers were stationed. Additionally, between 1966 and 1969, as many as 70,000 U.S. soldiers were sent to Thailand for R & R.[96]

In 1957, an estimated 20,000 prostitutes were working in Thailand. By 1964, that number had grown to 400,000, and by 1972, when the United States withdrew its main combat troops from Vietnam, there were at least 500,000 working prostitutes in the country.[97] From there on, the Thai sex industry simply exploded. By the end of the 1970s, Thailand, and most notably Bangkok, was the "sex capital" of the world.[98] By the end of the Vietnam War, Thai businesspeople and the Thai economy itself had become financially dependent on the sex industry. After the war, some American servicemen stayed in Thailand, themselves opening or investing in bar and club businesses there. These relocated entrepreneurs came to be known as MIBs (soldiers "missing in Bangkok").[99]

Today there are 2 million to 3 million prostitutes working in Thailand,[100] and an estimated 200,000 to 300,000 foreign women are trafficked into prostitution in Thailand from other countries every year.[101] Moreover, a reported 100,000 to 200,000 Thai women are currently working as prostitutes in other countries as disparate as the Netherlands, South Africa, the United States and Canada, Great Britain, Australia, India, Malaysia, Germany, Japan, and countries in the Middle East.[102]

The Thai sex industry continues to serve U.S. military personnel. In fact, during the 1991 Gulf War, U.S. soldiers were regularly sent to Thailand for R & R at sites still approved by the U.S. military.[103] In the 1990s, however, the real growth in consumers came from organized sex tours to the country. By the late 1990s, over 7 million tourists were coming to Thailand annually, and its tourism industry was valued at almost $8 billion. An estimated 65% of the tourists are single men on vacation.[104]

Tentacles of Organized Military Prostitution

As Kathleen Barry suggests, the "sexual demands of military men stationed in Third World countries have produced markets that are constantly replenished with women who are bought by traveling businessmen or military men on R & R leave."[105] Relatedly, she notes that sex industrialization follows from the "massive deployment of women for military prostitution during wars or foreign occupations," as well as from the "development of tourist industries that bring in foreign exchange for economic development."[106] It might be added that collective male demand for prostitution, or what I call "congregational prostitution," occurs in quasi-military as well as civilian settings, where it can also contribute to long-term sex industrialization.

Congregational Prostitution

It is almost a truism that wherever and whenever sizable groups of men congregate away from their homes and families—whether to fight or to seek refuge from fighting, to keep the peace, to work, or to play—demand for prostitution increases. To the extent that such congregations are regularized or institutionalized, the sex trade around them typically becomes organized. The well-documented emergence of a thriving prostitution industry in Cambodia following the arrival of 10,000 U.N. peacekeeping troops (including Europeans, Asians, and Africans) in the early 1990s provides one such example.[107] The number of women and girls working in prostitution in Cambodia grew from an estimated 1,500 in 1990 to 20,000 by 1993.[108] The demand for sexual services in Cambodia, spurred largely by the presence of the U.N. troops at this time, led to an increase in the trafficking of women to Cambodia for prostitution—most notably from Vietnam, but also from China and other East Asian source countries.[109] After the peacekeeping troops left Cambodia (in 1993), demand for, and thus the supply of, prostitutes initially declined. But a sex industry infrastructure lingered, and, as Donna Hughes points out, "economic liberalization" policies then provided an opportunity for "predatory entrepreneurs and increased forms of sexual exploitation" in the country.[110] By 1996, some 57,000 women and girls (many trafficked there from Vietnam, but also from other countries, including China, the Philippines, Moldova, and Romania) were working in prostitution in Cambodia.[111]

Cambodia's experience is clearly not the exception. As journalist Barbara Crossette wrote in 2003, one of "the uglier stories surrounding international peacekeeping in recent years is that U.N. operations too often fuel booms in local prostitution, frequently involving women abducted or duped by criminal trafficking gangs to be forced into brothels."[112] Following the end of the contentious civil conflict in the former Yugoslavia, 50,000 peacekeepers came to the region. The peacekeepers, mainly male, included about 36,000 military troops and over 2,000 U.N. International Police Task Force officers, along with civilian police, staff from other U.N. agencies, and staff from NGOs. According to Madeleine Rees, the head of the U.S. Office of the High Commissioner for Human Rights, there "is virtually no dispute any more that the issue of trafficking arose predominantly with the arrival of the peacekeeping troops in 1995."[113] Within a short time, hundreds of brothels opened, many of which were "staffed by girls and women from neighboring countries who had been kidnapped or lured by promises of respectable employment and sold into sexual slavery."[114] An officer investigating sex trafficking and forced prostitution in the area found that U.N. peacekeepers frequented clubs and bars where girls "as young as 15" were forced to do nude dancing and to have sex with customers. She also found evidence of some U.N. peacekeepers' involvement in prostitution rings in the region.[115]

Prostitution also soared in Mozambique following the arrival of peacekeeping troops there (including servicemen from countries as diverse as Bangladesh, Zambia, Italy, Portugal, Uruguay, and Botswana) in 1992. By 1993, the sex trade in Mozambique had become so big that a military officer among the peacekeepers was assigned as the "Liaison Officer," whose job was to mediate between the troops and the prostitutes and their trafficker–pimps.[116] In her 1996 study, Gracha Machel, the former first lady of Mozambique, found that some men in the peacekeeping forces were themselves recruiting girls (mainly between the ages of 12 and 18) for prostitution businesses.[117]

Peacekeepers in several other countries have also contributed to the expansion of prostitution there. Such was the case with the arrival of peacekeepers in Rwanda in 1995.[118] More recently, peacekeeping troops have prostituted women in parts of West Africa—especially Liberia, Guinea, and Sierra Leone—offering them food and medicine in exchange for sex. A sizable force of U.N. peacekeeping troops in Sierra Leone since 1999 (over 16,000 of them as of 2003) has contributed to the growth of the sex industry there. In newly independent East Timor, where U.N. peacekeepers are still stationed, the trafficking of Thai women into East Timorese brothels has become commonplace.[119]

In a U.N. report on the impact of armed conflict on women and women's role in "peacebuilding," authors Elisabeth Rehn (a former defense minister of Finland) and Ellen Johnson Sirleaf (a former Liberian minister) conclude that "rape, trafficking in women and children, sexual enslavement and child abuse often coexist alongside peacekeeping operations." They go on to say that U.N. policies are "extremely ambiguous in regulating interaction between U.N. peacekeeping personnel and the local female population."[120]

Congregational prostitution also occurs in settings where large groups of men live and work without families, often at some distance from their homes or home communities. The mining towns of Amazonia in Brazil are illustrative. Women and girls are regularly trafficked for prostitution into the relatively isolated mining towns scattered throughout the Amazonia region.[121] These job-specific towns are typically run by the mine owners, who set the "law" to their own advantage, which includes keeping employees happy. One strategy for doing so has been the provision of controlled prostitution, into which women and girls are trafficked and forced to live and work under the familiar debt bondage system. As described by one researcher, the towns are lined with bars and brothels, where owners offer "14-year-olds for sex on the menu."[122] Girls who refuse to cooperate or try to escape have in some instances been killed.[123]

In some places, the congregational consumer market includes a mix of military and civilian men, who may arrive and depart situationally or seasonally. Prostitution swells with the arrival and temporary stay of military troops in coastal towns. Prostitution demand increases, for example, whenever the U.S. Seventh Fleet docks at one of its liberty ports, such as in Kenya or the Philippines.[124] When sailors are not in port, working women and girls sometimes find a clientele among seasonal fishermen or some other situational workforce. Along the coast of Sierra Leone young girls sell sex—for as little as five cents a customer—to foreign soldiers or to fishermen from Portugal, Spain, and Russia.[125]

Women servicing varied foreign and local customer groups sometimes express preferences among them. Brazilian prostitutes who work around the port of Rio de Janeiro, for example, have reported that they favor Filipino clients over other sailor groups. Brazilian Denize Oliveira, who has made a living from prostitution for 15 years, explains that the Filipino sailors are considerate, "easy to do business with," and "treat us like equals." The "whites," on the other hand, Oliveira continues, "treat us like whores."[126] In spite of their own customer preferences, prostitutes servicing customers from different countries recognize that success in their business is enhanced through their familiarity with culture-specific masculinities. Many are aware of the role of militarized prostitution in shoring up masculine egos, in helping their male customers to feel "manly enough to act as soldiers."[127] Part of the trade with tricks, then, is to know which versions of masculinity apply to men of different cultures, races, or ethnicities.

In the reverse direction, the tricks often apply racist or cultural stereotypes to the women servicing them. Racism and ethnocentrism are ubiquitous in military life, but they are particularly blatant in the attitudes and behaviors of dominant-race men toward minority women.

Racist Images of Sexualized "Others"

"Bill," a Vietnam War veteran, says that he found the Vietnamese villagers to be friendly and that when he was wounded, "villagers saved his life." He believes that the military power of the North Vietnamese was superior to that of the South Vietnamese, but he admits to a hatred of the Viet Cong (North Vietnamese) and the atrocities he believes they committed during the war. As for respite from battle for the U.S. troops there, he reports, prostitutes and "blacklisted bars" were very popular. Prostitution, he says, was preferable to marrying a Vietnamese girl and "having to bring a gook back home."[128]

Western soldiers' sexual use of women of color in developing countries is backed by racist stereotypes of such women.[129] Long-standing among Americans and other Westerners are racist stereotypes of Asian women as sexually compliant and anxious to please. In her memoir of growing up in

Asia during the Vietnam War, Le Ly Hayslip writes that U.S. soldiers simply assumed that all Asian women with whom they came into contact were or were willing to be prostitutes.[130] Rita Nakashima Brock, an Asian-American who grew up on military bases around the world, including Germany, the United States, and Okinawa, reports that in her experience, any girl who even looked Asian was assumed by soldiers to be sexually available.[131]

Of course, sexualized racist stereotypes and beliefs are not limited to U.S. soldiers. According to several reports, the sexual enslavement and abuse of Chinese, Korean, and Filipina women by Japanese soldiers was made easier by Japanese feelings of racial superiority to their Asian neighbors.[132] Nor is such racism limited to soldiers. Researcher June Kane found that many of the racist stereotypes about Asian women described above were also expressed in her interviews with civilian sex tour customers from a variety of countries.[133]

Racism has also begun to play a role in the changing demand for foreign women in countries that have in the past relied on Asian women for the prostitution supply. Increased sex trafficking from the NIS and other Eastern European countries reflects a growing demand for white prostitutes in Western European and Middle Eastern countries, as well as in Asian countries such as Thailand and Japan.[134]

Sexual exploitation of women who have traveled or been trafficked from developing countries to more affluent ones also involves racial or ethnic hierarchies. Nepali women trafficked into Middle Eastern countries such as Jordan, Saudi Arabia, and Kuwait are reportedly viewed as lesser "others," allowing for a rationalization of their maltreatment.[135] In countries with oppressive racial policies, skin color figures into prostitution value. Under apartheid and its legacy in South Africa, for example, white and light-skinned women and girls work in brothels, whereas dark-skinned prostitutes typically work in the streets or the seedier bars.[136]

Racialized stereotypes have also cast women in Latin America in the role of sexual object for soldiers and sex tour customers. Moreover, within some Latin American countries, as in other regions, sexual hierarchies based on ethnicity or skin color reflect not only customer preferences, but also prostitution policies. The stationing of British-born and Nepali soldiers in Belize (in accordance with a Belize–British defense pact) has resulted in a more organized prostitution industry in that country. Brothels serving the base employ both Latina and Afro-Belizean prostitutes; and while the British soldiers appear to be customers of both, the Nepali soldiers prefer the Latina prostitutes. Moreover, officially approved brothels employ mainly Latina prostitutes.[137]

In other instances, soldiers themselves are segregated by race for R & R activities. Such is the case among U.S. soldiers in Okinawa. As one journalist reports, "the nightclub culture around the Okinawa bases is almost as segregated as the Jim Crow south."[138] And here the women often display their own racial preferences. Girls who prefer black men, known as *kokujo*, typically "paint their skin cocoa, weave their hair in cornrows," and "dress like Lil' Kim."[139]

In the summer of 2001, an African-American Air Force sergeant, Timothy Woodland, was charged with the rape of a young woman in an area of clubs and bars in Okinawa. At his trial, Woodland testified that the sex was consensual and that he frequently had sex with local women in bar parking lots. In March of 2002, Woodland was convicted of the rape and sentenced to 2 years and 8 months in a Japanese prison.[140] Some have contended that sexual assaults by military personnel occur regularly on the islands, but that racism toward African-Americans (on the part of both the United States and Japan) is reflected in selective law enforcement practices that privilege and protect the criminal behavior of white men.[141] As discussed previously, the Status of Forces Agreement between the United States and Okinawa protects U.S. servicemen from prosecution under Okinawan–Japanese jurisdiction. Woodland was only the second U.S. serviceman to be handed over to the Okinawans since the current SoFA took effect.[142]

Concluding Comments

Demand for prostitution is virtually always high when and where men gather collectively for war, as well as for peacekeeping and other kinds of work and play. However, in the last half of the twentieth century, it has been the buildup of organized *military* prostitution for soldiers' R & R—usually in a developing country where women have been objectified as foreign "others" by military customers—that has set the stage for a country's or city's sex industrialization. Once a prostitution economy has become firmly rooted in a town or country, sex trade entrepreneurs move in to either share in or take over the industry. GIven military *and* expanding civilian customer bases in poor countries with poor women (or given an expanding civilian customer base in affluent countries with poor women), sex industries flourish. And, as demand begins to outstrip supply, or demands for particular groups of women change, the trafficking of women into prostitution goes global.

Notes

1. Dara Colwell (2001), "Sex Industry Sent Topsy-Turvy by Terror," *Alternet.org,* November 16, available at http://www.alternet.org/story.html/StoryID=11928.
2. Anne-Marie Hilsdon (1995), *Madonnas and Martyrs: Militarism and Violence in the Philippines* (Quezon City: Ateneo de Manila University Press). [Cited in Jane Margold (2003), "Women, Violence, and the Reinvolvement of the U.S. Military in the Philippines," *Human Rights Dialogue* 2.10 (Fall):"Violence Against Women," available at http://www.cceia.org/viewMedia.php/prmID/1071 (4 pp.).]
3. Kathleen Barry (1995), *The Prostitution of Sexuality* (New York: New York University Press).
4. Ibid.
5. Gwyn Kirk, Rachel Cornwell, and Margo Okazawa-Rey (1999), "In Focus: Women and the U.S. Military in East Asia," *Foreign Policy in Focus* 4, A Joint Project of the Interhemispheric Resource Center and the Institution for Policy Analysis, ed. by Tom Barry (IRC) and Martha Honey (IPS), available at http://www.globalspin.org/women_asia_usmilitary.html.
6. Sister Mary Soledad Perpinan (1990), "Militarism and the Sex Industry in the Philippines," reproduced (slightly edited) from pp. 149–153 in *ISIS Women's World* 1990–1991, 24 (Winter).
7. Barry (1995), op. cit.; Aida Santos and Cecilia Hofmann (1997), "Prostitution and the Bases: A Continuing Saga of Exploitation," Coalition Against Trafficking in Women, available at http://www.ibon.org/news/if/02/65.htm (9 pp.).
8. Jane Margold (2003), "Women, Violence, and the Reinvolvement of the U.S. Military in the Philippines," *Human Rights Dialogue* 2.10 (Fall):"Violence Against Women," available at http://www.cceia.org/viewMedia.php/prmID/1071 (4 pp.); Cynthia Enloe (1993), *The Morning After: Sexual Politics at the End of the Cold War* (Berkeley: University of California Press).
9. "Stop Sex Trafficking of Filipino Women and Children!: A Primer on Sex Trafficking" (retrieved January 10, 2004), available at http://members.tripod.com/~gabriela_p/8-articles/990601_prose.html (8 pp.).
10. Gustavo Capdevilla (2002), "Filipinas, Russians Trafficked for US Military Bases in Korea," *Philippines Today*, November 9, available at http://www.philippinestoday.net/ofwcorner/ofw11_5.htm (2 pp.); Kanaga Raja (2002), "Trafficked Filipino Women Servicing American Soldiers in Korea," IBON Foundation, Inc., vol. VIII, no. 65, available at http://www.ibon.org/news/if/02/65.htm (2 pp.).

11. Raja (2002), op. cit.
12. Kirk et al. (1999), op. cit. The two agreement titles—Visiting Forces Agreement (VFA) and Status of Forces Agreement (SoFA)—are used interchangeably in the literature.
13. Dario Agnote (1998), "Sex Trade Key Part of S.E. Asian Economies," *Kyodo News*, August 18; Diana Mendoza (1998), "RP Has 400,000 Prostitutes," *Today*, February 25. [Sources cited in Donna M. Hughes, Laura Joy Sporcic, Nadine Z. Mendelsohn, and Vanessa Chirgwin (1999), *Factbook on Global Sexual Exploitation*, "The Philippines" (Coalition Against Trafficking in Women), available at http://www.uri.edu/artsci/wms/hughes/factbook.htm (12 pp.).]
14. Kirk et al. (1999), op. cit.
15. Mendoza (1998), op. cit.; GABRIELA (1997), "Statistics and the State of the Philippines," July 24. [Cited in Hughes et al. (1999), op. cit., "The Philippines."]
16. Mendoza (1998), op. cit.
17. Halinah Todd (retrieved February 3, 2004), "Prostitution," *Mobilizer* (Summer) (New York: National Mobilization for Survival, Campaign Against Military Prostitution), available at http://eserver.org/feminism/prostituion.txt; Liz Kelly (2000), "Wars Against Women: Sexual Violence, Sexual Politics and the Militarised State," pp. 45–65 in *States of Conflict: Gender, Violence and Resistance*, ed. by Susie Jacobs, Ruth Jacobson, and Jennifer Marchbank (New York: Zed Books); Santos and Hofmann (1997), op. cit.; Barry (1995), op. cit.
18. Barry (1995), op. cit., pp. 150–151.
19. "Demonstrators at Los Angeles International Airport Target Sex Tour to the Philippines" (1998), Captive Daughters (April 18), available at http://www.captivedaughters.org/press-4-18-98.htm. [Cited in Hughes et al. (1999), op. cit., "The Philippines."]
20. Perpinan (1990), op. cit.
21. Sol F. Juvida (1997), "Philippines—Children: Scourge of Child Prostitution," *IPS*, October 12. [Cited in Hughes et al. (1999), op. cit., "The Philippines."]
22. Ibid.
23. Margold (2003), op. cit.
24. "Visiting Forces Agreement" (1998) (signed by Domingo L. Siazon, Jr. and Thomas C. Hubbard in Manila), available at http://senate.hypermart.net/vfa_text.html (12 pp.). For criticisms of and concerns about VFA/SoFAs more generally, see Kirk et al. (1999), op. cit.
25. William Pomeroy (1997), "US Moves to Restore Its Military in Philippines," *People's Weekly World*, November 1.
26. Margold (2003), op. cit.

27. Santos and Hofmann (1997), op. cit., p. 8.
28. Ibid., p. 8.
29. Kelly (2000), op. cit., pp. 57–58.
30. Joshua S. Goldstein (2001), *War and Gender: How Gender Shapes the War System and Vice Versa* (Cambridge: Cambridge University Press)
31. Ibid.; Susan Brownmiller (1975), *Against Our Will: Men, Women and Rape* (New York: Fawcett Columbine).
32. Ryan Masaaki Yokota (1998), "Okinawans Fight for End to U.S. Occupations," Okinawan Peace Network of Los Angeles (October 6), available at http://www.uchinanchu.org/resources/bruin)article_100698.htm (p. 2 of 3).
33. Suzuyo Takazato (2001), "Sisters in Okinawa," pp. 260–263 in *Women's Lives: Multicultural Perspectives*, 2nd ed., by Gwyn Kirk and Margo Okazawa-Rey (Mountain View, CA: Mayfield).
34. [Quoted in Lisa Takeuchi Cullen (2001), "Sex and Race in Okinawa," *Time*, August 27, p. 41.]
35. Takazato (2001), op. cit.
36. Ibid.
37. Gwyn Kirk, Rachel Cornwell, and Margo Okazawa-Rey (retrieved September 9, 2002), "Women and U.S. Military Presence" [KAISA-KA study], East Asia-US Women's Network Against Militarism, available at www.vonip.com/main/articles/womenmilitary.html.
38. Ibid.
39. Enloe (1993), op. cit.
40. Ibid.
41. Ibid.
42. Ibid.
43. Saundra Sturdevant and Brenda Stoltzfus (1992), *Let the Good Times Roll: Prostitution and the U.S. Military in Asia* (New York: New Press).
44. Teresa Bill (retrieved February 6, 2004), "Into the Marketplace: Working Class Women in 20th Century Hawaii," available at http://www.soc.hawaii.edu/hwhp/hawork/itm.overview.html; Jodi Tilsner (retrieved February 6, 2004), "Rosie the Riveter and Other Women World War II Heroes," available at http://www.u.arizona.edu/~kari/rosie.htm; Colwell (2001), op. cit; Enloe (2003), op. cit.
45. Beth Bailey and David Farber (1992), "Hotel Street: Prostitution and the Politics of War," *Radical History Review* (Winter), pp. 54–77.
46. Beth Bailey and David Farber (1992), *The First Strange Place: The Alchemy of Race and Sex in World War II Hawaii* (New York: Free Press).
47. Bill (2004), op. cit.; Tilsner (2004), op. cit.
48. Enloe (1993), op. cit.
49. Ibid.

50. George Abraham (2001), "Sex in World War II: The European Front," The History Channel, July 10.
51. There are numerous works on the "comfort women." See, for example, "Japan's Mass Rape and Sexual Enslavement of Women and Girls from 1932–1945: The 'Comfort Women' System" (retrieved December 27, 2003), *Case Watch,* available at http://www.cmht.con/casewatch/cases/cwcomfort2.htm (6 pp.); Helen Durham and Bebe Loff (2001), "Japan's 'Comfort Women,'" *Lancet* 357, p. 302; Nelia Sancho, ed. (1998), "The Case of the Filipino Comfort Women, Part II," *War Crimes on Asian Women: Military Sexual Slavery by Japan During World War II* (Manila: Asian Women's Human Rights Council); Mi Mi-Gyeong (1993), "Realities of the 'Comfort Women' in South Korea," in *War Victimization and Japan: Proceedings of the International Public Hearing Concerning Post-War Compensation of Japan* (Japan: Toho Shuppan).
52. Bailey and Farber (1992), "Hotel Street."
53. Sancho (1998), op. cit.
54. Durham and Loff (2001), op. cit.
55. "Japan's Mass Rape" (2003), op. cit. pp. 2–3.
56. Ibid., p. 3.
57. Ibid., p. 3.
58. Sancho (1998), op. cit.; Alice Yun Chai (1993), "Asian Pacific Feminist Coalition Politics: The *Chongshindae/Jugunianfu* ('Comfort Women') Movement," *Korean Studies* 17, pp. 67–91.
59. "Japan's Mass Rape" (2003), op. cit.
60. Yoshimi Yoshiaki (2000), *"Comfort Women": Sexual Slavery in the Japanese Military During World War II,* translated by Suzanne O'Brien (New York: Columbia University Press).
61. "Japan's Mass Rape" (2003), op. cit.
62. Joyce Howard Price (2003), "Rebuilding After War Takes Time," *The Washington Times,* available at http://washingtontimes.com/national/200330903-115834-9905r.htm.
63. For years, the Japanese government denied that it or its military had any part in the "comfort women" system (and at times, denied that it even existed), or that women were abducted and abused, let alone murdered, as part of organized military prostitution in World War II. Given the vast number of victims and witnesses, the government's continuing denials up until the early 1990s are shocking. As of 2001, history textbooks in schools in Japan did not mention the comfort women or the system of organized military prostitution ["Japan's Mass Rape" (2003)].
64. Durham and Loff (2001), op. cit.

65. Nelia Sancho (1997), "The 'Comfort Women' System during World War II: Asian Women as Targets of Mass Rape and Sexual Slavery by Japan," pp. 144–154 in *Gender and Catastrophe*, ed. by Ronit Lentin (London: Zed Books). [From testimony of Tomasa Salinog, cited in *Philippine "Comfort Women" Compensation Suit, Excerpts of the Complaint* (1993) (Manila: Task Force on the Filipino Comfort Women), p. 19.]
66. Sheila Coronel and Ninotchka Rosca (1993), "For the Boys: Filipinas Expose Years of Sexual Slavery by the U.S. and Japan," *Ms.* (November–December), pp. 11–15.
67. Ibid., p. 12.
68. Sancho (1998), op. cit.; Coronel and Rosca (1993), op. cit.
69. Angel Wilson (2000), " 'Comfort Women' Sue Japan," *The Oregonian*, September 19, A5.
70. Nicholas D. Kristof (1996), "Asian Brothels Force Ever-Younger Children to Serve AIDS-Wary Men," *The Oregonian*, June 12, A12.
71. Mainchi Shimbun (2000), "High Court Says Ex-Sex Slaves Not Entitled to Compensation," *Mainichi Daily News*, December 7, available at http://www.mainichi.co.jp/english/news/archive/200012/07/news03.html (3 pp.).
72. "Japan's Mass Rape" (2003), p. 3.
73. "WHO Notes Lucrative Asian Sex Trade" (2001), *Business World*, August 31.
74. Sources cited in Hughes et al. (1999), op. cit., "Japan"; Elif Kaban (1998), "UN Labour Body Urges Recognition of Sex Industry," Reuters 18 (August); Vladmir Isachenkov (1997), "Soviet Women Slavery Flourishes," Associated Press, November 6. For additional statistics, see "Worst Forms of Child Labour—Japan: Global March Against Child Labour," available at http://www.globalmarch.org/worstformsreport/world/japan.html.
75. Capdevilla (2002), op. cit.; Katharine H. S. Moon (1997), *Sex Among Allies: Military Prostitution in U.S.-Korea Relations* (New York: Columbia University Press).
76. Moon (1997), op. cit.
77. Mire Koikari (1999), "Rethinking Gender and Power in the U.S. Occupation of Japan, 1945–1952," *Gender & History* 11 (July), p. 320.
78. Elim Kim, "Research for the Reform of the Law on the Prevention of Prostitution," p. 89 (in Korean). [Cited in Moon (1997), op. cit., p. 28.]
79. Ibid.
80. Ibid., p. 30.
81. Peter Kloepping (2000), "The Korean/U.S. Status of Forces Agreement Under Scrutiny," *Asia Solidarity Quarterly* (Autumn), available at

http://www.pspd.org/pspd/asq/asq2/the.html (5 pp.). Kloepping argues that the wording of the U.S. SoFA with South Korea makes it much more difficult for the Korean government to prosecute American soldiers than do similar agreements that the United States has with Germany and Japan.

82. "United States—U.S. Military Bases—ROK-US Status of Forces Agreement (SoFA)" (retrieved February 6, 2004), available at http://sofa.jnbo.net/eng_sofa.html (3 pp.). See also East Asia/US Women's Network Against Militarism, "Korea" (retrieved September 9, 2002), available at http://www.apcjp.org/womens_network/skorea.htm (5 pp.); this source states that there are from 120 to 180 U.S. military bases and installations in South Korea.
83. Barry (1995), op. cit.
84. See references and citations in Hughes et al. (1999, retrieved September 8, 2002), op. cit., "Korea" (3 pp.). Kathleen Barry [(1995), op. cit.] states that there were from one to one-and-a-half-million prostitutes working in South Korea in the mid-1990s. Donald Macintyre [(2002), "Base Instincts," *Time–Asia*, August 12, available at http://www.time.com/time/asia/magazine/article/0,13673,50102812-333899,00.html (6 pp.)] believes that the numbers of prostitutes working around bases and in Korea overall are much higher than official estimates. Macintyre points out that in 2001 alone, 8,500 foreign women, mostly Filipinas and Russians, entered South Korea on entertainment visas.
85. Capdevilla (2002), op. cit.; Kirk et al. (2002), op. cit.
86. Macintyre (2002), op. cit.
87. Ibid., p. 1.
88. Ibid., p. 2 (both quotes).
89. For Vietnam War troop deployment data, see http://members.aol.com/warlibrary/vwatl.htm.
90. Barry (1995), op. cit.; Perpinan (1990), op. cit.
91. Barry (1995), op. cit., p. 133.
92. Mohamed Awad (1966), *Report on Slavery* (New York: United Nations), p. 198. [Cited in Barry (1995), op. cit., p. 132.]
93. Brownmiller (1975), op. cit., pp. 93–95.
94. Rita Nakashima Brock and Susan Brooks Thistlewaite (1996), *Casting Stones: Prostitution and Liberation in Asia and the United States* (Minneapolis, MN: Fortress Press); Meredeth Turshen and Briavel Holcomb, eds. (1993), *Women's Lives and Public Policy: The International Experience* (Westport, CT: Praeger).
95. Brock and Thistlewaite (1996), op. cit., p. 116.
96. Nantawan Boonprasat Lewis (1999), "Remembering Conquest: Religion, Colonization and Sexual Violence: A Thai Experience," pp. 4–17

in *Remembering Conquest; Feminist/Womanist Perspectives on Religion, Colonization, and Sexual Violence*, ed. by Nantawan Boonprasat Lewis and Marie M. Fortune (New York: Haworth).

97. Catherine Hill (1993), "Planning for Prostitution: An Analysis of Thailand's Sex Industry," pp. 133–134 in *Women's Lives and Public Policy: The International Experience*, ed. by Meredeth Turshen and Briavel Holcomb (Westport, CT: Praeger).
98. Perpinan (1990), op. cit.
99. Corie Hammers (2001), "International Trafficking in Women in the Asian Region in the Era of Globalization," unpublished master's thesis, Portland State University, Portland, OR.
100. Lewis (1999), op. cit.; Barry (1995), op. cit.
101. Lin Lean Lim (1998), *The Sex Sector: The Economic and Social Bases of Prostitution in Southeast Asia* (Geneva: International Labour Office).
102. Ibid.; also refer to sources in The Protection Project (2002), *Human Rights Report on Trafficking in Persons, Especially Women and Children: A Country-by-Country Report on a Contemporary Form of Slavery*, 2nd ed., "Thailand" (The Paul H. Nitze School of Advanced International Studies, Johns Hopkins University), pp. 535–544.
103. Turshen and Holcomb (1993), op. cit., p. 135. [Cited in Jennifer Latsetter (2000), "American Military-Base Prostitution," available at http://www.wm.edu/SO/monitor/spring2000/paper6.htm.]
104. Todd (2004), op. cit.; Lewis (1999), op. cit.
105. Barry (1995), op. cit., p. 126.
106. Ibid., pp. 122–123.
107. Felicity Hill (retrieved February 19, 2004), "Gender and Frontline Perspectives on Peacekeeping and the Brahimí Report," Women's International League for Peace and Freedom (March 1), available at www.wilpf.int.ch/publications/brahimireport.htm; Thalif Deen (2002), "UN Cracks Down on Sexual Exploitation by Peacekeepers," Inter Press Service, July 31, available at http://www.codewan.com.ph/CyberDyaryo/features/f2002_0731_05.htm (3 pp.); Donna M. Hughes (2000), "Welcome to the Rape Camp: Sexual Exploitation and the Internet in Cambodia," *Journal of Sexual Aggression*, available at http://www.uri/edu/artsci/wms/hughes/rapecamp.htm (26 pp.); Eva Arnvig (1993), "Child Prostitution in Cambodia: Did the UN Look Away?" *International Monitor* 10, pp. 4–6.
108. UNICEF–Cambodia (1996), "Towards a Better Future—An Analysis of the Situation of Children and Women in Cambodia," p. 145. [Cited in Hughes (2000), "Welcome to the Rape Camp," p. 5.]
109. Kelly (2000), op. cit.; June Kane (1998), *Sold for Sex* (Brookfield, VT: Ashgate).

110. Keo Kang and Im Phally (1995), "Notes on the March–April 1995 Rapid Appraisal of the Human Rights Vigilance of Cambodia on Child Prostitution and Trafficking," Human Rights Task Force on Cambodia, Phnom Penh, p. 3. [Cited in Hughes (2000), "Welcome to the Rape Camp," p. 5.]
111. Ibid. See also sources in The Protection Project (2002), op. cit., "Cambodia," pp. 96–101.
112. Barbara Crossette (2003), "Peacekeeping's Unsavory Side," *U.N. Wire*, June 11, available at http://www.unwire.org/Features/Columns/522_4898.asp (3 pp.).
113. [Quoted in Julia Stuart (2003), "Dark Side of Peacekeeping," *The Independent*, July 10, available at http://www.obv.org.uk/reports/2003/rpt20030710g.htm (p. 2 of 5).]
114. Ibid., p. 2 of 5.
115. Ibid.
116. Kane (1998), op. cit.
117. Deen (2002), op. cit.
118. Crossette (2003), op. cit.
119. Ibid.
120. Elisabeth Rehn and Ellen Johnson Sirleaf (2002), "Women, War and Peace: The Independent Experts' Assessment on the Impact of Armed Conflict on Women and Women's Role in Peacebuilding," U.N. Development Program for Women (UNIFEM). [Referred to and quoted in Crossette (2003), op. cit., p. 1.]
121. Carlos Bendana (1992), "Latin America: Alternatives for Latin American Street Children," Inter Press Service, June 16. [Cited in The Protection Project (2002), op. cit., "Brazil," p. 79.]
122. Kane (1998), op. cit., p. 13.
123. Ibid.
124. Mario Osava (2002), "Sex During Port Calls," Inter Press Service (October), available at http://www.philippinestoday.net/prelease/prelease2_1002.htm (2 pp.).
125. Kane (1998), op. cit.
126. Osava (2002), op. cit., p. 1.
127. Enloe (1993), op. cit., p. 145.
128. Paul Moore [Interviewer] (1974) (retrieved December 17, 2003). Interview: Americans in Vietnam Project, T. Harry Williams Center for Oral History Collection, Tape 1411, Side A, available at http://www.lib/lsu.edu/special/williams/abstracts/vietnam/marshall.html (2 pp.).
129. Barry (1995), op. cit.
130. Le Ly Hayslip, with Jay Wurts (1989), *When Heaven and Earth Changed Places* (New York: Doubleday).

131. Rita Nakashima Brock (1992), "Japanese Didn't Invent Military Sex Industry?" *The New York Times*, February 23 (Letter to the Editor). [Cited in Enloe (1993), op. cit.]
132. "Japan's Mass Rape" (2003); Cullen (2001), op. cit.; Sancho (1997), op. cit.
133. Kane (1998), op. cit.
134. Donna M. Hughes (2000), "The 'Natasha' Trade: The Transnational Shadow Market of Trafficking in Women," *Journal of International Affairs*, Special Issue: "In the Shadows: Promoting Prosperity or Undermining Stability?" 53 (Spring), pp. 625–651; Michael Specter (1998), "Traffickers' New Cargo: Naive Slavic Women," *The New York Times*, January 11, pp. 1, 6.
135. Kane (1998), op. cit.
136. Ibid.
137. Enloe (1993), op. cit.
138. Cullen (2001), op. cit.
139. Ibid., p. 39.
140. David Allen (2002), "Woodland Convicted of Rape, Sentenced to 32 Months in Japanese Prison," Portland Independent Media Center, March 28, available at http://portland.indymedia.org/en/2002/03/8657.shtml.
141. Cullen (2001), op. cit.
142. Allen (2002), op. cit.

8

Tackling Sex Trafficking and Enslaved Prostitution Now and into the Future

Tackling sex trafficking—now and into the future—is no small task. Sex trafficking is a well-established, highly profitable industry that operates not only with considerable impunity, but with very little citizen awareness of its existence. "Sex trafficking—what exactly *is* that?" became a familiar query as I talked to friends and colleagues about the research for this book. Those who did know what sex trafficking was were usually shocked to learn of its size and scope, and of its system of debt bondage and sexual enslavement.

In fairness, though, the question "What exactly is that?" is not so easily answered. While researchers and activists agree that forced trafficking and enslaved prostitution are harmful, they sometimes disagree about the framing and parameters of sex trafficking. Is sex trafficking, for example, *always* a violation of women's human rights, or is it even an act *inherently* harmful to women? What about cases in which women choose to migrate for prostitution and don't see themselves as victims of traffickers? Janice Raymond, a prominent researcher and activist in the Coalition Against Trafficking in Women, argues that sex trafficking *and* the sex trade (or, as she thinks of it, the prostituting of women) are both harmful to women and violations of their human rights, and that the distinction between involuntary and voluntary traffic is an artificial one. Raymond laments the fact that prostitution is sometimes treated as a woman's (human) right or a legitimate job choice, and that some groups working to curb "involuntary" sex trafficking (e.g., the Dutch Foundation Against Trafficking in Women and its "offshoot," the Global Alliance Against Trafficking in Women) resist efforts to name prostitution itself as a violation of human rights.[1] This division muddies legal and law enforcement strategies, as some argue for legalization of prostitution but criminalization of "involuntary" trafficking, while others argue that legalizing prostitution and registering prostitutes not only does not improve the lives of prostitutes, but also makes it even more difficult to curb sex trafficking.[2]

Defining Sex Trafficking and Sexual Exploitation as Universal Harms

International Conventions

Although the above issues remain divisive among feminist/womanist groups, most official international constructions view both trafficking *and* prostitution as harmful. The 1950 U.N. Convention for the Suppression of the Traffic in Persons and of the Exploitation of the Prostitution of Others makes its position clear in its initial declaration that "prostitution and the accompanying evil of the traffic in persons for the purpose of prostitution are incompatible with the dignity and worth of the human person and endanger the welfare of the individual, the family and the community."[3]

There is also international precedent for considering the trafficking of women into enslaved prostitution as a violation of their human rights. The Universal Declaration of Human Rights, adopted by the U.N. General Assembly in 1948, states in Article 4 that "no one shall be held in slavery or servitude; slavery and the slave trade shall be prohibited in all their forms."[4] And, in Article 8 of the 1966 U.N. Covenant on Civil and Political Rights, the enslavement prohibition is reinforced, in that "no one shall be held in slavery; slavery and the slavery-trade in all their forms shall be prohibited."[5] Both prostitution and trafficking into prostitution have been framed as discrimination as well. Article 6 of the U.N. Convention on the Elimination of All Forms of Discrimination Against Women obliges state parties to "take all measures, including legislation, to suppress all forms of traffic in women and exploitation of the prostitution of women."[6]

Finally, trafficking women into enslaved prostitution has been treated as an act of violence against women, a framing about which there is considerable consensus, at least among women activists around the world. At the Fourth World Conference on Women in Beijing in 1995, combating violence against women was a goal strongly shared by conference attendees. And, in the "Violence Against Women" section of the conference's

Platform for Action, one "strategic objective" was to "eliminate trafficking in women and assist victims of violence due to prostitution and trafficking."[7]

While there is variation in emphases, official definitions of human trafficking are beginning to merge, with most recognizing trafficking as a crime even when the victim is not taken by force, or against her will. Adopted by the U.N. General Assembly in 2000, the Convention Against Transnational Organized Crime's Protocol defines trafficking inclusively, as

> the recruitment, transportation, transfer, harbouring or receipt of persons, by means of the threat or use of force or other forms of coercion, of abduction, of fraud, of deception, of the abuse of power or of a position of vulnerability or of the giving or receiving of payments or benefits to achieve the consent of a person having control over another person, for the purposes of exploitation. Exploitation shall include, at a minimum, the exploitation of the prostitution of others or other forms of sexual exploitation, forced labour or services, slavery or practices similar to slavery, servitude or the removal of organs.[8]

Similarly, the U.N. Convention for the Suppression of the Traffic in Persons and of the Exploitation of the Prostitution of Others states in Article 1 that those states or nations agreeing to abide by this convention are to "punish any person who, to gratify the passions of another," "procures, entices or leads away, for purposes of prostitution, another person, *even with the consent of that person,*" or "exploits the prostitution of another person, *even with the consent of that person*" [italics mine].[9] A separate Convention on the Abolition of Slavery, the Slave Trade, and Institutions and Practices Similar to Slavery, adopted in 1956, further criminalizes sex trafficking. This latter convention states in Article 3 that "the act of conveying or attempting to convey slaves from one country to another by whatever means of transport, or of being accessory thereto, shall be a criminal offence under the laws of the state parties to this Convention."[10]

Concerns remain, however, about hegemonic rule making in the U.N., along with the expectation that one definition or standard will be applied across the board. Nowhere is this point made more sharply than in the "debate" over cultural relativism versus universal human rights.

Cultural Relativism Versus Universal Human Rights

The arguments around cultural relativism both raise legitimate concerns *and* threaten the fight against sex trafficking and enslaved prostitution. The cultural relativist argument holds that traditional cultural practices and norms of some countries are being constructed by outsiders as acts of violence against women or violations of women's human rights. Clearly, the argument that declarations of human rights are often dominated by affluent Western powers that degrade and dismiss the cultures of others has merit. And, all too often, the ethnocentrism of powerful nations and global entities has been revealed in their failure to understand the varying needs of women in different cultures and with different social statuses. The complaint that international conferences on women "tend to globalize" the trafficking issue and thus fail to recognize the diversity of women's situations in relation to the trafficking phenomenon also warrants consideration.[11]

On the other hand, as Arati Rao suggests, "no group has suffered greater violation of its human rights in the name of culture than women."[12] Certainly, the discussion in Chapter 6 of patriarchal belief systems is consistent with Rao's claim. Rao goes even further in her analysis, pointing out that "culture is not a static, unchanging, identifiable body of information, against which human rights may be measured for compatibility and applicability." Instead, she continues, "culture is a series of constantly contested and negotiated social practices whose meanings are influenced by the power and status of their interpreters and participants."[13] Rao suggests that a more critical assessment of cultural claims be made—who is the speaker, and what is her or his status? What social group is affected by a particular claim, and to what extent has that group been able to participate in claims making? A related concern is that the cultural relativist argument "implies that there is a homogeneous culture upon which there is agreement," but all too often, diverse and minority voices within a culture—any culture—are simply not heard.[14]

Are there human rights about which we can all agree—are there, in one author's words, certain values that "transcend culture"?[15] The poser of that question answers it in the affirmative and offers slavery as one example. To the extent, then, that women are trafficked into enslaved prostitution, would (or should) all agree that their human rights have been violated? Another suggested absolute human right is the "impartial promotion of the interests of everyone alike,"[16] an equality-and-justice right that is probably acceptable to most *in principle*. To actually uphold it, however, would be a formidable task that would require the obliteration of ethnocentrism, racism, classism, and sexism, all of which are relevant to sex trafficking. It seems obvious that discrimination against women and women's subordination around the world must be addressed in any effort to curb sex trafficking. But is even this a shared belief? These are heavy questions and not likely to be agreed upon anytime soon. Nevertheless, each is important in thinking about the cultural and political feasibility of strategies for combating sex trafficking and enslaved prostitution.

Immediate Needs and Long-Term Changes

Complex social problems can be addressed at (at least) two levels. The first involves identifying immediate needs and possible solutions, then implementing the most feasible corrective policies or programs while continuing to work on others. The second involves tackling root causes of the problem, which are often culturally embedded and institutionalized and thus more resistant to change. At this second level, change efforts need to be multipronged, and change is more likely to occur incrementally. The two levels are not necessarily mutually exclusive; that is, some strategies work both to satisfy immediate needs and to achieve long-term solutions.

Sex trafficking and sexual enslavement is a complex, global social problem that presents both immediate needs and underlying change-resistant causes. Among the former are various kinds of support and help for victims of trafficking, especially for the growing number of child victims, better law enforcement, and greater cooperation from legitimate groups—both public and private. Greater citizen awareness of sex trafficking and sexual enslavement is both an immediate need and a long-term goal. That is, broader awareness and education campaigns should be undertaken immediately, with the goal of eventually persuading the public to take a strong stand against sex trafficking. More basic, long-term structural and normative change efforts should focus on global and national inequities in income, employment, and other social resources; globalization policies; and patriarchal structures that facilitate the exploitation of and discrimination against women.

Support and Help for Victims of Trafficking

Legal Services and Resources

Trafficking victims often arrive in a country without legitimate identification papers, unable to speak the language, and forced into an illegal trade. Should they escape and seek help, they may be arrested and placed in jail, deported, or both. Moreover, they often lack protection from retribution by their traffickers should they agree to testify against them.[17] These problems can be *relatively* easily remedied. At the least, states can give legal recognition to trafficked women as victims of crime, regardless of the legality of the work into which they have been trafficked; implement stays of deportation; and provide victim (and other witness) protection services.[18] Victims' rights can often be protected under existing legal statutes or policies that target migrant workers. Victims can also be given financial and technical assistance in getting new identification papers, assistance with immigration and repatriation processes, and access to hotlines for immediate help and information about victims' rights and options.[19] In fact, a number of these remedies are currently being applied in countries around the world, and international bodies are encouraging their expansion.

The 2000 U.N. Protocol to Prevent, Suppress and Punish Trafficking in Persons, Especially Women and Children asks states to adopt many of the above practices, including assistance with identification and travel documents, the granting of special residency status, and protection for victims who are willing to testify against their traffickers.[20] Many states are implementing such services. A number of countries, including Australia, Austria, Belgium, Canada, the Czech Republic, Hungary, Italy, Lithuania, the Netherlands, and Spain, now offer trafficking victims some form of temporary residence and a special visa that allows victims to stay in the country under the protection of the host government. Some of these "protection visas" are restricted, stipulating, for example, that they are only for victims who have agreed to testify against their traffickers, and limiting the amount of time for which they are good. Some, on the other hand, provide protection until it is determined that the victim can safely return home.[21]

In the United States, the Victims of Trafficking and Violence Protection Act of 2000 provides victims of trafficking with assistance in establishing residency and temporary access to services. It also acknowledges that trafficking victims "are repeatedly punished more harshly than the traffickers themselves," and that the emphasis should be on prosecuting the traffickers, rather than on prosecuting the victims for "unlawful acts committed as a direct result of being trafficked, such as using false documents, entering the country without documentation, or working without documentation."[22]

Services Provided by Groups and Organizations

A number of government bodies, nongovernmental organizations (NGOs), and other groups have formed alliances to provide myriad services to victims of trafficking, including not only legal assistance but medical, psychological, and job training services, help in getting housing, money to meet survival needs, and referrals for special needs. In some cases, multiple services are mandated through national legislation. Under its Combating of Trafficking in Persons and Sexual Exploitation of Children Law of 2000, for example, Cyprus must give protection and support to trafficking victims, including temporary shelter, medical care, psychiatric services, and "arrangements for maintenance."[23] And, through a similar law, Thailand requires "appropriate assistance" to victims of trafficking, including food, housing, and repatriation to their home country.[24]

The most successful undertakings in the provision of multiple services to trafficking victims are typically cooperative ones, often pairing governments with NGOs and their extensive networks. Among the countries in which the government works closely with local NGOs to provide shelter and access to legal, psychological, medical, and other material resources are Albania, Bangladesh, Bosnia–Herzegovina, Côte d'Ivoire, the Czech Republic, Estonia, Switzerland, and Thailand.[25] In Switzerland, the government works most closely with one NGO that provides services to women trafficked into the country from Africa, Latin America, and Eastern Europe, although it networks with other organizations as well.[26] Similarly, the Estonian government contracts with one comprehensive-service NGO, and also has contract relationships with several others for the delivery of consultation and crisis services.[27] The government in Côte d'Ivoire cooperates with NGOs to repatriate trafficking victims.[28] In Albania, the police regularly refer victims to NGOs, and with help from local businesses, the police and NGOs have set up two temporary shelters for trafficking victims.[29]

NGOs themselves often engage in activism on several fronts. One such example is the Polaris Project. Founded by two individuals in Rhode Island, the Polaris Project works "on the streets and in brothel locations" to do "direct victim outreach and community-based investigation in partnership with communities and law enforcement." The Project, which now has over 1,000 members and supporters, describes itself as a grassroots network whose mission is to "address the vital need for direct intervention, grassroots advocacy, and action-oriented research to combat trafficking in women and children."[30]

In Bombay, India, the NGO Apne Aap "works to end sex trafficking and to assist the women and children caught up in the sex trade." Apne Aap runs a center in Bombay that offers trafficking victims a "safe space," literacy classes, and a record of their health files. As a strategy for protecting women from arrest, Apne Aap gives the women identification cards signifying their affiliation with the organization. Most recently, Apne Aap has developed a program for trafficking victims who are living with AIDS and is assisting other NGOs in India in setting up their own such programs.[31]

The Cambodian Women's Crisis Center (CWCC), founded in 1997, now has several drop-in centers, along with confidential centers where trafficking victims can get counseling and skills training. The CWCC works with local factories, restaurants, and other work sites to find jobs for women who want to stay in the country; it also works extensively with the Cambodian government to help Cambodian women who have been trafficked out of the country and are now being repatriated. The CWCC role includes not only helping the women to return to their villages, but also preparing their families and communities for the women's return and reintegration. Together with the Cambodian Ministry of Social Affairs, Labor, and Vocational & Youth Rehabilitation, the CWCC monitors the progress of repatriated women. In addition to helping returning women, the CWCC also helps in the repatriation of women who have been trafficked *to* Cambodia for prostitution. In this task, the CWCC partners with the International Organization for Migration (IOM).[32]

Many other organizations and programs around the world provide assistance to and advocate for victims of sex trafficking. Through local and global networking, such efforts have been successful in reaching a number of victims and in bringing about greater awareness of the trafficking problem. Given the huge volume of trafficked women and their continual movement around the globe, however, even the best victim service efforts are limited. Moreover, the hold of the traffickers is strong. Profits in the trafficking industry depend on keeping victims under control, and traffickers themselves have dense networks to assist them toward this end. Thus, in addition to providing victims with services once they are out of their traffickers' grasp, there are ongoing efforts to "rescue" groups of women from the brothels and clubs in which they are confined.

Rescues

Many rescues are part of a law enforcement raid on a brothel or related business in which both the trafficker–pimps and the prostituted women are picked up. To the extent that the prostituted women are actually treated as victims and offered assistance, these raids also qualify as rescues. Missions in which the only goal is to free women victims are sometimes organized by government entities, NGOs, and private activist groups. One example of the last in the United States is Shared Hope International, an organization that rescues women from forced prostitution. Shared Hope was founded in 1999 by a former U.S. Congresswomen, Linda Smith, who set up its office in a small town in her home state of Washington.[33] In addition to organizing rescues, Shared Hope works to bring about public awareness of the global hold of sex trafficking.

Law enforcement agencies, NGOs, and other groups commonly cooperate within and across national borders to effect a rescue and to see it through successful repatriations. An example of a large-scale, cross-national, and cross-agency arrest and rescue mission was the joint effort in 2003 of law enforcement groups in 12 Central and Eastern European countries[34] working together with the IOM. Altogether, this network sought out traffickers and their victims at over 20,000 sites, an effort culminating in the identification of 831 traffickers (criminal proceedings were initiated against almost 500 of them) and 696 trafficking victims. The joint effort was enhanced by the IOM's role in assisting and advocating for the provision of assistance to the trafficking victims. Also part of the network was the Southeast European Cooperative Initiative (operating out of Bucharest, a transborder crime center), which documented and evaluated the raid and rescue mission.[35]

To rescue Kosovar women living in enslaved prostitution, a special operation was set up in the early 2000s under the Trafficking and Prostitution Investigation Unit of the U.N. International Police Force, known as CIVPOL. Within a 9-month period, this unit rescued 270 women.[36] The task of rescuing Cambodian women who have been trafficked into Thailand, Malaysia, and Taiwan is given to the Cambodian Immigration Office, which works closely with the CWCC, described earlier, to ensure that the women they rescue make it home and are accepted back into their communities.[37]

It should be noted that there are criticisms of rescue missions, in particular from some activists for sex workers' rights, who claim that many women in prostitution are forced into "rescues" that they neither asked for nor want. For these women, the claim goes, prostitution is a work choice, and "rescue" from it is akin to abduction. Sometimes, in this view, women are held indefinitely against their will by "rescuers," losing valuable work time. Furthermore, critics continue, while it may not be an ideal work choice, given the lack of alternative opportunities for women in some countries, prostitution should be granted equal labor rights and protections.[38]

Such criticisms are far less forthcoming when it comes to the trafficking and prostitution of children and adolescents. Some law enforcement raid and rescue missions have focused specifically on finding and freeing children, often victims of internal trafficking. In Colombia, for example, law enforcement officers raided "sex shops" throughout the country in 1998, arresting 29 adult trafficker–pimp suspects and freeing 370 children between the ages of 12 and 16. The children were typically found living under conditions of abuse and enslavement and forced to work as prostitutes. Close to 40% of the enslaved children were found in the major city of Cartagena, known as a "busy sex-tourist destination."[39]

Author Hnin Hnin Pyne writes about young girls from Myanmar (Burma) trafficked into prostitution in Thailand, with whom she spoke following their rescue during a raid on their brothel. In all, 19 women were rescued in this raid; 17 of them were HIV-positive, and all of them had at least one STD. One 17-year-old girl was "coughing and shivering" as the author sat next to her. She had been promised work as a maid when, at age 14, she was trafficked into Thailand and then immediately sold to a brothel owner. She had spent the last 3 years in two different brothels, where she serviced from 12 to 20 men a day and contracted the HIV virus.[40] Hers is one of many stories of women and girls for whom rescue comes too late. Living with HIV/AIDS is increasingly common among prostitutes in all regions of the world.

The HIV/AIDS Crisis and Approaches to It

As of 2003, approximately 47 million people worldwide were living with HIV or AIDS. In 2003 alone, there were 5 million new cases of HIV (an average of about 14,000 a day)—the most ever. Of the new cases, 3.4 million were in sub-Saharan Africa, another 1.1 million were in South or Southeast Asia, and 270,000 were in East Asia and the Pacific. Eastern and Central Europe had 280,000 new cases.[41] In both Botswana and Swaziland, an astounding 39% of adults are HIV-positive;[42] and in Africa overall, at least 6,500 people die from AIDS-related causes every day.[43] Although Africa still has the highest number of people living with HIV/AIDS, other "hotspots" have emerged in recent years. The HIV rate is skyrocketing in many parts of South and Southeast Asia,[44] and Eastern Europe, the NIS, and Central Asia are showing record numbers of new infections as well.[45] Over 90% of people with HIV/AIDS are from developing countries.[46]

Also for the first time, in 2002, half of all the adults with HIV/AIDS were women. Their rise to parity was largely due to the number of infected women in sub-Saharan Africa: by the end of the 1990s, women accounted for almost 60% of all those with HIV/AIDS in that region. Women also account for half or more of all cases in the Caribbean, North Africa, and the Middle East.[47] Age is also a factor. Young women, in the 16–24 age group, have a higher rate of HIV/AIDS worldwide than do men in that age group.[48]

Studies have long shown that prostitutes are at particularly high risk for STD infections, and HIV/AIDS is no exception. In fact, today, prostitution is seen as a primary HIV transmission route in all regions of the world.[49] While the numbers of HIV-positive prostitutes are estimates at best, and sometimes vary from study to study, even the lowest estimates are frightening. In Central Africa, 66% of all prostitutes are HIV-positive,[50] as are 50% to 60% of prostitutes in Bombay,[51] and 40% in Myanmar.[52] In Georgetown, the capital of Guyana in South America, prostitutes have a 46% HIV-positive rate,[53] and studies in northern Thailand have found 36% of prostitutes there to be HIV-positive.[54] Other places show lower—but still very high—rates of HIV infection among prostitutes:

at least 20% in Germany,[55] 20% in some cities in Honduras,[56] and 20% in Vietnam.[57]

Among women trafficked into prostitution who contract HIV/AIDS, additional problems arise. Based on their study of Nepali girls trafficked to India for prostitution, Human Rights Watch reports that girls "who test positive for AIDS are immediately dismissed [by the brothel or pimp] and, visibly sick and without money, are either ostracized by their families or unwilling to go home." Stuck in a foreign country, without family or other friendly faces, some of these girls simply stay in India and wait to die. Without intervention, even those who make it back to Nepal typically work the streets until they also die.[58] One report estimates that 60% of the Nepali girls working in prostitution in India are HIV-positive.[59]

The dismissal of HIV-positive prostitutes to "protect" customers stems from a particular framing of the HIV/AIDS (or other STD)–prostitution link. From militarized prostitution to commercial sex tourism, the constructed "reality" has been that customers are at risk of getting HIV or some other STD from prostitutes, when in fact the typical pattern, particularly in developing countries and military base or sex tour sites, is that customers are transmitting the infections to women and girls.[60] Even in the general population, male-to-female transmission of the HIV virus through sexual contact is *far* more common (in some countries, two to four times more common) than is female-to-male transmission.[61] Moreover, there is some evidence that men with HIV or other STD infections are more likely than uninfected men to have sex with prostitutes.[62]

While today there is a better international understanding of the AIDS crisis in developing and transitional countries than there was just a decade ago, prevention strategies still tend to be based on the above transmission frame; and prevention services and medical treatment don't even begin to meet the need. Prostitutes, and particularly women and girls trafficked into prostitution, who contract HIV/AIDS are among the least likely to receive medical treatment. In addition to the usual strategies—education about HIV transmission, access to condoms, access to treatment and adequate supplies of medication—a different frame calls forth another approach to the problem. As succinctly stated by Janice Raymond: "If AIDS programs are serious about eradicating AIDS, they must challenge the sex industry."[63] Raymond points out that "women in prostitution industries have been blamed for this epidemic of STDs when, in reality, studies confirm that it is men who buy sex who carry the disease from one prostituted woman to another and ultimately back to their wives and girlfriends."[64] Additionally, she continues, "70% of female infertility" in developing countries is caused by STDs that husbands and boyfriends have transmitted to their female partners. And one problem leads to another, Raymond suggests, in that this pattern of transmission creates "a whole new segment of women who are abandoned by their husbands due to infertility," and may then be "propelled into prostitution for survival."[65]

When prostitutes are seen as the causal agents in the transmission of HIV/AIDS and other STDs, the inclination is to focus monitoring and punitive measures on them and to ignore the role of their customers. Tactics such as forced routine medical testing or the placement of other restrictions on prostitutes' behavior have not been particularly successful, and can even have the opposite effect—driving prostitutes "underground" where they receive no health education, assistance, or medical treatment at all.[66] For women who have been trafficked into enslaved prostitution, the likelihood of getting help is even lower. While outreach, education, and the provision of medical and related services for prostituted women are important in addressing immediate needs, the longer-range effort should focus more on customers, and on curbing and controlling the sex industry itself.

Problems and Special Needs of Trafficked Children

"They all get pregnant by the age of 13," a 52-year-old Canadian man told researcher Julia O'Connell Davidson. "This is such an open, natural culture. Girls are so willing and open, they want to please. They're sexual from the age of six."[67] In his remarks, this man expresses the anti-child ethnocentrism common among many sex tourists who use the bodies of children from developing countries for sex. Beyond the rationalizations, the question that begs an answer is the one posed by researcher June Kane: "Who wants to sleep with a ten-year-old?"[68]

The Volume of Child Trafficking

While there is a sizable "pedophile market" for the sex trade worldwide, the fact is that literally millions of men *not ever described as or thought to be pedophiles* seek prostituted sex from children. In fact, the distinction between a "pedophile" and a "normal" sex market is increasingly blurred as sex customers demand younger and younger girls. (It could be argued that the term "pedophile" is actually a euphemism for, or at least is believed by some to refer to, an adult seeking same-sex children for prostitution, which is seen in a homophobic sense as more "abnormal" than heterosexual sex with children.)

Today, an estimated 1.2 million children are trafficked from their homes to foreign cities or countries every year for prostitution or other labor.[69] In the decade of the 1990s, for example, some 200,000 Bangladeshi girls were sold into prostitution in several countries in South Asia and the Middle East, including Pakistan, India, and Persian Gulf countries.[70] One estimate places the number of 10- to 15-year-old children who have been forced into prostitution in Brazil at 2 million.[71] Young girls are continually trafficked from Vietnam to Cambodia, and young Cambodian girls "have been trafficked out of Cambodia by the thousands to meet the demand for child prostitutes in Thailand."[72] In addition, according to several reports, hundreds of young girls are regularly trafficked from Nigeria into the European sex industry—to Italy, Germany, Belgium, and Holland, as well as to Persian Gulf countries such as Saudi Arabia.[73]

At least 250,000 children are in prostitution in China; 100,000 children work as prostitutes in India's major cities alone; and the majority of prostitutes in Bangladesh are under 18.[74] In fact, in the late 1990s, according to the co-coordinator of End Child Prostitution, Pornography and Trafficking in Children for Sexual Exploitation (ECPAT), one of the largest and most active NGOs working against the trafficking and prostitution of children, over a million children in Asia were providing sexual services for adults, including an estimated 60,000 to 100,000 in the Philippines, 60,000 in Taiwan, 40,000 in Vietnam, 40,000 in Indonesia, 40,000 in Pakistan, and 30,000 in Sri Lanka.[75] But the child sex trade is certainly not limited to Asia. An estimated 26,000 children are sold on the streets to sex customers in Johannesburg in South Africa.[76] Some 16,000 children are in prostitution in Mexico.[77] Of the women trafficked for sex to the Netherlands, who were assisted by one NGO in the mid-1990s, 57% were under the age of 21.[78] And an estimated 19,000 Pakistani children have been trafficked in recent years to the United Arab Emirates.[79]

The trafficking of children into the sex trade seems to be steadily and dramatically increasing, indicating a problem in need of immediate attention. A number of reports state that wherever sex tourism is growing, so is the demand for child prostitutes—in Latin American countries such as Cuba, Costa Rica, the Dominican Republic, Colombia, Brazil, Honduras, and Nicaragua,[80] as well as in Sri Lanka, a well-known destination for pedophile sex tourism.[81]

A significant rise in the trafficking of girls between the ages of 8 and 15 to and through Pakistan has occurred in the last decade;[82] the same pattern has been found in sex trafficking from Nepal to India, where the average age of trafficked Nepali girls decreased (by over about 2 years, in the late 1990s) from between 14 and 16 to between 12 and 14. The highest prices are for girls between the ages of 10 and 12.[83] Also documented has been a substantial increase in young girls, mainly in the 11–16 age group, trafficked from Bangladesh to various destinations.[84]

The Why(s) of Child Sex Trafficking: Myths and Myth Breaking

As indicated at the beginning of this section, myths about the "natural sexuality" of children in cultures of "the other" allow many customers to rationalize their abuse of children for sexual gratification. There are other myths that legitimate the sexual exploitation of children, particularly female children. A patriarchal myth in several cultures is that sex with a young virgin restores and invigorates adult male libido.[85] A related myth holds that a man can be cured of an STD by having sex with a young virgin.[86] Another reported male motivation in seeking a young girl for sex is the desire to dominate[87]—that is, to have as one's sexual object not just a childlike or subordinate woman, but an actual child, who truly has no voice of her own. Some male consumers of sex with female children, then, appear to be playing out one or another form of narcissistic masculinity on the bodies of children, who are usually desperately poor and almost always very frightened.

Investigative journalist Nicholas Kristof first saw Nguyen, a "shy" 14-year-old Vietnamese girl, as she sat in a brothel in a Cambodian town waiting to be sold for the first time. The brothel owner had purchased Nguyen several days earlier and was holding her back for a customer who would be willing to pay a high price—$500—for Nguyen's virginity. Kristof gives her voice: "Nguyen shuddered and leaned against a 15-year-old friend who had been sold for the first time just a few days earlier. 'I'm scared,' she said softly, 'I'm scared.' "[88]

While many of the young virgins expected to bring a good price are in their early teens, there are more and more who are much younger. In the mining towns of Brazil, mine operators have authorized "virginity auctions," for which girls as young as 9 are trafficked into the town, displayed, and sold to the highest bidder.[89] And, in his investigative report, journalist Peter Landesman tells the story of "Andrea," the name her traffickers gave her (and the only name she knows). Andrea, of Mexican heritage, was born in the United States, where she was either sold or abandoned when she was about 4 years old. For the following 12 years, Andrea was enslaved in a sex-trafficking ring that moved her back and forth across the border, servicing customers both in Mexico and in the United States.[90] When Landesman met Andrea, then in her early to mid-20s (she didn't know her birth date), she had been rescued and was living free of her traffickers for the first time since she was little more than a toddler. Because of fears of retribution from Andrea's traffickers, the rescue operators arranged for Landesman to meet her "at a secret location" in the United States.[91]

Another reason for the higher demand for very young girls is the mistaken belief that they are unlikely to have been infected with HIV/AIDS or any other STD.[92] And here lies one of the great tragedies for trafficked children. The reality is that the younger the girl, the greater her risk of being infected by a customer. There is considerable expert agreement that due to the less mature development of the genital tract, including a "less protective" cervical mucous and lower levels of antibodies, young girls are biologically more vulnerable than adult women to HIV and other STD infections.[93] Additionally, while virtually all women who are trafficked into enslaved prostitution lack the power to negotiate the terms of their sexual encounters (e.g., getting the customer to use a condom), young girls are even less powerful and less knowledgeable in this regard.[94]

In many developing countries, the prevalence rates of HIV infection in young women and girls are particularly high. After examining studies of HIV rates in Africa, the author of one report said that rates of HIV infection among teen girls and women under age 25 throughout Africa "defy belief." Almost six of every ten women in their early 20s in the South African town of Carletonville, for example, were found to be HIV-infected. Moreover, in 11 population-based studies in Africa, the average rates of HIV infection were more than five time higher in teen girls than in teen boys.[95]

Of course, even before AIDS was a recognized disease, STD infection of male customers (but not of the young girls!) was a concern. During their ruthless "conscriptions" of comfort women, the Japanese army, hoping to protect soldiers from STDs, abducted girls as young as 11 from their elementary schools.[96] In fact, during this period, young girls were not safe anywhere. In a speech she gave in Geneva, U.N. Special Rapporteur on Violence Against Women, Radhika Coomaraswamy, read the following excerpt from an interview with a former Korean comfort woman:

> One day in June, at the age of 13, I had to prepare lunch for my parents who were working in the field and so I went to the village well to fetch water. A Japanese garrison soldier surprised me there and took me away so that my parents never knew what happened to their daughter. I was taken to the police station in a truck, where I was raped by several policemen. After 10 days or so I was taken to the Japanese army garrison barracks. . . . There were about 400 other Korean young girls with me and we served 5,000 Japanese soldiers as sex slaves every day.[97]

Efforts to End Child Sex Trafficking

In 1996, a World Congress Against Commercial Sexual Exploitation of Children—with representatives from 122 countries, 105 representatives from the U.N and other governmental groups, 471 representatives from NGOs, 47 youth delegates, and over 500 news media attendees—was convened in Stockholm to work toward combating all forms of commercial sexual exploitation of children.[98] The resultant "Agenda for Action" included strategies to prevent the sexual exploitation of children and to protect and help recover and reintegrate exploited children. In the case of sex trafficking specifically, the agenda included the development of laws and policies protecting children from both cross-border and internal trafficking, as well as cross-national cooperative efforts to ensure children's safe return to their homelands and communities.[99] Emerging from this World Congress as a major anti–child trafficking NGO was ECPAT (End Child Prostitution, Pornography and Trafficking in Children for Sexual Exploitation). Prior to the World Congress, ECPAT consisted of four groups in Asia; as of 2003, the ECPAT network included 69 groups in 61 countries, with every region of the world represented. The groups are all "independent organisations or coalitions working against commercial sexual exploitation of children." ECPAT's activities include doing their own research, sharing relevant information about what governments are doing, offering models for prevention work, and developing tools for police and caregiver training.[100]

Many other organizations and networks actively work against global child trafficking and child prostitution. The U.N. Children's Fund (UNICEF), the IOM, and the International Labour Organization (ILO) all have ongoing campaigns to fight child trafficking and protect its victims. One such ILO campaign, known as the "Worst Forms of Child Labour," provides data and regularly shares pertinent information on child sex trafficking.[101] Another active NGO, Captive Daughters, is specifically committed to ending the sex trafficking of children, especially girls.[102]

Legal remedies for child trafficking have been strengthened in various countries and regions. In an attempt to face its growing problem with child and pedophile sex tourism and child pornography, for example, Sri Lanka has increased criminal penalties for sex offenders and made pedophilia a "non-bailable offense." It has also raised the age of (minors') consent from 12 to 16.[103] Bangladesh, with a poor record of rescuing trafficked children and arresting their traffickers, set up in 2002 a special anti–child trafficking cell within the Women and Children Affairs Ministry.[104] While these and other efforts seem to be on the right track, some express concern about the limitations of legal remedies, pointing to the many factors that work against proactive investigations and rigorous law enforcement in poor countries with few resources and many other pressing problems. Additionally, pay for law enforcement and related work is typically very low, leaving such "guardians" vulnerable to corruption by traffickers.

National Laws on Prostitution and Sex Trafficking

Laws on prostitution vary between and within regions of the world and with countries' trafficking roles. As shown in Table 1, prostitution is illegal in only 40% of the 99 countries actively involved in trafficking (listed in Chapter 5); moreover, keeping a brothel is illegal in just over half of those countries.[105] The legal statuses of two other prostitution-related crimes, pimping and solicitation, are more uniform, but in opposite directions from each other. Just under 84% of the trafficking countries have laws against pimping, but soliciting a prostitute is illegal in only 25% of the countries.[106]

Table 1 gives breakdowns by countries' trafficking role and by region regarding the legal status of prostitution, keeping a brothel, and having

Table 1

Percentage of Countries Taking Legal Measures Against Prostitution and Trafficking, by Trafficking Role Type and by Region

	Prostitution illegal	Brothels illegal	U.N. antitrafficking protocol signed
Total (*N* = 99)	40.0	55.6	52.5
BY TRAFFICKING ROLE TYPE			
Destination countries (*n* = 37)	35.1	70.3	62.2
Source countries (*n* = 37)	37.8	51.4	54.1
Bidirectional countries (*n* = 16)	50.0	31.3	25.0
Hub countries (*n* = 9)	55.6	55.6	55.6
BY REGION			
Africa (*n* = 11)	45.5	72.7	54.5
Asia, East/Southeast (*n* = 13)	53.8	38.5	15.4
Asia, South (*n* = 5)	60.0	40.0	20.0
Central/Eastern Europe (*n* = 13)	38.5	23.1	69.2
Latin America (*n* = 12)	33.3	41.7	50.0
Middle East (*n* = 9)	88.9*	77.8	11.1
Russia and NIS (*n* = 15)	40.0	66.7	46.7
OECD [Westernized bloc] (*n* = 21)	14.3	61.9	90.5

Source: The Protection Project (2002), *Human Rights Report on Trafficking in Persons, Especially Women and Children,* 2nd ed.

*Israel is the only Middle Eastern country in which prostitution is legal.

signed the U.N. Protocol to Prevent, Suppress and Punish Trafficking in Persons, Especially Women and Children (which, as of 2002, slightly over half of the trafficking countries had signed). As the table shows, prostitution is much more likely to be illegal in hub and bidirectional countries than in destination and source countries. On the other hand, brothels are highly likely (and far more likely than in other types of countries) to be illegal in destination countries. While brothels are illegal in 70% of destination countries, they are illegal in only 31% of bidirectional countries. The same pattern is found for signing of the U.N. antitrafficking protocol. About two-thirds of destination countries have signed it—the most of any trafficking type. The least likely to have signed the protocol are the bidirectional countries, only one-fourth of which have done so.

Some of these findings appear to be related to regional differences. In the Middle East, prostitution is illegal in all but one country (Israel), and brothels are illegal in all but two countries. Yet, as of 2002, only one Middle Eastern country (Syria) had signed the antitrafficking protocol. The Westernized OECD countries are far *less* likely than any other region to classify prostitution as a crime (it is illegal in only 3 of 21 OECD countries), but by far the most likely (over 90%) to have signed the antitrafficking protocol. The legal approach, then, in the (mainly) destination Middle Eastern countries is quite different from that in the destination Westernized OECD countries. The Central and Eastern European and NIS countries (only one of which is a destination site) are far *less* likely than any other region to have laws against keeping a brothel, but the second most likely to have signed the antitrafficking protocol. One interpretation of these findings is that affluent Westernized and transitional European countries have greater trust in, or feel more closely bound to, policies set by the United Nations, or perhaps to the United Nations itself.

Quite clearly, whether or not prostitution is against the law makes little difference in regard to the volume or pervasiveness of sex trafficking and the sex trade. Prostitution is illegal, for example, in the hub countries of Thailand, the Philippines, Albania, Mexico, and Pakistan, all of which have active and expansive sex trades. And in the Persian Gulf destination countries of Bahrain, Kuwait, Qatar, Saudi Arabia, and the United Arab Emirates, all of the prostitution-related activities are illegal.

In most nations, at least one prostitution-related behavior—prostitution itself, soliciting, or keeping a brothel—is legal and thus leaves a door open. Yet virtually all nations also have something in their penal code that prohibits some prostitution-related or trafficking-related activity. Moreover, as of 2002, 14 nations had legislated a special act that protects women and children from trafficking and other commercial sexual exploitation. The 11 sex-trafficking countries with such an act are regionally mixed; in alphabetical order, they are Australia, Bangladesh, Bulgaria, Cyprus, India, Ireland, Malaysia, Russia, Sri Lanka, Thailand, and the United States.[107]

In the United States, one of only three Westernized OECD destination countries in which prostitution is illegal,[108] the Victims of Trafficking and Violence Protection Act of 2002, referred to earlier, recognizes trafficking in humans as a form of slavery, and notes that its modern-day victims are mainly women and children. The act's purposes are "to combat trafficking in persons, a contemporary manifestation of slavery whose victims are predominantly women and children, to ensure just and effective punishment of traffickers, and to protect their victims."[109] The act supplements other national laws and conforms to the U.N. conventions that address trafficking and enslaved prostitution. It outlines strategies for enforcing the law and prosecuting traffickers, and it urges international cooperation to fight trafficking. Also in 2000, Executive Order 13257 set up an Interagency Task Force to Monitor and Combat Trafficking in Persons.[110] The effectiveness of the U.S. Victims of Trafficking and Violence Protection Act, and others like it around the world, however, has yet to be validated.

While there is law enforcement and judicial activity around the world, compared to the volume of business in the sex industry, trafficker prosecution and conviction rates are dismal. A glance at the trafficking cases reported by most countries to the U.S. State Department for its 2003 "Trafficking in Persons Report" is informative. (Data were requested for April 2002 through March 2003, but are referred to below, as they are in the report, as "2003 data" or "data from the last year.")[111]

Take Moldova, for example, one of the poorest and most prolific source countries in Eastern Europe. (An estimated 1,000 Moldovan women are annually trafficked into prostitution, primarily in Western Europe.) While prostitution is legal in Moldova, pimping and keeping a brothel are not, and Moldova has signed the U.N. antitrafficking protocol. Of the 44 criminal trafficking cases opened in Moldova in 2003, 13 were dismissed, and 21 were suspended or still pending by the end of the year. Only 8 were referred to the courts, and of those, only 2, both for child trafficking, resulted in convictions. In nearby Belarus, the Interior Ministry opened 110 cases of trafficking and recruitment for sexual exploitation, and 35 people were convicted of those trafficking crimes.

In the hub country of Pakistan, the Federal Investigative Agency reported that 11 people had been arrested in the last year under a new law criminalizing "all aspects" of trafficking, but that because courts were seriously backlogged, there were few prosecutions. Data from another hub country, the Philippines, were incomplete, but its reports indicated 18 arrests and 1 conviction for trafficking in 2003. And in the hub country of

Albania, 144 trafficking cases were prosecuted by the General Prosecutor's Office, ending in 17 convictions.

In Poland, a bidirectional country, 149 trafficking investigations were opened in 2003, resulting in 47 arrests, 18 prosecutions, and 8 convictions. In Lithuania, another bidirectional country, 22 criminal cases against mostly international traffickers were initiated, and 6 convictions were won. In the last year, Israel, an active destination country, opened 67 trafficking investigations, involving 138 people, 92 of whom were arrested. Thirty of the cases were prosecuted, 28 of which were resolved through a plea bargain. Sentences resulted in incarceration time ranging from 6 months to 9 years.

Trafficking crime sentences vary considerably from country to country and case to case. While some are relatively long—10 to 20 years—a number are lighter than might be expected. In 2003, for example, Japan convicted Koichi "Sony" Hagiwara, a "kingpin" trafficker in the country. A repeat offender, who operated a major criminal trafficking operation that had trafficked hundreds of victims from Colombia, Hagiwara was sentenced to 2 years in prison.[112]

The annual "Trafficking in Persons Report," from which the above data come, was another mandate of the U.S. Victims of Trafficking and Violence Protection Act of 2000. In addition to providing "country narratives," the report places countries in one of three tiers, based on their efforts to combat trafficking. Tier 1 countries "fully comply with minimum standards for the elimination of trafficking"; Tier 2 countries do "not yet fully comply with minimum standards for the elimination of trafficking" but are "making significant efforts to do so"; and Tier 3 countries do not "fully comply with minimum standards for the elimination of trafficking" and are "not making significant efforts" toward compliance.[113] The 2002 report listed 18 Tier 1 countries, 51 Tier 2 countries, and 19 Tier 3 countries.[114] By 2003, there were 26 Tier 1 countries, a gain of 8 over the prior year. And, when the 2003 report was released in June of that year, there were 15 Tier 3 countries; however, in September of 2003, by executive order, 10 of those countries were elevated to Tier 2: Belize, Bosnia–Herzegovina, the Dominican Republic, Georgia, Greece, Haiti, Kazakhstan, Suriname, Turkey, and Uzbekistan. Of the 5 remaining Tier 3 countries, only one, Myanmar, is a prominent global sex trafficking country. (The other Tier 3 countries are Cuba, Liberia, North Korea, and Sudan.)[115]

It is good news to learn that nearly all of the major sex trafficking countries are now judged to at least be taking steps to curb trafficking; and the country narratives in the report do show some government antitrafficking activity in the great majority of countries. However, as noted, given the volume of trafficking, arrest and prosecution rates should be much higher. Global trafficking cases can be extremely complex, and police and court resources in many countries are stretched to their limits. However, part of the problem is that the net is often not cast widely enough, and thus the passive or active complicity of "corrupt guardians" and other players in legitimate positions is missed. Without the assistance of numerous enforcers of the law, including police officers, border guards, and immigration officials, sex trafficking would be far more difficult. And the problem is not restricted to lower-level "guardians." Judicial officers, embassy officials, and government executives have also been found to be in on the take. In addition, there are many private-sector persons, from high-level executives on down, who are intentionally involved in and profiting from sex trafficking—bankers, investors, travel and employment agents, taxi drivers, and so on.

In spite of the many international conventions and protocols, the national laws criminalizing one or another prostitution-related or trafficking-related activity, special legislative acts that outlaw trafficking in persons, new international, regional, and local investigative units, and numerous police raids and investigations, the sex trafficking industry just continues to pick up steam, getting bigger and more profitable every year. The need for services for sex trafficking victims, as described earlier, is urgent and critical; and the provision of those services is important work that needs to be encouraged and supported with public and private resources. In addition, more attention and support needs to be given to the improvement of antitrafficking law enforcement and prosecution. However, the undoing of the trafficking industry itself will require long-term societal changes and a willingness to commit to them. The next section offers some recommendations.

Tackling Sex Trafficking and Enslaved Prostitution Through Social Change

Activating Social Change

Public Awareness and Education

Here I return to where I started at the beginning of this chapter: to the urgent need for public awareness of and education about sex trafficking and sexual enslavement. While NGOs and other organizations share their findings, frequently this communication is only *among* the groups already working against sex trafficking. In collaboration with state governments, such groups could disseminate information much more broadly.[116] Educating law enforcement officers and other government officials is an essential part of such an undertaking. But the general public also needs to be convinced that sex trafficking is a major social problem affecting virtually all countries in the world.

More people need to know about debt-bonded prostitution and the enslaved conditions under which so many trafficked women and girls live and work; about the very young children trafficked into the sex industry, and the diseases, including HIV/AIDS, that they contract from customers; about the organization of the sex trafficking and sex trade industries—how traffickers operate, who the parties to sex trafficking are, how high their profits and how low their risks are, who the customers are, and how much sex tourism has grown.

A public awareness campaign introduced in Brazil in 1997 provides one model. This campaign, with full cooperation from the government and antitrafficking groups, focused on sex tourism, and in particular on the child sex market. The campaign theme was reflected in the headline words on promotional materials—"Beware, Brazil is watching you"—accompanied by a "pair of alert, menacing eyes," and encouraging public protection of children from sex tourists.[117]

Good media coverage is essential to any effective public campaign. Like the general public, the mainstream media need to be convinced that sex trafficking is a widespread and serious problem before they can be expected to give it the coverage it needs.[118] Moreover, the kind of media coverage given to sex trafficking, including featured pictures, is important. For example, as researcher June Kane notes, sometimes media pictures on trafficking "compromise the dignity" of the victim and "leave the exploiter untouched."[119] Media exposure to the industry, the traffickers, and the customers are important parts of the public's education.

Potential Private-Sector Allies

Many private individuals and organizations use their legitimate status to serve and advance the trafficking industry. They include, among others, banks and bankers who transfer, launder, or harbor illegally gained funds or who knowingly loan money for illegal purposes; business investors who make money by investing in trafficking-related operations or accept trafficking profits as investments in their own businesses; travel and employment agencies that advertise and arrange for trips and "jobs" abroad; and providers of a whole array of services that the trafficking industry relies on (e.g., making counterfeit identity and travel papers, renting out properties for brothel businesses, transporting victims to and from various work sites in taxis or private cars).

While vigorous prosecution of people and groups who commit trafficking-related crimes is necessary, it is not sufficient. There is no good reason why business and industry cannot become antitrafficking advocates, getting the word out to their clients. For example, the Swedish Save the Children campaign against the sexual exploitation of children helped make cards that Swedish Travel Agency Association members agreed to place in the airline ticket packets they dispersed to customers. On one side of the card was a picture of a beautiful, white-sand beach, described as the "bright side" of tourism; the other side was black, and the caption described the "dark side" (i.e., child sex tourism).[120] Similarly, the Australian Customs Office gives foreign travelers a leaflet on child sex tourism produced by ECPAT-Australia.[121]

Research and Data Analysis

Understanding sex trafficking and enslaved prostitution requires ongoing research. Again, trafficking is a complex, global phenomenon, with underground networks that intentionally hide what they are doing and how they are doing it. There is no way to combat sex trafficking effectively unless we understand it. A number of solid research projects are already under way, many of which have supplied information for this book. Several bring together research findings from around the world and put out new editions annually or continually add to their original work. Prominent among the former are The Protection Project's country-by-country *Human Rights Report on Trafficking in Persons, Especially Women and Children*, the second edition of which was published in 2002; and the U.S. State Department's "Trafficking in Persons Report," which provides country-by-country narratives along with general information on trafficking, and the third edition of which was published in 2003. An example of a continually updated project is the Global Survival Network's *Factbook on Global Sexual Exploitation*, edited by Donna M. Hughes, Laura Joy Sporcic, Nadine Z. Mendelsohn, and Vanessa Chirgwin, published in 1999, but with regular additions. The *Factbook* provides brief synopses of research findings on prostitution and trafficking in individual countries. All of these resources are available on the Internet.

Additionally, there are any number of research reports put out by NGOs and government units that focus on sex trafficking in particular countries or regions. Among the many products provided by NGOs are bibliographical and annotated lists, not only of research reports on trafficking, but also of various resources that are available for victims in different parts of the world.

Finally, there are Web sites that provide general information on trafficking, some of which comes from e-mails sent to the sites by various interested parties. In fact, one, the Stop-Traffic listserv, is described as an e-mail service (stop-traffic@friends-partners.org; http://www.friends-partners.org/partners/stop-traffic) that provides an outlet for updated information from around the world on trafficking in persons. A regional information-providing Web site, *Libertad Latina* (http://www.libertadlatina.org), focuses on Latinas, but casts a global net in its mission statement: "We stand up to light a path out of the abyss of criminal sex trafficking, rape with impunity and severe sexual harassment that plagues the lives of many millions of women and minor children around the world." From a slightly different slant, another Latino/a-focused Web site, *Derechos Human Rights* (http://www.derechos.org), describes itself as an Internet-based human rights organization that offers human rights information, including violations, actions, documents, and links.

NGOs, Networks, and Alliances

The role played by NGOs in antitrafficking initiatives cannot be overstated, and virtually all recommendations for combating sex trafficking emphasize the importance of including NGOs in any kind of plan.[122] The most effective and far-reaching NGOs are networks or alliances themselves, are part of a larger network, or have formed important alliances with other organizations. Networking to deal with a global phenomenon should come as no surprise. Indeed, the very success of the sex trafficking industry itself has been predicated on its ability to develop and operate through flexible, sometimes overlapping, networks.

Some global NGOs, such as Human Rights Watch (http://www.hrw.org), Global Survival Network (http://www.globalsurvival.net), the International Organization for Migration (http://www.iom.int), and the International Labour Organization (http://www.ilo.org), have broader mandates, but have directed an enormous amount of attention to sex trafficking in recent years, producing some of the most frequently cited studies and reports on the issue. Other global groups, such as Amnesty International's Women's Human Rights Network (http://www.amnesty.org/women) and Vital Voices (a global partnership supporting women's efforts in building strong democracies and economies and working toward peace) (http://www.vitalvoices.org), are focused more generally on women's issues, but again have contributed generously to the exposure of sex trafficking.

Some NGOs and other groups take on a special sex trafficking campaign or project as part of a larger agenda. For example, GABRIELA (http://www.members.tripod.com/~gabriela_p), an alliance of women's organizations in the Philippines, launched the Purple Rose Campaign in 1999, described as a "massive global campaign to expose and fight sex trafficking perpetrators." This activist campaign engaged in "awareness-raising and mass actions, worldwide."[123] In 2001, Terre des Hommes (http://www.terredeshommes.org), an international network of ten organizations working for children's rights, opened the Campaign to Stop Child Trafficking, dedicated to improving protection for children at risk of being trafficked and ensuring that traffickers are effectively prosecuted. Another is the Burma Trafficking Project (http://www.apccjp.org/Burma/burma.htm), initiated by the Asia Pacific Center for Justice and Peace and based in Washington D.C., which works with Asian and Pacific groups and organizations advocating for political and economic justice.

One of the most specific and most active of the global NGOs working on sex trafficking is the Coalition Against Trafficking in Women (CATW) (http://www.catwinternational.org), "composed of regional networks and of affiliated individuals and groups," which "serves as an umbrella that coordinates and takes direction from its regional organizations and networks." CATW "works internationally to combat sexual exploitation in all its forms, especially prostitution and trafficking in women and children, in particular girls." Other active networks specifically dedicated to combating trafficking in women and children include the Coalition to Abolish Slavery and Trafficking (http://www.trafficked-women.org), "an alliance of nonprofit service providers, grassroots advocacy groups and activists dedicated to providing human services and human rights advocacy to victims of modern-day slavery"; the Global Alliance Against Traffic in Women (http://www.inet.co.the/org/gaatw), a Thailand-based NGO working internationally to fight trafficking; the Foundation Against Trafficking in Women (STV) (http://www.qweb.kvinnoforum.se/trafficking.htm), based in the Netherlands and devoted to the prevention of trafficking in women and support of trafficked persons; and La Strada (http://www.brama.com/lastrada/about.html), a coalition of NGOs from Poland, the Czech Republic, Ukraine, and Bulgaria that works to prevent trafficking in women from the Central and Eastern European region.

The work of many of these organizations and alliances also addresses the root causes of sex trafficking. They recognize, for example, that until there is greater economic opportunity and justice for developing and poorer countries, and especially for women from those countries, we cannot hope to truly topple sex trafficking and the sex trade.

Substantive Societal Change

Economic Opportunity and Justice

Even more difficult to combat than sex trafficking itself is the poverty of source countries and the women who live in them that make both so vulnerable—the former to the revenues that sex trafficking can bring in, and the latter to the promise of income to survive. As we saw earlier, the most active source countries are either developing countries with high levels of poverty and low levels of human development, or transitional countries with stagnant economies and high rates of unemployment. In one way or another, women's economic status in source countries is particularly poor. While there are fewer job opportunities in source countries for women than for men, poverty and unemployment rates are also high for many men as well. Low-level trafficking jobs are filled by both men and women in source countries, in sex-industrialized hub countries, and in some developing countries that have become popular sites for sex tourism. At the least, dismantling sex trafficking and the sex trade will require the provision of education and job opportunities for women (and men) that will allow them to support themselves and their families.

Although helping in some ways, globalization policies have often added to the economic woes of developing and transitional countries, leaving them debt-ridden and even more dependent on affluent countries. Globalization policies also frequently work against women, passing them by for loans and other resources that might help them become more economically stable.

The building of globalization-guided market economies needs to be examined in order to determine what actually does help or harm countries struggling to sustain themselves and become economically viable. Just as important as strengthening economies overall, however, is the distribution of resources within them—whether we're talking about the global economy or that of individual countries. "Free market" economic systems do not typically equalize on their own, so the question is whether there is a will, or whether a will can be mobilized, to achieve a more equitable distribution of resources across and within nations.

The will or attitudinal piece is also critical to success in curbing the demand that fuels sex trafficking and the sex trade. Without the enormous male demand that seems never to recede, sex trafficking and the sex trade would of course not be so profitable. What can be done about this final piece?

Patriarchal Belief Systems

As Charlotte Bunch suggests, the subordination of women "runs so deep that it is still viewed as inevitable or natural rather than as a politically constructed reality maintained by patriarchal interests, ideology and institutions."[124] We have looked at the ways in which one patriarchal institution, the military, has all too often encouraged forms of masculinity that include the degradation of the feminine, hyper-heterosexuality among men, and the use of women's bodies for male recreation and pleasure. However, similar beliefs are embedded in many institutions, across cultures, and they tend to be resistant to change.

Public awareness and education campaigns about sex trafficking and enslaved prostitution should include materials introducing or reinforcing egalitarian belief systems regarding gender, class, and ethnic relations; such materials could be differently shaped for specific cultures with input from local and regional groups and organizations. As has been discussed, sex trafficking can be framed in different ways—as a human rights violation, as a form of discrimination against women, as an act of violence against women, or even as a health-related problem—and the framing for one culture or situation may not be the best for another. Attitudinal perhaps change through persuasion alone, however, can be slow going. And, sometimes, attitudinal change occurs only *after* actions to curb behaviors have been implemented and enforced.

Stricter monitoring and enforcement of international conventions and national laws on trafficking, along with more certain prosecution of and punishment for traffickers, can de-normalize sex trafficking and perhaps change public attitudes toward it. The law can also be used to deliver a message of nonacceptance for old ways of thinking about male entitlement,the sexual exploitation of women, and structured gender relations more generally.

In Conclusion

Without concerted and carefully planned activism against it, the trafficking of women and girls into enslaved prostitution is likely to continue to expand. We have moved beyond the decade of the 1990s, during which many research organizations, Web sites, NGOs, campaigns, and projects were initiated or activated. Research is continually adding to our knowledge about the sex trafficking industry and the experiences of those who have been exploited by it. Moreover, we have network power with which to fuel a global antitrafficking machine. As we have seen, some are already tackling sex trafficking, but the job requires greater resolve and activism on the part of governments and individuals alike.

Notes

1. Janice G. Raymond (1998), "Prostitution as Violence Against Women: NGO Stonewalling in Beijing and Elsewhere," *Women's Studies International Forum* 21 (June), pp. 1–9.
2. Ibid., for a fuller discussion of this debate.
3. United Nations Convention for the Suppression of the Traffic in Persons and of the Exploitation of the Prostitution of Others (1950), Article 24, United Nations, available at http://www.unhchr.ch/html/menu3/b/33.htm.
4. United Nations Universal Declaration of Human Rights (1948), Article 4, United Nations, available at http://www.hrweb.org/legal/udhr.html.
5. United Nations Covenant on Civil and Political Rights (1966), Article 8, United Nations, available at http://www.hrweb.org/legal/cpr.html.
6. United Nations Convention on the Elimination of All Forms of Discrimination Against Women (1979), Article 6, United Nations, available at http://www.unhchr.ch.html/menu3b/elcedaw.htm.
7. Fourth World Conference on Women Platform for Action (1995), "Violence Against Women," Strategic objective D.3., 130.
8. United Nations Convention Against Transnational Organized Crime (2000), Protocol, available at http://www.un.org/crime_cicp_convention_documents.htm.
9. United Nations Convention for the Suppression of Traffic (1950), Article 1.
10. United Nations Convention on the Abolition of Slavery, the Slave Trade, and Institutions and Practices Similar to Slavery (1956), Article 3, available at http://www.untreaty.un.org/English/TreatyEvent_2001/22.htm.
11. Barbara Borst (2003), "Documentary on Thai Sex Trade Explores Complexities of Anti-trafficking Efforts," *PhillyBurbs.com*, June 12, available at http://www.phillyburbs.com/pb-dyn/news/103-06122003-106123.htm.
12. Arati Rao (1995), "The Politics of Gender and Culture in International Human Rights Discourse," pp. 161–175 in *Women's Rights Human Rights: International Feminist Perspectives*, ed. by Julie Peters and Andrea Wolper (New York: Routledge), p. 169.
13. Ibid., p. 172–173.
14. Shawn Meghan Burn (2000), Chapter 4, "Women's Rights as Human Rights," in *Women Across Cultures: A Global Perspective* (Mountainview, CA: Mayfield), p. 266.

15. Ibid., p. 266.
16. Ibid., p. 267.
17. Linda Smith and Mohamed Mattar (2003), "Creating International Consensus on Combating Trafficking in Persons: U.S. Policy, the Role of the UN, and Global Responses and Challenges," *The Fletcher Forum of World Affairs* 281 (Winter), pp. 155–178.
18. Gillian Caldwell, Steven Galster, and Nadia Steinzor (1997), "Crime and Servitude: An Exposé of the Traffic in Women for Prostitution from the Newly Independent States," report presented at conference on "The Trafficking of Women Abroad" (Washington D.C.: Global Survival Network).
19. Katharina Knaus, Angelika Kartusch, and Gabriele Reiter (1999 [revised May 2000]), "Combat of Trafficking in Women for the Purpose of Forced Prostitution: International Standards" (May) (Vienna: Ludwig Boltzmann Institution of Human Rights).
20. United Nations Protocol to Prevent, Suppress and Punish Trafficking in Persons, Especially Women and Children, Supplementing the United Nations Convention Against Transnational Organized Crime (2000), United Nations, available at http://www1.umn.edu/humanrts/instree/trafficking.html.
21. Smith and Mattar (2004), op. cit.; Andra Jackson (2003), "Visas for Sex Victims Who Help Nail Traffickers," *The Age*, October 25, available at http://www.theage.com.au/articles/2003/10/24/1066974316603.html.
22. Victims of Trafficking and Violence Protection Act (2000), United States Congress, H.R. 3244.
23. Combating of Trafficking in Persons and Sexual Exploitation of Children Law (2000), Section 53. [Cited in The Protection Project (2002), *Human Rights Report on Trafficking in Persons, Especially Women and Children: A Country-by-Country Report on a Contemporary Form of Slavery*, 2nd ed., "Cyprus" (The Paul H. Nitze School of Advanced International Studies, Johns Hopkins University).]
24. Trafficking Act, Sections 4, 11. [Cited in The Protection Project (2002), op. cit., "Thailand."]
25. United States State Department (2003, 2002), *Trafficking in Persons Report*, "Country Narratives" (Washington D.C.: Office to Monitor and Combat Trafficking in Persons), available at http://www.state.gov/g/tip/rls/tiprpt/2003/21275pf.htm, and http://www.state.gov/g/tip/rls/tiprpt/2002/10679.htm, respectively. Here, as elsewhere, I am providing examples rather than a comprehensive list of laws, programs, or antitrafficking NGOs in particular countries or regions. There are many active projects in addition to those I describe. For more

extensive lists and Web sites, see the Coalition Against Trafficking in Women, at http://www.catwinternational.org.

26. United States State Department (2003, 2002), op. cit., "Switzerland."
27. United States State Department (2003, 2002), op. cit., "Estonia."
28. United States State Department (2003, 2002), op. cit., "Côte d'Ivoire."
29. United States State Department (2003, 2002), op. cit., "Albania."
30. Polaris Project: Combating Trafficking in Women and Children (retrieved March 15, 2004), "Introduction." Available at http://www.polarisproject.org/polarisproject/ (2 pp.).
31. "Bombay, India, NGO Creates Program for Trafficking Victims Living with AIDS" (2002), *Vital Voices Trafficking Alert* (October), Vital Voices Global Partnership, p. 4.
32. Perla Aragon-Choudhury (2001), "Successful (Uphill) Battle Against Exploiting Women," *Business World* 28 (September). [Cited in The Protection Project (2002), op. cit., "Cambodia."]
33. Kelly Adams (2003), "Smith Spearheads Forum on Sexual Slavery," *The Columbian*, February 26, available at http://www.anti-slavery.com/news/general%20news/coverage/tc02-26-03.htm (1 p.).
34. David Binder (2003), "Sex-Trade Smuggling Crackdown," *International Herald Tribune*, available at http://www.iht.com/cgi-bin/generic.cgi?template=articleprint.tmplh&ArticleID=114378 (2 pp.). The 12 countries taking part in the raid were Albania, Bosnia–Herzegovina, Bulgaria, Croatia, Macedonia, Greece, Hungary, Moldova, Romania, Serbia–Montenegro, Slovenia, and Ukraine.
35. Ibid.
36. "Canadian Detective on Mission to Rescue Kosovo Sex Slaves" (2001), *Oliviathestar.com*, December 7.
37. Aragon-Choudhury (2001), op. cit.
38. See, for example, Maggie Jones (2003), "Thailand's Brothel Busters," *MotherJones.com* (November/December), available at http://www.mojones.com/news/outfron/2003/11/ma_570_01.html; Phelim McAleer (2003), "Happy Hookers of Eastern Europe," *The Spectator*, April 5, available at http://www.walnet.org/csis/news/world_2003/spectator-030405.html.
39. "Colombia Launches Crackdown on Child Prostitution" (1998), Reuters 26. [Cited in Donna M. Hughes, Laura Joy Sporcic, Nadine Z. Mendelsohn, and Vanessa Chirgwin (1999), *Factbook on Global Sexual Exploitation*, "Colombia" (Coalition Against Trafficking in Women), available at http://www.uri.edu/artsci/wms/hughes/factbook.htm.]
40. Hnin Hnin Pyne (1995), "AIDS and Gender Violence: The Enslavement of Burmese Women in the Thai Sex Industry," pp. 215–223 in *Women's Rights Human Rights: International Feminist Perspectives*, ed.

by Julie Peters and Andrea Wolper (New York: Routledge).

41. Rose Mestel (2003), "U.N. Report: Global AIDS Epidemic Still Spreading," *The Oregonian*, November 27, A17. [Mestel's data source is the *U.N. AIDS Report*, available at http://www.unaids.org/en/default.asp.]
42. Ibid.
43. "Prostitution Rife in Nigerian Capital as AIDS Rates Soar" (2003), *Terra Daily*, December 7, available at http://www.terradaily.com/2003/031207060117.jrtolrxx.html (4 pp.).
44. David Seddon (1998), "HIV-AIDS in Nepal: The Coming Crisis," *Bulletin of Concerned Asian Scholars* 30, p. 35.
45. Mestel (2003), op. cit.
46. "The Decriminalization of Prostitution in South Africa: Medical and Social Reasons for Keeping Prostitution Illegal" (1997), Doctors for Life, available at http://www.dfl.org.za/issues/Prostitution/dfl_prostitution.htm (22 pp.).
47. Lawrence K. Altman (2002), "Women Now Half of HIV Victims," *The Oregonian*, November 27, pp. 1, 10.
48. "The Decriminalization of Prostitution in South Africa" (1997), op. cit.
49. Ibid.; see pp. 4–5 for a referenced list of countries in which prostitutes have been found to be a high-risk group for HIV/AIDS.
50. W. A. Haseltine (1986), "HTLV-II/LAV-Antibody-Positive Soldiers in Berlin," *New England Journal of Medicine* 314. [Cited in "The Decriminalization of Prostitution in South Africa" (1997).]
51. Human Rights Watch–Asia (1995), "Rape for Profit: Trafficking of Nepali Girls and Women to India's Brothels" (New York).
52. "The Status and Trends of the HIV/AIDS Epidemic in Asia and the Pacific" (2001), UNAIDS, available at http://www.unaids.org/hivaids-info/statistics/MAP/MAP2001.doc.
53. "AIDS in a New Millennium: A Grim Picture with Glimmers of Hope" (2000), *Report on the Global HIV/AIDS Epidemic*, UNAIDS (June), available at http://www.hivinsight.org/InSite.jsp/doc=2098.478d.
54. "The Decriminalization of Prostitution in South Africa" (1997), op. cit.
55. Haseltine (1986), op. cit., p. 55.
56. "AIDS in a New Millennium" (2000), op. cit.
57. "Vietnam-Prostitute-AIDS: Vietnam Reports Explosion of HIV Infection Among Prostitutes" (2002), Agence France Presse, September 17, available at http://www.walnet.org/csis/news/world_2002/afp-020917.html (2 pp.).
58. Human Rights Watch–Asia (1995), op. cit.
59. Ishwarprasad Gilada (1993), *Tulasa and the Horrors of Child Prostitution: Sold and Resold Body and Soul* (Bombay: Indian Health Organization).

60. Janice G. Raymond (1998), "Health Effects of Prostitution," Coalition Against Trafficking in Women (July 1), available at http://www.hsph.harvard.edu/Organizations/healthnet/gender/docs/Raymond.PDF (7 pp.); Human Rights Watch–Asia (1995), op. cit.
61. A. Farag, ed. (1995), Interdenominational Summit Conference on AIDS for Church Women Leaders in Zimbabwe, January 23–27 [cited in "The Decriminalization of Prostitution in South Africa" (1997), op. cit.]; "Women in Mekong Region Faced with Higher Rates of HIV Infection Than Men: China, Cambodia, Laos, Thailand, and Vietnam Showing Similar Trends" (2002), Mekong Leaders' Consultative Meeting on Women and AIDS, press release, UNAIDS.
62. M. Sassan-Morokro, A. E. Greenberg, I. M. Couilbaly et al. (1996), "High Rates of Sexual Contact with Female Sex Workers, Sexually Transmitted Diseases, and Condom Neglect Among HIV-Infected and Uninfected Men with Tuberculosis in Abidjan, Côte d'Ivoire," *Journal of Acquired Immune Deficiency Syndromes and Human Retrovirology* 11, February 1, pp. 183–187. [Cited in "The Decriminalization of Prostitution in South Africa" (1997), op. cit.]
63. Raymond (1998), "Health Effects of Prostitution," p. 5.
64. Ibid., p. 4.
65. Ibid., p. 4.
66. "The Decriminalization of Prostitution in South Africa" (1997), op. cit.
67. [Quoted in June Kane (1998), *Sold for Sex* (Brookfield, VT: Ashgate).]
68. Kane (1998), op. cit., p. 93.
69. "Trafficking Is a Violation of Fundamental Rights" (retrieved March 18, 2004), UNICEF, available at http://www.unicef.org/protection/index_exploitation.html (2 pp.).
70. Tabibul Islam (1998), "Rape of Minors Worries Parents," Inter Press Service 8 (April). [Cited in Hughes et al. (1999), op. cit., "Bangladesh."]
71. "Brazilian Street Children" (retrieved September 10, 2003), Jubilee Action, available at http://www.jubileeaction.co.uk/reports/Brazilian%20Street%20Children.pdf.
72. Malcolm Macalister Hall (2003), "Global Industry Fed by Child-Traffickers," *The Telegraph*, September 12, available at http://www.ecpatorg.uk/Global%20%industry%20press.htm (2 pp.).
73. "Trafficking in Children for Sexual Purposes" (2000), *Looking Back, Thinking Forward—The 4th Report on Commercial Sexual Exploitation of Children*, ECPAT International Newsletters 33, December 1.
74. Kane (1998), op. cit.
75. Hall (2003), op. cit.; Kane (1998), op. cit.
76. Kane (1998), op. cit.

77. "Trafficking Is a Violation of Fundamental Rights" (2004), op. cit.
78. Caldwell et al. (1997), op. cit.
79. Indrani Sinha (retrieved November 19, 2002), "Paper on Globalization and Human Rights," SANLAAP India. [Cited in Hughes et al. (1999), op. cit., "Pakistan."]
80. See, for example, "Latin American Women, Children at Risk: Within Latin America—HIV/AIDS" (retrieved January 30, 2004), *LibertadLatina.org*, available at http://www.libertadlatina.org/Crisis_Latin-America_US_HIV-AIDS.htm (2 pp.); "Trafficking Is a Violation of Fundamental Rights" (2004), op. cit.; Charles M. Goolsby (2003), "Dynamics of Prostitution and Sex Trafficking from Latin America into the United States," Libertad Latina 2003 Report on Latin American to U.S. Sex Trafficking, available at http://www.libertadlatina.org/LL_LatAM_US_Slavery_Report_01_2003.htm; Hall (2003), op. cit.
81. Susannah Price (1999), "South Asia: '100 Kids Abused Daily' in Sri Lanka," BBC News, February 9, available at http://news.bbc.co.uk/2hi/world/south_asia/276054.stm; "Global Law to Punish Sex Tourists Sought by Britain and EU" (1997), *The Indian Express*, November 21 [cited in Hughes et al. (1999), op cit., "Sri Lanka"]; Julian West (1997), "Sri Lankan Children for Sale on the Internet," *London Telegraph*, October 26 [cited in Hughes et al. (1999), op. cit., "Sri Lanka."]
82. Coalition Against Trafficking in Women–Asia Pacific (retrieved October 31, 2002), *Trafficking in Women and Prostitution in the Asian Pacific*. [Cited in Hughes et al. (1999), op. cit., "Pakistan."]
83. Raymond (1998), "Prostitution as Violence Against Women"; Jon E. Rhode (1996), "Child Prostitution in India," UNICEF Report, available at http://www.jubileeaction.co.uk/reports/CHILD96; Human Rights Watch–Asia (1995), op. cit.
84. "Child Trafficking Creates Panic" (2002), *The Independent* [Associated Press], September 6, available at http://www.walnet.org/csic/news/world_2002/independent-020906.html (3 pp.).
85. Kane (1998), op. cit.
86. Rhode (1996), op. cit.
87. Kane (1998), op. cit.
88. Nicholas D. Kristof (1996), "Asian Brothels Force Ever-Younger Children to Serve AIDS-Wary Men," *The Oregonian*, June 12, A12.
89. Jack Epstein (1996), "Nine Year Old Girls Sold to Miners in Sex Auctions," *Christian Science Monitor*, available at http://www.libertadlatina.org/Crisis_Latin_America_Brazil.htm.
90. Peter Landesman (2004), "The Girls Next Door," *The New York Times Magazine*, January 25, pp. 30–39, 66–67, 72, 75.
91. Ibid., p. 38.

92. Rhode (1996), op. cit.; Human Rights Watch–Asia (1995), op. cit.
93. Human Rights Watch (2002), "Forced Prostitution and HIV/AIDS" (November 26), available at http://www.hrw.org/about/projects/womenrep/General-137.htm; "The Decriminalization of Prostitution in South Africa" (1997), op. cit.; Human Rights Watch–Asia (1995), op. cit.
94. Raymond (1998), "Health Effects of Prostitution"; Human Rights Watch–Asia (1995), op. cit.
95. "AIDS in a New Millennium" (2000), op. cit.
96. David Andrew Schmidt (2000), *Ianfu—The Comfort Women of the Japanese Imperial Army of the Pacific War: Broken Silence* (Lewiston: The Edwin Mellon Press).
97. Radhika Coomaraswamy (1999), lecture delivered at the Third Minority Rights Lecture on May 25, 1999, Geneva, United Nations High Commissioner for Human Rights, p. 3 of 12.
98. Kane (1998), op. cit.
99. Ibid.
100. Available at EPCAT Web site, http://www.ecpat.net/eng/Ecpat_network/history.asp.
101. Web sites, respectively, are http://www.unicef.org/about/who/index_mission.html; http://www.iom.int; http://www.ilo.org.
102. Web site is http://www.captivedaughters.org.
103. Feizal Smith (1998), "Sri Lanka: Tightening Screws on Paedophiles," *IPS*, February 20 [cited in Hughes et al. (1999), op. cit., "Sri Lanka"]; West (1997), op. cit.
104. "Child Trafficking Creates Panic" (2002), op. cit.
105. The data on national laws come from The Protection Project's *Human Rights Report on Trafficking in Persons, Especially Women and Children* (The Paul H. Nitze School of Advanced International Studies, Johns Hopkins University), published in 2002. Thus, changes in or additions to national laws after 2002 are not recorded here.
106. Data on prostitution-related laws other than those presented in Table 1 and data for individual countries can be found in The Protection Project (2002), op. cit., "Tabulations."
107. Ibid.
108. The one exception is the state of Nevada, where prostitution is legal in certain counties, and in certain cities or areas. With the exception of Clark County (in which Las Vegas is located), all Nevada counties have the right to legalize and regulate brothel prostitution. As of January 2003, brothels had been legalized in 11 Nevada counties.
109. Victims of Trafficking and Violence Protection Act (2000), op. cit.
110. Ibid.

111. United States State Department (2003), op. cit. Time periods to which the data refer are not always clearly stated (and occasionally are not stated at all) in the report. Clearly, though, the time periods, although roughly similar, are not the same across countries.
112. Ibid.
113. United States State Department (2003), op. cit., "Tier Placements."
114. United States State Department (2002), op. cit.
115. United States State Department (2003), op. cit.
116. Caldwell et al. (1997), op. cit.
117. Kane (1998), op. cit.
118. "Reporting Female Trafficking" (2001), *Africa News*, September 27, Africa News Service, available at http://www.protectionproject.org/t/ne928.htm (1 p.). This article makes the point that for too many in the "established media," the trafficking focus is still on prostitution—whether young girls are prostitutes by choice, and if so, how to dissuade them from it. Instead, the article continues, the media must "convince itself that female trafficking is no longer a moral problem but an international crime against humanity."
119. Kane (1998), op. cit., p. 113.
120. Ibid.
121. Ibid.
122. "Pathbreaking Strategies in the Global Fight Against Sex Trafficking" (2003), Recommendations from Trafficking Conference held February 23–26, Washington, D.C., released by the U.S. Department of State, May 29, available at http://www.state.gov/g/tip/rls/rpt/20834.htm.
123. "Purple Rose Campaign" (retrieved March 8, 2004), available at http://www.purplerosecampaign.org.
124. Charlotte Bunch (1995), "Transforming Human Rights from a Feminist Perspective," pp. 11–17 in *Women's Rights Human Rights: International Feminist Perspectives*, ed. by Julie Peters and Andrea Wolper (New York: Routledge), pp. 14–15.

Index